OMNIVM
LVX
CIVIVM
MDCCCLII
MDCCC
LXXVIII

The Muses' Library

★

IRISH POETS OF THE NINETEENTH CENTURY

IRISH POETS OF THE NINETEENTH CENTURY

selected

with introductions

by

GEOFFREY TAYLOR

HARVARD UNIVERSITY PRESS

CAMBRIDGE, MASSACHUSETTS

68–74 Carter Lane, London, E.C.4

First published in U.S.A. 1951
by Harvard University Press
Cambridge, Massachusetts

Printed in Great Britain

CONTENTS

Preface *page* vii

I. Selections from the Poetry of

WILLIAM ALLINGHAM 1

J. J. CALLANAN 55

AUBREY DE VERE 71

SIR SAMUEL FERGUSON 107

T. C. IRWIN 145

J. C. MANGAN 209

J. F. O'DONNELL 261

II. Anthology of the best poems by less important poets 295

Notes 387

Index of First Lines 399

PREFACE

In this volume of *The Muses' Library* I have set out to do two things: first, to make a substantial selection from each of the more important nineteenth-century Irish poets; second, to make an anthology of the better poems by other Irish writers of the same period.

At the very start a question had, of course, to be begged. It had to be taken for granted that there really is such a thing as an Irish poet in a strictly literary sense. On this point there can, as a matter of fact, be no doubt. Thirty-one years ago Thomas MacDonagh, who was killed by the English for taking part in the Easter-week Rising, published an anthology of *Poems of the Irish Mode*. It demonstrated to anyone who had an ear that there is such a thing as Anglo-Irish poetry in its own right. But MacDonagh's anthology contained only thirty poems. *The Muses' Library* no less than local patriotism demands more than this, and there is plenty of precedent for giving more. For this 'more', however, some rather arbitrary criterion had to be invented. The test that I have applied to poets is that they must have been Irish by birth, and they must have written poetry with some Irish reference, either historical or topographical. The second part of this rule excludes such poets as George Darley and Arthur O'Shaughnessy who were in some sense Irish by birth but who did not even pay lip service to Ireland in their poetry.

On the other hand, for particular poems, I have not insisted that they should be concerned with Ireland. Irish poetry is inevitably and not dishonourably Provincial; but there is no need to make it seem parochial.

In the period covered, also, I have had to exclude

our two best poets—Tom Moore at one end and W. B. Yeats at the other—because, though they both wrote in the nineteenth century, the first belongs rather to the eighteenth, and the second to the twentieth. For the anthology section I have been rather less stringent and have included several poems in a decidedly eighteenth-century style.

Within my illogical but necessary limits, I hope I have left out no poem that is startlingly good, and put in none that has not some poetic excellence.

GEOFFREY TAYLOR

Dublin
May 1947

WILLIAM ALLINGHAM

1824–1889

WILLIAM ALLINGHAM
1824–1889

William Allingham's ancestors had come from England and settled at Ballyshannon, County Donegal, in the reign of Queen Elizabeth. By tradition, therefore, he belonged neither to the original wave of Anglo-Norman invaders who became more Irish than the Irish themselves, nor to the last great plantation under Cromwell which, the Irish memory being elephantine but without historical perspective, has never been permitted to assimilate itself with the heroic mythology of the 'mere Irish'. And so, with no drop of Celtic blood but with behind him three centuries of the most potent climate in the world except the Egyptian, his position was likely to be anomalous. He was never quite sure what his nationality was, and this doubtless affected his personal relationships and also his poetic reputation.

He was born in Ballyshannon in 1824, 'in a little house, the most westerly of a row of three, in a street running down to the Harbour. Opposite was a garden wall, with rose-bushes hanging over.' The note struck even in those few words of autobiography is markedly un-Irish. Your typical Irishman thinks of 'Ireland', an Emerald Isle, a mystical entity suffering violation, suffering partition. Your typical Englishman thinks of his native village, or at most, like Hudson, of the Wylye Valley, or like Hardy, of Egdon Heath. But Allingham felt for Donegal as Matthew Arnold felt for Oxford. That garden—and the Irish, as George Moore acidly pointed out, do not care for gardens—that garden, with its wall and its roses occurs again, this time in verse:

On the garden side
Our wall being low, the great Whiterose-bush lean'd
A thousand tender little heads, to note
The doings of the village all day long.

Allingham's attitude to Ireland was completely objective. He was that almost impossible thing, an Irish Liberal. His attitude to Ballyshannon was nostalgically affectionate.

Allingham's father was a merchant who owned a small fleet of trading ships importing timber from Canada and the Baltic. He was well-to-do but not wealthy, and Allingham at the age of fourteen was taken from the local Protestant school to become a clerk in the Ballyshannon branch of the Provincial Bank. After serving the Bank in various North of Ireland towns for seven years he obtained, at the age of twenty-two, a civil-service post in the Customs. He was stationed at Belfast and later at Donegal town and seems from the first to have found his new job more congenial than the old. 'I talked to the clerks about literature and poetry . . . I preached Tennyson to them, hitherto an unknown name', he writes. And already, in 1843, he had struck up a friendship by post with Leigh Hunt, whom he met on a visit to London in 1847 and who launched him on the literary world. It was about then that his life-long friendship with Rossetti began. In 1851 he met the admired Tennyson. Twelve years later, still in the Customs service, he was transferred to Lymington in Hampshire. 'You will be near Tennyson,' said Carlyle. 'Yes, yes, you are sure to come together.'

Carlyle spoke with, perhaps, a dyspeptic shrewdness. Allingham and Tennyson did indeed come together and the long association did not bring out the best in either of them. Allingham idolized Tennyson, and

Tennyson's behaviour to Allingham varied between condescension and rudeness. It is all there, in the Diary which Allingham kept and which his wife published after his death:

'He (Tennyson) paused at a weed of goatsbeard, saying "It shuts up at three." Then we went down the garden, past a large fig-tree growing in the open—"It's like a breaking wave", says I. "Not in the least", says he. Such contradictions, *from him*, are no way disagreeable. In parting he said to me, "We shall see you sometimes", which gladdened me.'

On another occasion Tennyson publicly corrected Allingham's pronunciation. But such was Allingham's adoration that he never seems to have felt in the least humiliated—even on Tennyson's account. This Diary, kept in great detail for various dates between 1863 and 1889, is exceedingly entertaining, and valuable for the light it throws on informal aspects, not only of Tennyson, but of many of the other great Victorians. As a self-portrait it shows Allingham as almost morbidly self-effacing, morbidly grateful for any crumbs of recognition. It shows a thinness in the texture of his personality which is all too often reflected in his poetry.

After 1863 Allingham lived in England, seldom revisiting his native country. In 1874 he married Helen Paterson, a water-colour painter of some charm. Three children were born to them. He resigned from the Customs and became assistant editor of *Fraser's Magazine.* From 1850 onwards he published a book of poems every few years. He died at his home in Hampstead on November 17th, 1889. His last words were 'I see such things as you cannot dream of!' It would have pleased him to know that they brought some comfort to the Poet Laureate who had once interrupted him with 'What I want is an assurance of immortality.'

Tennyson, one hopes, enjoys immortality in the next world: certainly his poems have gained it for him in this one. On the other hand, whatever assurance Allingham may have had about the next, this world has hardly done him justice. There has never been a collected edition of his poems, and all his separate books have long been out of print. Such reputation as he may have had was knocked on the head by Professor Saintsbury in the *Cambridge History of English Literature*—'He has the fluency and ease of verse which has been again and again noticed as common in Irish poets; but he has been allowed by competent critics to be dull, tame and uninventive.' Saintsbury then misquotes 'Up the airy mountain'. More recently, Professor H. J. C. Grierson has told us that Allingham has been 'somewhat obscured by the superior lustre of the Sinn Feiners'. Both these critics may be suspected of an anti-Irish bias. Both, it will be noticed, reckon him an Irish poet. The Irish, on the other hand, who are quite as apt to be biased and who are even less inclined to read poetry unless it is patriotic, have rejected and forgotten him.

One may admit that Allingham wrote much second-rate lyric verse, that his use of words is frequently undistinguished and that his music is often tinkling. The same is true of many minor poets whose memories are greener than Allingham's and who yet produced nothing comparable, either in quantity or quality, with his best work. So far as his shorter poems are concerned the selection I have made must speak for him. But there are also several longer poems which I have not had room to include, one of which, *Laurence Bloomfield*, is essential to his reputation. I have included a few descriptive extracts from this poem, but some further brief account of it must be given here.

In Allingham's own opinion *Laurence Bloomfield* was his masterpiece, and according to Lionel Johnson it was praised by the Russian Turgenev. The poem, published in book form in 1864, consists of twelve chapters containing in all some 4,700 lines in heroic couplets. It is a picture of life in the west of Ireland as Allingham knew it exactly a hundred years ago; yet much of its realism, even now, is not more than three decades out of date. The characters will still be remembered as types by anyone over forty. Laurence Bloomfield is a young Irish landlord, educated in England and imbued with English liberalism, who returns to his estate at Lismoy. The popular patriots of the time were the Ribbonmen. The story concerns the wholesale eviction of 'tenants-at-will' from the village of Ballytullagh, the destruction by police and bailiffs of their miserable hovels, and the consequences that ensued. The picture is not overdrawn nor heightened in colour. George Moore, writing twenty years later, describes an eviction of equal brutality—they were normal. The villain of the piece is the shrewd, hard-working, desperately unimaginative, and deservedly hated Land Agent of several great estates. He is drawn with understanding and not without sympathy. The nominal hero, I suppose, is Bloomfield; but the real hero is a young peasant who joins the Ribbon Lodge. It is a grim enough story, ending on a note of slightly incongruous, slightly forced-fairytale optimism. Allingham in his preface disclaims all partisan intention, but it is clear that his own position was that of a cautious, romantic, Social Reformer. The book can be read as a poem (and it is primarily that), as a novel, as a social document, or as a pamphlet which was not without its effect on Gladstone and other English politicians. It is also a full gallery of portraits and landscapes—generally interwoven and so not easily detached in quotation.

Allingham seems to have fallen between two stools. Tennyson and his other English friends were always twitting him about Ireland—they would not let him forget that he was in some degree alien; whereas his own literary ambition, and to some extent his literary instinct, was to be entirely and essentially English. The resulting slight ambiguity made him difficult to classify and, in a poetic literature so fantastically rich as that of England, easy to neglect.

WILLIAM ALLINGHAM
BIBLIOGRAPHY

Poems, 1850.
Day and Night Songs, 1854.
The Music Master, 1855.
Laurence Bloomfield in Ireland, 1864.
Fifty Modern Poems, 1865.
Rambles by Patricius Walker (prose), 1873.
Songs, Ballads and Stories, 1877.
Evil May-Day, 1882.
Ashby Manor, a play, 1883.
Blackberries, 1884.
Rhymes for the Young, 1886.
Irish Songs and Poems, 1887.
Flower Pieces, 1888.
Life and Phantasy, 1889.
Thought and Word, 1890.
Varieties in Prose, 1893.
By the Way, 1912.

William Allingham, A Diary, 1907.
Letters, 1911.
Letters of Rossetti to Allingham, 1897.

Kate o' Belashanny

I

SEEK up and down, both fair and brown,
We've purty lasses many, O;
But brown or fair, one girl most rare,
The Flow'r o' Belashanny, O.
As straight is she as poplar-tree
(Tho' not as aisy shaken, O),
And walks so proud among the crowd,
For queen she might be taken, O.
From top to toe, where'er you go,
The loveliest girl of any, O,—
Ochone! your mind I find unkind,
Sweet Kate o' Belashanny, O!

II

One summer day the banks were gay,
The Erne in sunshine glancin' there,
The big cascade its music play'd
And set the salmon dancin' there.
Along the green my Joy was seen;
Some goddess bright I thought her there;
The fishes, too, swam close, to view
Her image in the water there.
From top to toe, where'er you go,
The loveliest girl of any, O,—
Ochone! your mind I find unkind,
Sweet Kate o' Belashanny, O!

III

My dear, give ear!—the river's near,
And if you think I'm shammin' now,

To end my grief I'll seek relief
Among the trout and salmon, now;
For shrimps and sharks to make their marks,
And other watery vermin there;
Unless a mermaid saves my life,—
My wife, and me her merman there.
From top to toe, where'er you go,
The loveliest girl of any, O,—
Mavrone! your mind I find unkind,
Sweet Kate o' Belashanny, O!

IV

'Tis all in vain that I complain;
No use to coax or chide her there;
As far away from me as Spain,
Although I stand beside her there.
O cruel Kate! since that's my fate,
I'll look for love no more in you;
The seagull's screech as soon would reach
Your heart, as me implorin' you.
Tho' fair you are, and rare you are,
The loveliest flow'r of any, O,—
Too proud and high,—good-bye, say I,
To Kate o' Belashanny, O!

The Milkmaid

O WHERE are you going so early? he said;
Good luck go with you, my pretty maid;
To tell you my mind I'm half afraid,
But I wish I were your sweetheart.
When the morning sun is shining low,
And the cocks in every farmyard crow,

I'll carry your pail,
O'er hill and dale,
And I'll go with you a-milking.

I'm going a-milking, sir, says she,
Through the dew, and across the lea;
You ne'er would even yourself to me,
Or take me for your sweetheart.
When the morning sun, etc.

Now give me your milking-stool awhile,
To carry it down to yonder stile;
I'm wishing every step a mile,
And myself your only sweetheart.
When the morning sun, etc.

Oh, here's the stile in-under the tree,
And there's the path in the grass for me,
And I thank you kindly, sir, says she,
And wish you a better sweetheart.
When the morning sun, etc.

Now give me your milking-pail, says he,
And while we're going across the lea,
Pray reckon your master's cows to me,
Although I'm not your sweetheart.
When the morning sun, etc.

Two of them red, and two of them white,
Two of them yellow and silky bright,
She told him her master's cows aright,
Though he was not her sweetheart.
When the morning sun, etc.

She sat and milk'd in the morning sun,
And when her milking was over and done,

She found him waiting all as one
 As if he were her sweetheart.
  When the morning sun, etc.

He freely offer'd his heart and hand;
Now she has a farm at her command,
And cows of her own to graze the land;
 Success to all true sweethearts!
  When the morning sun is shining low,
  And the cocks in every farmyard crow,
   I'll carry your pail
   O'er hill and dale,
  And I'll go with you a-milking.

The Girls' Lamentation

WITH grief and mourning I sit to spin;
My Love passed by, and he didn't come in;
He passes by me, both day and night,
And carries off my poor heart's delight.

There is a tavern in yonder town,
My Love goes there and he spends a crown;
He takes a strange girl upon his knee,
And never more gives a thought to me.

Says he, 'We'll wed without loss of time,
And sure our love's but a little crime';—
My apron-string now it's wearing short,
And my Love he seeks other girls to court.

O with him I'd go if I had my will,
I'd follow him barefoot o'er rock and hill;

I'd never once speak of all my grief
If he'd give me a smile for my heart's relief.

In our wee garden the rose unfolds,
With bachelor's-buttons and marigolds;
I'll tie no posies for dance or fair,
A willow-twig is for me to wear.

For a maid again I can never be,
Till the red rose blooms on the willow tree.
Of such a trouble I've heard them tell,
And now I know what it means full well.

As through the long lonesome night I lie,
I'd give the world if I might but cry;
But I mus'n't moan there or raise my voice,
And the tears run down without any noise.

And what, O what will my mother say?
She'll wish her daughter was in the clay.
My father will curse me to my face;
The neighbours will know of my black disgrace.

My sister's buried three years, come Lent;
But sure we made far too much lament.
Beside her grave they still say a prayer—
I wish to God 'twas myself was there!

The Candlemas crosses hang near my bed[1];
To look at them puts me much in dread,
They mark the good time that's gone and past:
It's like this year's one will prove the last.

[1] Little crosses woven of straw. A new cross is added each year, and the old ones are left till they fall to pieces.

The oldest cross it's a dusty brown,
But the winter winds didn't shake it down;
The newest cross keeps the colour bright;
When the straw was reaping my heart was light.

The reapers rose with the blink of morn,
And gaily stook'd up the yellow corn;
To call them home to the field I'd run,
Through the blowing breeze and the summer sun.

When the straw was weaving my heart was glad,
For neither sin nor shame I had,
In the barn where oat-chaff was flying round,
And the thumping flails made a pleasant sound.

Now summer or winter to me it's one;
But oh! for a day like the time that's gone.
I'd little care was it storm or shine,
If I had but peace in this heart of mine.

Oh! light and false is a young man's kiss,
And a foolish girl gives her soul for this.
Oh! light and short is the young man's blame,
And a helpless girl has the grief and shame.

To the river-bank once I thought to go,
And cast myself in the stream below;
I thought 'twould carry us far out to sea,
Where they'd never find my poor babe and me.

Sweet Lord, forgive me that wicked mind!
You know I used to be well-inclined.
Oh, take compassion upon my state,
Because my trouble is so very great.

My head turns round with the spinning-wheel,
And a heavy cloud on my eyes I feel.
But the worst of all is at my heart's core;
For my innocent days will come back no more.

The Ruined Chapel

By the shore, a plot of ground
Clips a ruin'd chapel round,
Buttress'd with a grassy mound;
  Where Day and Night and Day go by,
And bring no touch of human sound.

Washing of the lonely seas,
Shaking of the guardian trees,
Piping of the salted breeze;
  Day and Night and Day go by
To the endless tune of these.

Or when, as winds and waters keep
A hush more dead than any sleep,
Still morns to stiller evenings creep,
  And Day and Night and Day go by;
Here the silence is most deep.

The empty ruins, lapsed again
Into Nature's wide domain,
Sow themselves with seed and grain
  As Day and Night and Day go by;
And hoard June's sun and April's rain.

Here fresh funeral tears were shed;
Now the graves are also dead;

And suckers from the ash-tree spread,
While Day and Night and Day go by;
And stars move calmly overhead.

The Fairies

Up the airy mountain,
Down the rushy glen,
We daren't go a-hunting
For fear of little men;
Wee folk, good folk,
Trooping all together;
Green jacket, red cap,
And white owl's feather!

Down along the rocky shore
Some make their home,
They live on crispy pancakes
Of yellow tide-foam;
Some in the reeds
Of the black mountain lake,
With frogs for their watch-dogs,
All night awake.

High on the hill-top
The old King sits;
He is now so old and gray
He's nigh lost his wits.
With a bridge of white mist
Columbkill he crosses,
On his stately journeys
From Slieveleague to Rosses;
Or going up with music
On cold starry nights,

To sup with the Queen
Of the gay Northern Lights.

They stole little Bridget
For seven years long;
When she came down again
Her friends were all gone.
They took her lightly back,
Between the night and morrow,
They thought that she was fast asleep,
But she was dead with sorrow.
They have kept her ever since
Deep within the lake,
On a bed of flag-leaves,
Watching till she wake.

By the craggy hill-side,
Through the mosses bare,
They have planted thorn-trees
For pleasure here and there.
Is any man so daring
As dig them up in spite,
He shall find their sharpest thorns
In his bed at night.

Up the airy mountain,
Down the rushy glen,
We daren't go a-hunting
For fear of little men;
Wee folk, good folk,
Trooping all together;
Green jacket, red cap,
And white owl's feather!

The Fairy King

THE Fairy King was old.
He met the Witch of the wold.
'Ah ha, King!' quoth she,
'Now thou art old like me.'
'Nay, Witch!' quoth he,
'I am not old like thee.'

The King took off his crown,
It almost bent him down;
His age was too great
To carry such a weight.
'Give it me!' she said,
And clapt it on her head.

Crown sank to ground;
The Witch no more was found.
Then sweet spring-songs were sung,
The Fairy King grew young,
His crown was made of flowers,
He lived in woods and bowers.

The Nobleman's Wedding

I ONCE was a guest at a Nobleman's wedding;
  Fair was the Bride, but she scarce had been kind,
And now in our mirth, she had tears nigh the shedding;
  Her former true lover still runs in her mind.

Attired like a minstrel, her former true lover
  Takes up his harp, and runs over the strings;
And there among strangers, his grief to discover,
  A fair maiden's falsehood he bitterly sings.

'Now here is the token of gold that was broken;
Seven long years it was kept for your sake;
You gave it to me as a true lover's token;
No longer I'll wear it, asleep or awake.'

She sat in her place by the head of the table,
The words of his ditty she mark'd them right well:
To sit any longer this bride was not able,
So down at the bridegroom's feet she fell.

'O one, one request, my lord, one and no other,
O this one request will you grant it to me?
To lie for this night in the arms of my mother,
And ever, and ever thereafter with thee.'

Her one, one request it was granted her fairly;
Pale were her cheeks as she went up to bed;
And the very next morning, early, early,
They rose and they found this young bride was dead.

The bridegroom ran quickly, he held her, he kiss'd her,
He spoke loud and low, and listen'd full fain;
He call'd on her waiting-maids round to assist her,
But nothing could bring the lost breath back again.

O carry her softly! the grave is made ready;
At head and at foot plant a laurel-bush green;
For she was a young and a sweet noble lady,
The fairest young bride that I ever have seen.

Lovely Mary Donnelly

OH, lovely Mary Donnelly, my joy, my only best!
If fifty girls were round you, I'd hardly see the rest;

Be what it may the time o' day, the place be where it will,
Sweet looks o' Mary Donnelly, they bloom before me still.

Her eyes like mountain water that's flowing on a rock,
How clear they are, how dark they are! they give me many a shock;
Red rowans warm in sunshine and wetted with a show'r,
Could ne'er express the charming lip that has me in its pow'r.

Her nose is straight and handsome, her eyebrows lifted up,
Her chin is very neat and pert, and smooth like a china cup.
Her hair's the brag of Ireland, so weighty and so fine;
It's rolling down upon her neck, and gather'd in a twine.

The dance o' last Whit-Monday night exceeded all before,
No pretty girl for miles about was missing from the floor;
But Mary kept the belt o' love, and O but she was gay!
She danced a jig, she sung a song, that took my heart away.

When she stood up for dancing, her steps were so complete
The music nearly kill'd itself to listen to her feet;
The fiddler moan'd his blindness, he heard her so much praised,
But bless'd his luck to not be deaf when once her voice she raised.

And evermore I'm whistling or lilting what you sung,
Your smile is always in my heart, your name beside my
  tongue;
But you've as many sweethearts as you'd count on
  both your hands,
And for myself there's not a thumb or little finger
  stands.

'Tis you're the flower o' womankind in country or in
  town;
The higher I exalt you, the lower I'm cast down.
If some great lord should come this way, and see your
  beauty bright,
And you to be his lady, I'd own it was but right.

O might we live together in a lofty palace hall,
Where joyful music rises, and where scarlet curtains
  fall!
O might we live together in a cottage mean and small,
With sods o' grass the only roof, and mud the only
  wall!

O lovely Mary Donnelly, your beauty's my distress.
It's far too beauteous to be mine, but I'll never wish it
  less.
The proudest place would fit your face, and I am poor
  and low;
But blessings be about you, dear, wherever you may go!

George Levison

OR, THE SCHOOLFELLOWS

THE noisy sparrows in our clematis
Chatted of rain, a pensive summer dusk

Shading the little lawn and garden-ground
Between our threshold and the village-street;
With one pure star, a lonely altar-lamp
In twilight's vast cathedral. But the clouds
Were gravely gathering, and a fitful breeze
Flurried the window-foliage that before
Hung delicately painted on the sky,
And wafted, showering from their golden boss,
The white-rose petals.
On the garden side
Our wall being low, the great Whiterose-bush lean'd
A thousand tender little heads, to note
The doings of the village all day long;
From when the labourers, trudging to their toil
In earliest sunshine, heard the outpost cocks
Whistle a quaint refrain from farm to farm,
Till hour of shadow, silence, and repose,
The ceasing footstep, and the taper's light.
Up to the churchyard rail, down to the brook,
And lifted fields beyond with grove and hedge,
The Rose-bush gazed; and people, as they pass'd,
Aware of sweetness, look'd aloft in turn;
School-children, one arm round a comrade's neck,
Would point to some rich cluster, and repay
A flying bloom with fairer glance of joy.
In that warm twilight, certain years ago,
At sunset, with the roses in a trance,
And many another blossom fast asleep,
One Flow'r of Flow'rs was closing like the rest.
Night's herald star which look'd across the world
Saw nothing prettier than our little child
Saying his evening prayer at mother's knee,
The white skirt folding on the naked feet,
Too tender for rough ways, his eyes at rest
On his mother's face, a window into heaven.
Kiss'd now, and settled in his cot, he's pleased

With murmuring song, until the large lids droop
And do not rise, and slumber's regular breath
Divides the soft round mouth. So Annie's boy
And mine was laid asleep. I heard her foot
Stir overhead; and hoped there would be time
Before the rain to loiter half an hour,
As far as to the poplars down the road,
And hear the corncrakes through the meadowy vale,
And watch the childhood of the virgin moon,
Above that sunset and its marge of clouds
A floating crescent.
Sweetheart of my life!—
As then, so now; nay, dearer to me now,
Since love, that fills the soul, expands it too,
And thus it holds more love, and ever more,—
O sweetheart, helpmate, guardian, better self!
Green be those downs and dells above the sea,
Smooth-green for ever, by the plough unhurt,
Nor overdrifted by their neighbouring sands,
Where first I saw you; first since long before
When we were children at an inland place
And play'd together. I had often thought,
I wonder should I know that pleasant child?—
Hardly, I fear'd. I knew her the first glimpse;
While yet the flexile curvature of hat
Kept all her face in shadow to the chin.
And when a breeze to which the harebells danced
Lifted the sun a moment to her eyes,
The ray of recognition flew to mine
Through all the dignity of womanhood.
Like dear old friends we were, yet wondrous new.
The others chatted; she and I not much.
Hearing her ribbon whirring in the wind
(No doubting hopes nor whimsies born as yet)
Was pure felicity, like his who sleeps
Within a sense of some unknown good-fortune,

True, or of dreamland, undetermined which;
My buoyant spirit tranquil in its joy
As the white seamew swinging on the wave.
Since, what vicissitude! We read the past
Bound in a volume, catch the story up
At any leaf we choose, and much forget
How every blind to-morrow was evolved,
How each oracular sentence shaped itself
For after comprehension.
                                        Thus I mused,
Then also, in that buried summer dusk,
Rich heavy summer, upon autumn's verge,
My wife and boy upstairs, I leaning grave
Against the window; and through favourite paths
Memory, as one who saunters in a wood,
Found sober joy. In turn that eve itself
Rises distinctly. Troops of dancing moths
Brush'd the dry grass. I heard, as if from far,
The tone of passing voices in the street.
Announced by cheerful octaves of a horn,
Those rapid wheels flew, shaking our white-rose,
That link'd us with the modern Magic-Way,
And all the moving million-peopled world.
For every evening, done our little darg
To keep the threads of life from tanglement,
In happy hour came in the lottery-bag,
Whose messenger had many a prize for us:
The multifarious page ephemeral,
The joy at times of some brave book, whereby
The world is richer; and more special words,
Conveying conjured into dots of ink
Almost the voice, look, gesture that we knew,—
From Annie's former house, or mine, from shore
Of murky Thames, or rarer from hot land
Of Hindoo or Chinese, Canadian woods,
Or that huge isle of kangaroos and gold,

Magnetic metal,—thus to the four winds
One's ancient comrades scatter'd through the world.
Where's Georgy now, I thought, our dread, our pride,
George Levison, the sultan of the school?
With Greek and Latin at those fingers' ends
That sway'd the winning oar and bat; a prince
In pocket-money and accoutrement;
A Cribb in fist, a Cicero in tongue;
Already victor, when his eye should deign
To fix on any summit of success.
For, in his haughty careless way, he'd hint—
'I've got to push my fortune, by and-bye.'
How we all worshipp'd Georgy Levison!
But when I went to college he was gone,
They said to travel, and he took away
Mentor conjoin'd with Crichton from my hopes,—
No trifling blank. George had done little there,
But could—what could he not? . . . And now, perhaps,
Some city, in the strangers' burial-ground,
Some desert sand, or hollow under sea,
Hides him without an epitaph. So men
Slip under, fit to shape the world anew;
And leave their trace—in schoolboy memories.
  Then I went thinking how much changed I was
Since those old school-times, not so far away,
Yet now like pre-existence. Can that house,
Those fields and trees, be extant anywhere?
Have not all vanish'd, place, and time, and men?
Or with a journey could I find them all,
And myself with them, as I used to be?
Sore was my battle after quitting these.
No one thing fell as plann'd for; sorrows came
And sat beside me; years of toil went round;
And victory's self was pale and garlandless.
Fog rested on my heart; till softly blew
The wind that clear'd it. 'Twas a simple turn

Of life,—a miracle of heavenly love,
For which, thank God!
When Annie call'd me up,
We both bent silent, looking at our boy;
Kiss'd unaware (as angels, may be, kiss
Good mortals) on the smoothly rounded cheek,
Turn'd from the window, where a fringe of leaves,
With outlines melting in the darkening blue,
Waver'd and peep'd and whisper'd. Would she walk?
Not yet a little were those clouds to stoop
With freshness to the garden and the field.
I waited by our open door; while bats
Flew silently, and musk geranium-leaves
Were fragrant in the twilight that had quench'd
Or tamed the dazzling scarlet of their blooms.
Peace, as of heaven itself, possess'd my heart.
A footstep, not the light step of my wife,
Disturb'd it; then, with slacker pace, a man
Came up beside the porch. Accosting whom,
And answering to my name: 'I fear,' he said,
'You'll hardly recollect me now; and yet
We were at school together long ago.
Have you forgotten Georgy Levison?'

He in the red arm-chair; I not far off,
Excited, laughing, waiting for his face:
The first flash of the candles told me all:
Or, if not all, enough, and more. Those eyes,
When they look'd up at last, were his indeed,
But mesh'd in ugly network, like a snare;
And though his mouth preserved the imperious curve,
Evasion, vacillation, discontent,
Warp'd every feature like a crooked glass.
His hair hung prematurely grey and thin;
From thread-bare sleeves the wither'd tremulous hands
Protruded. Why paint every touch of blight?

Tea came. He hurried into ceaseless talk;
Glanced at the ways of many foreign towns;
Knew all those men whose names are on the tongue,
And set their worths punctiliously; brought back
Our careless years; paid Annie compliments
To spare; admired the pattern of the cups;
Lauded the cream,—our dairy's, was it not?
A country life was pleasant, certainly,
If one could be content to settle down;
And yet the city had advantages.
He trusted, shortly, underneath his roof
To practise hospitality in turn.
But first to catch the roof, eh? Ha, ha, ha!
That was a business topic he'd discuss
With his old friend by-and-bye—
For me, I long'd
To hide my face and groan; yet look'd at him;
Opposing pain to grief, presence to thought.

Later, when wine came in, and we two sat
The dreary hours together, how he talk'd!
His schemes of life, his schemes of work and wealth,
Intentions and inventions, plots and plans,
Travels and triumphs, failures, golden hopes.
He was a young man still—had just begun
To see his way. I knew what he could do
If once he tried in earnest. He'd return
To Law, next term but one; meanwhile complete
His great work, '*The Philosophy of Life,*
Or, Man's Relation to the Universe',
The matter lying ready to his hand.
Forty subscribers more, two guineas each,
Would make it safe to publish. All this time
He fill'd his glass and emptied, and his tongue
Went thick and stammering. When the wine came in
(Perhaps a blame for me—who knows?) I saw

The glistering eye; a thin and eager hand
Made the decanter chatter on the glass
Like ague. Could I stop him? So at last
He wept, and moan'd he was a ruin'd man,
Body and soul; then cursed his enemies
By name, and promised punishment; made vaunt
Of genius, learning; caught my hand again,—
Did I forget my friend—my dear old friend?
Had I a coat to spare? He had no coat
But this one on his back; not one shirt—see!

'Twas all a nightmare; all plain wretched truth.
And how to play physician? Where's the strength
Repairs a slow self-ruin from without?
The fall'n must climb innumerable steps,
With humbleness, and diligence, and pain.
How help him to the first of all that steep?

Midnight was past. I had proposed to find
A lodging near us; for, to say the truth,
I could not bid my wife, for such a guest
In such a plight, prepare the little room
We still call'd 'Emma's' from my sister's name.
Then with a sudden mustering up of wits,
And ev'n a touch of his old self, that quick
Melted my heart anew, he signified
His bed was waiting, he would say good-night,
And begg'd me not to stir, he knew his road.
But arm in arm I brought him up the street,
Among the rain-pools, and the pattering drops
Drumming upon our canopy; where few
Or none were out of doors; and once or twice
Some casement from an upper story shed
Penurious lamplight.
Tediously we kept
The morning meal in vain expectancy.

Our box of clothes came back; the people said
He paid without a word, and went his way,
They knew not whither. He return'd no more.
He now is dead.
                    Through all the summer-time
The touch of that unhappy visit lay,
Like trace of frost on gardens, on our life.
Great cities give events to every hour;
Not so that ancient village, small, remote,
Half-hid in boscage of a peaceful vale,
With guardian hills, but welcoming the sun,
And every group of seasonable stars
That rise upon the circle of the year;
Open to natural influences; far
From jostling crowds of congregated men.
   That village also lies behind us now;
Midst other fields abide we, other faces.
Annie, my darling, we were happy there,
And Heaven continues happiness and hope
To us and to our children. May their steps
Keep the good pathway through this perilous world.
That village is far-off, that year is fled.
But, still, at many a meditative hour
By day or night, or with memorial flash,
I see the ghost of Georgy Levison;
A shifting phantom,—now with boyhood's face
And merry curls; now haggard and forlorn,
As when the candles came into the room.

   One sells his soul; another squanders it;
The first buys up the world, the second starves.
Poor George was loser palpably enough;
Supernal Wisdom only knows how much.

Late Autumn

OCTOBER,—and the skies are cool and grey
O'er stubbles emptied of their latest sheaf,
Bare meadow, and the slowly falling leaf.
The dignity of woods in rich decay
Accords full well with this majestic grief
That clothes our solemn purple hills to-day,
Whose afternoon is hush'd, and wintry brief.
Only a robin sings from any spray.
And night sends up her pale cold moon, and spills
White mist around the hollows of the hills,
Phantoms of firth or lake; the peasant sees
His cot and stackyard, with the homestead trees,
In-islanded; but no vain terror thrills
His perfect harvesting; he sleeps at ease.

Song

O SPIRIT of the Summertime!
Bring back the roses to the dells;
The swallow from her distant clime,
The honey-bee from drowsy cells.

Bring back the friendship of the sun;
The gilded evenings, calm and late,
When merry children homeward run,
And peeping stars bid lovers wait.

Bring back the singing; and the scent
Of meadowlands at dewy prime;—
Oh, bring again my heart's content,
Thou Spirit of the Summertime!

After Sunset

THE vast and solemn company of clouds
Around the Sun's death, lit, incarnadined,
Cool into ashy wan; as Night enshrouds
The level pasture, creeping up behind
Through voiceless vales, o'er lawn and purpled hill
And hazèd mead, her mystery to fulfil.
Cows low from far-off farms; the loitering wind
Sighs in the hedge, you hear it if you will,—
Though all the wood, alive atop with wings
Lifting and sinking through the leafy nooks,
Seethes with the clamour of ten thousand rooks.
Now every sound at length is hush'd away.
These few are sacred moments. One more Day
Drops in the shadowy gulf of bygone things.

Song—'Across the Sea'

1

I WALK'D in the lonesome evening,
  And who so sad as I,
When I saw the young men and maidens
  Merrily passing by.
    To thee, my Love, to thee—
    So fain would I come to thee!
While the ripples fold upon sands of gold
    And I look across the sea.

2

I stretch out my hands; who will clasp them?
  I call,—thou repliest no word:

O why should heart-longing be weaker
Than the waving wings of a bird!
To thee, my Love, to thee—
So fain would I come to thee!
For the tide's at rest from east to west,
And I look across the sea.

3

There's joy in the hopeful morning,
There's peace in the parting day,
There's sorrow with every lover
Whose true-love is far away.
To thee, my Love, to thee—
So fain would I come to thee!
And the water's bright in a still moonlight,
As I look across the sea.

The Winding Banks of Erne:

OR, THE EMIGRANT'S ADIEU TO BALLYSHANNON

A Local Ballad

1

ADIEU to Ballyshannon! where I was bred and born;
Go where I may, I'll think of you, as sure as night and morn,
The kindly spot, the friendly town, where everyone is known,
And not a face in all the place but partly seems my own;
There's not a house or window, there's not a field or hill,

But, east or west, in foreign lands, I'll recollect them
still.
I leave my warm heart with you, though my back I'm
forced to turn—
So adieu to Ballyshannon, and the winding banks of
Erne!

2

No more on pleasant evenings we'll saunter down the
Mall,
When the trout is rising to the fly, the salmon to the
fall.
The boat comes straining on her net, and heavily she
creeps,
Cast off, cast off!—she feels the oars, and to her berth
she sweeps;
Now fore and aft keep hauling, and gathering up the
clue,
Till a silver wave of salmon rolls in among the crew.
Then they may sit, with pipes a-lit, and many a joke
and 'yarn';—
Adieu to Ballyshannon, and the winding banks of
Erne!

3

The music of the waterfall, the mirror of the tide,
When all the green-hill'd harbour is full from side to
side—
From Portnasun to Bulliebawns, and round the Abbey
Bay,
From rocky Inis Saimer to Coolnargit sandhills grey;
While far upon the southern line, to guard it like a
wall,
The Leitrim mountains, clothed in blue, gaze calmly
over all,

And watch the ship sail up or down, the red flag at her stern;—
Adieu to these, adieu to all the winding banks of Erne!

4

Farewell to you, Kildoney lads, and them that pull an oar,
A lug-sail set, or haul a net, from the Point to Mullaghmore;
From Killybegs to bold Slieve-League, that ocean-mountain steep,
Six hundred yards in air aloft, six hundred in the deep;
From Dooran to the Fairy Bridge, and round by Tullen strand,
Level and long, and white with waves, where gull and curlew stand;—
Head out to sea when on your lee the breakers you discern!—
Adieu to all the billowy coast, and winding banks of Erne!

5

Farewell Coolmore,—Bundoran! and your summer crowds that run
From inland homes to see with joy th' Atlantic-setting sun;
To breathe the buoyant salted air, and sport among the waves;
To gather shells on sandy beach, and tempt the gloomy caves;
To watch the flowing, ebbing tide, the boats, the crabs, the fish;
Young men and maids to meet and smile, and form a tender wish;

The sick and old in search of health, for all things have
  their turn—
And I must quit my native shore, and the winding
  banks of Erne!

6

Farewell to every white cascade from the Harbour to
  Belleek,
And every pool where fins may rest, and ivy-shaded
  creek;
The sloping fields, the lofty rocks, where ash and holly
  grow,
The one split yew-tree gazing on the curving flood
  below;
The Lough, that winds through islands under Turaw
  mountain green;
And Castle Caldwell's stretching woods, with tranquil
  bays between;
And Breesie Hill, and many a pond among the heath
  and fern,—
For I must say adieu—adieu to the winding banks of
  Erne!

7

The thrush will call through Camlin groves the live-
  long summer day;
The waters run by mossy cliff, and bank with wild
  flowers gay;
The girls will bring their work and sing beneath a
  twisted thorn,
Or stray with sweethearts down the path among the
  growing corn;
Along the river side they go, where I have often
  been,—
O, never shall I see again the days that I have seen!

A thousand chances are to one I never may return,—
Adieu to Ballyshannon, and the winding banks of
Erne!

8

Adieu to evening dances, when merry neighbours
meet,
And the fiddle says to boys and girls, 'Get up and
shake your feet!'
To 'shanachus'[1] and wise old talk of Erin's days gone
by—
Who trench'd the rath on such a hill, and where the
bones may lie
Of saint, or king, or warrior chief; with tales of fairy
power,
And tender ditties sweetly sung to pass the twilight
hour.
The mournful song of exile is now for me to learn—
Adieu, my dear companions on the winding banks of
Erne!

9

Now measure from the Commons down to each end of
the Purt,
Round the Abbey, Moy, and Knather,—I wish no one
any hurt;
The Main Street, Back Street, College Lane, the Mall,
and Portnasun,
If any foes of mine are there, I pardon every one.
I hope that man and womankind will do the same by
me;
For my heart is sore and heavy at voyaging the sea.
My loving friends I'll bear in mind, and often fondly
turn
To think of Ballyshannon, and the winding banks of
Erne.

[1] *Shanachus*, old stories,—histories, genealogies.

10

If ever I'm a money'd man, I mean, please God, to cast
My golden anchor in the place where youthful years were pass'd;
Though heads that now are black and brown must meanwhile gather grey,
New faces rise by every hearth, and old ones drop away—
Yet dearer still that Irish hill than all the world beside;
It's home, sweet home, where'er I roam, through lands and waters wide.
And if the Lord allows me, I surely will return
To my native Ballyshannon, and the winding banks of Erne.

Sunday Bells

SWEET Sunday Bells! your measured sound
Enhances that repose profound
Of all the golden fields around,
And range of mountain, sunshine-drown'd.

Amid the cluster'd roofs outswells,
And wanders up the winding dells,
And near and far its message tells,
Your holy song, sweet Sunday Bells!

Sweet Sunday Bells! ye summon round
The youthful and the hoary-crown'd,
To one observance gravely bound;
Where comfort, strength, and joy are found.

The while, your cadenced voice excels
To waken memory's tender spells;
Revives old joy-bells, funeral-knells,
And childhood's far-off Sunday Bells.

O Sunday Bells! your pleading sound
The shady spring of tears hath found,
In one whom neither pew nor mound
May harbour in the hallow'd ground:

Whose heart to your old music swells;
Whose soul a deeper thought compels;
Who like an alien sadly dwells
Within your chime, sweet Sunday Bells!

Among the Heather

(An Irish Song)

1

One evening walking out, I o'ertook a modest *colleen*,
When the wind was blowing cool, and the harvest leaves were falling.
'Is our road, by chance, the same? Might we travel on together?'
'O, I keep the mountain side, (she replied) among the heather.'

2

'Your mountain air is sweet when the days are long and sunny,
When the grass grows round the rocks, and the whin-bloom smells like honey;

But the winter's coming fast, with its foggy, snowy
weather,
And you'll find it bleak and chill on your hill, among
the heather.'

3

She praised her mountain home: and I'll praise it too,
with reason,
For where Molly is, there's sunshine and flow'rs at
every season.
Be the moorland black or white, does it signify a
feather,
Now I know the way by heart, every part, among the
heather?

4

The sun goes down in haste, and the night falls thick
and stormy;
Yet I'd travel twenty miles to the welcome that's
before me;
Singing hi for Eskydun, in the teeth of wind and
weather!
Love'll warm me as I go through the snow, among the
heather.

In a Spring Grove

Here the white-ray'd anemone is born,
Wood-sorrel, and the varnish'd buttercup;
And primrose in its purfled green swathed up,
Pallid and sweet round every budding thorn,
Gray ash, and beech with rusty leaves outworn.
Here, too, the darting linnet hath her nest
In the blue-lustred holly, never shorn,

Whose partner cheers her little brooding breast,
Piping from some near bough. O simple song!
O cistern deep of that harmonious rillet,
And these fair juicy stems that climb and throng
The vernal world, and unexhausted seas
Of flowing life, and soul that asks to fill it,
Each and all these,—and more, and more than these!

The Mowers

WHERE mountains round a lonely dale
Our cottage-roof enclose,
Come night or morn, the hissing pail
With fragrant cream o'erflows;
And roused at break of day from sleep,
And cheerly trudging hither,—
A scythe-sweep, and a scythe-sweep,
We mow the grass together.

The fog drawn up the mountain-side
And scatter'd flake by flake,
The chasm of blue above grows wide,
And richer blue the lake;
Gay sunlights o'er the hillocks creep,
And join for golden weather,—
A scythe-sweep, and a scythe-sweep,
We mow the dale together.

The goodwife stirs at five, we know,
The master soon comes round,
And many swaths must lie a-row
Ere breakfast-horn shall sound;

Sweet vernal-grass, and foxtail deep,
  The spike or silvery feather,—
A scythe-sweep, and a scythe-sweep,
  We mow them down together.

The noon-tide brings its welcome rest
  Our toil-wet brows to dry;
Anew with merry stave and jest
  The shrieking hone we ply.
White falls the brook from steep to steep
  Among the rocks and heather,—
A scythe-sweep, and a scythe-sweep,
  We mow the dale together.

For dial, see, our shadows turn;
  Low lies the stately mead:
A scythe, an hour-glass, and an urn—
  All flesh is grass, we read.
To-morrow's sky may laugh or weep,
  To Heav'n we leave it whether:
A scythe-sweep, and a scythe-sweep,
    We've done our task together.

An Evening

A SUNSET'S mounded cloud;
  A diamond evening-star;
  Sad blue hills afar;
    Love in his shroud.

Scarcely a tear to shed;
  Hardly a word to say;
  The end of a summer day;
    Sweet Love dead.

Nanny's Sailor Lad

Now fare-you-well! my bonny ship,
For I am for the shore.
The wave may flow, the breeze may blow,
They'll carry me no more.

And all as I came walking
And singing up the sand,
I met a pretty maiden,
I took her by the hand.

But still she would not raise her head,
A word she would not speak,
And tears were on her eyelids,
Dripping down her cheek.

Now grieve you for your father?
Or husband might it be?
Or is it for a sweetheart
That's roving on the sea?

It is not for my father,
I have no husband dear,
But oh! I had a sailor lad
And he is lost, I fear.

Three long years
I am grieving for his sake,
And when the stormy wind blows loud,
I lie all night awake.

I caught her in my arms,
And she lifted up her eyes,
I kiss'd her ten times over
In the midst of her surprise.

Cheer up, cheer up, my Nanny
And speak again to me;
O dry your tears, my darling,
For I'll go no more to sea.

I have a love, a true true love,
And I have golden store,
The wave may flow, the breeze may blow,
They'll carry me no more!

In Snow

O English mother, in the ruddy glow
Hugging your baby closer when outside
You see the silent, soft, and cruel snow
Falling again, and think what ills betide
Unshelter'd creatures,—your sad thoughts may go
Where War and Winter now, two spectre-wolves,
Hunt in the freezing vapour that involves
Those Asian peaks of ice and gulfs below.
Does this young Soldier heed the snow that fills
His mouth and open eyes? or mind, in truth,
To-night, *his* mother's parting syllables?
Ha! is't a red coat?—Merely blood. Keep ruth
For others; this is but an Afghan youth
Shot by the stranger on his native hills.

A Wealthy Man

All landscapes are his land;
His gold's in sky and sea;
Fair Idea his mistress,
Child of Eternity.

Earth's Night

EARTH'S night is where she rolls
 In her own shade;
And even thus the Soul's
 Dark hours are made.

Three Fragments

I

AND from a northern coast the Lovers watch'd
Midsummer sunset crimsoning the sea,
A bath of colours 'twixt the sky and sand
From east to furthest west. The ripple broke
Like azure flame along the level shore,
And every dimple, every ridge that nets
The glassy film was variably dyed
With floating brilliance of prismatic hues,
Green, orange, golden, exquisitely gay,
Like delicate music. Ever in the north
The dusking splendour crept behind the hills
Eastwards, and one cloud waited for the Dawn
To drink its fill of glory. To the beach,
Meanwhile, ran wave on wave in lovely sport,
Whispering a message to the dewy fields
Far-spread and hush'd beneath a dark-blue dome.

II

THE night a spongy dimness fill'd with moonshine,
Gray river-course, black boats based on their shadows,
The river, misty trees, the night, the world—
A sudden meteor in the zenith flew,
 As though great Night gave signal for some wonder;

Then all was still and motionless, no sound,
No stir in starry heav'n or dark earth under.

III

BLACK texture of the leafy trees, engraved
On the clear, solemn, pearly blue of dawn;
No bird as yet awake, no star asleep,
Though some look drowsy.
Ocean lies tranquil in the arms of night,
Uncurtain'd by Dawn's airy heralds; far
On every hand, up to the mountain mist,
Fields, hills, and cots, and every forest brake
Slumber in dew.

Fragment

—you see
Nestled into a hollow of the downs,
Where sheep stray widely o'er the short green turf,
A little gray-wall'd church with lichen'd roof;
A farmyard and a huge old barn whose stacks
O'er-top the spire, the farmhouse lattices
Embower'd with vine; a figtree'd garden wall;
And one clump of rook-nested elms above
Gables and red tiled roofs and twisted chimneys.

Fragment

THE wing'd seeds with decaying wings
That lie upon the cold moist ground
Know this mild breath is heavenly Spring's.

And every germen hath unwound
His little coil of green, and put
A pale point forth, a timid shoot
A slowly clasping spreading root,
A rising stem, a twig, a bud,
A thousand veins of pure green blood
Through breathing leaves, to stand one day,
When suns and moons have roll'd away,
A new Tree bearing flow'rs and fruit,
And many seeds like that one seed.

A Mill

Two leaps the water from its race
Made to the brook below,
The first leap it was curving glass,
The second bounding snow.

Fragment

Near where the riotous Atlantic surge
Booms heavily in storm, far-heard at night,
And flings ashore the bones of murder'd ships,
Or, in a gentler time, the milky wave,
The whispering weary wave, lies down to rest,
Lives a calm Well of water, a large Spring,
Pure and perennial. Often have I watch'd
Its crystal heart with ever tremulous pulse
Dim the green lining of the hollow'd sand,
Thick-platted cress within a spacious cup
Full at the solstice and for ever cold,
A soft pulsation scarcely to be heard

Save by a loving ear. Whole caravans
Creeping in torture through a burning waste
By one such Fount were saved. But here it brims,
With purest overflow for barefoot girls
Who tread the mossy track to dip their pails
Into the lonely Spring—

from

Laurence Bloomfield in Ireland

BALLYTULLAGH

THE hamlet Ballytullagh, small and old,
Lay negligently cluster'd in a fold
Of Tullagh Hill, among the crags and moor;
A windy dwelling-place, rough, lonesome, poor;
So low and weather-stain'd the walls, the thatch
So dusk of hue, or spread with mossy patch,
A stranger journeying on the distant road
Might hardly guess that human hearts abode
In those wild fields, save when a smoky wreath
Distinguish'd from huge rocks, above, beneath,
Its huddled roofs. A lane goes up the hill,
Cross'd, at one elbow, by a crystal rill,
Between the stepping-stones gay tripping o'er
In shallow brightness on its gravelly floor,
From crags above, with falls and rocky urns,
Through sward below, in deep deliberate turns,
Where each fine evening brought the boys to play
At football, or with *camuns* drive away
The whizzing *nagg*; a crooked lane and steep,
Older than broad highways, you find it creep,
Fenced in with stooping thorn-trees, bramble-brakes,
Tall edge-stones, gleaming, gay as spotted snakes,

With gold and silver lichen; till it bends
Between two rock-based rough-built gable ends,
To form the street, if one may call it street,
Where ducks and pigs in filthy forum meet;
A scrambling, careless, tatter'd place, no doubt;
Each cottage rude within-doors as without;
All rude and poor; some wretched,—black and bare
And doleful as the cavern of Despair.
  And yet, when crops were good, nor oatmeal high,
A famine or a fever-time gone by,
The touch of simple pleasures, even here,
In rustic sight and sound the heart could cheer.
With voice of breezes moving o'er the hills,
Wild birds and four-foot creatures, falling rills,
Mingled the hum of huswife's wheel, cock-crow,
The whetted scythe, or cattle's evening low,
Or laugh of children. Herding went the boy,
The sturdy diggers wrought with spade and *loy*,
The tether'd she-goat browsed the rock's green ledge,
The clothes were spread to dry on sloping hedge,
The *colleens* did their broidery in the shade
Of leafy bush, or gown-skirt overhead,
Or wash'd and *beetled* by the shallow brook,
Or sung their ballads round the chimney-nook
To speed a winter night, when song and jest
And dance and talk and social game are best:
For daily life's material good enough
Such trivial incidents and homely stuff.
Here also could those miracles befall
Of wedding, new-born babe, and funeral;
Here, every thought and mood and fancy rise
From common earth, and soar to mystic skies.

WILLIAM ALLINGHAM

THE LOUGH

AMONG those mountain-skirts a league away
Lough Braccan spread, with many a silver bay
And islet green; a dark cliff, tall and bold,
Half-muffled in its cloak of ivy old,
Bastion'd the southern brink, beside a glen
Where birch and hazel hid the badger's den,
And through the moist ferns and firm hollies play'd
A rapid rivulet from light to shade.
Above the glen, and wood, and cliff, was seen,
Majestically simple and serene,
Like some great soul above the various crowd,
A purple mountain top, at times in cloud
Or mist, as in celestial veils of thought,
Abstracted heavenward.
Creeps a little boat,
Along the path of evening's golden smile,
To where the shatter'd castle on its isle
May seem a broad-wing'd ship; two massive tow'rs
Lifted against the yellow light that pours
On half the lough and sloping fields,—half-laid,
Creek, bush, and crag, within the mountain shade.
Dark bramble-leaves now show a curling fringe,
And sallies wear the first autumnal tinge;
With speckled plumes high wave the crowded reeds,
Amongst whose watery stems the mallard feeds.

RUINS AT SUNSET

South-westward, where th' autumnal sun went
down,
A lake-reflected headland heaved its crown
Of darkling trees, and, knew you where to search,
The hoary ruins of a little church,
That mingled there with human skulls and bones
The mossy downfall of its sculptured stones;
While, like one poem scatheless and sublime
Amid the vast forgetfulness of Time,
Slender and tall a Round Tower's pointed crest
Rose dimly black against the gorgeous west.

IRISH HISTORY

Island of bitter memories, thickly sown
From winding Boyne to Limerick's treaty-stone,
Bare Connaught Hills to Dublin Castle wall,
Green Wexford to the glens of Donegal,
Through sad six hundred years of hostile sway,
From Strongbow fierce to cunning Castlereagh!
These will not melt and vanish in a day.
These can yet sting the patriot thoughts which turn
To Erin's past, and bid them weep and burn.

WILLIAM ALLINGHAM

SPRING

But haste we!—'Tis that merry time of year,
Once more brought round upon our whirling sphere,
(The days of darkness and of snow gone past,
Of chilly sunbeams and the freezing blast),
When eager skylarks at the gate of morn
Keep singing to the sower of the corn
In his brown field below; the noisy rooks
Hold council in the grove-top; shelter'd nooks
Bring forth young primroses and violets;
The woodland swarms with buds, the ash-tree sets
Dark lace upon his bough,—with tenderest green
The larch-spray tufted, pallid leaflets seen
Unfolding and uncrumpling day by day.
Nigh Croghan Hall the herons lean and grey
Hover and float upon those wide-spread wings
Around their lofty cradles, with the Spring's
Breath rocking slowly.

MIDSUMMER

Now early sink away the starry Twins,
Pursuing sunset; eastern heaven begins
To lift Arcturus, with that Coronet
Upon the brow of Summer glittering set;
And rich the country now, with shady roads
And hollow lanes embank'd with fern; white loads
Of fragrant hawthorn-bloom, but when this bloom
Grows fainter, bramble-roses in its room;
And sunny paths for milkmaids, winding through
The grass thick-set with yellow flow'rs and blue,
Millions of little blue and yellow flow'rs;
Rich are the warm, long, lustrous, golden hours,

That nourish the green javelins of the wheat,
The delicate flax, the tufted clover sweet,
And barley's drooping beard, and speckled oats.
The yorlin's trembling sigh of pleasure floats
On sultry wind; the landrails hoarse crake-crake
Still keeps the meadows and cornfields awake
When two clear twilights mingle in the sky
Of glowing June.

GIRLS GOING TO THE FAIR

'Tis where the road-side rivulet expands,
And every stone upon its image stands,
The country maidens finish their attire,
Screen'd by the network of a tangled briar;
On grassy bank their shapely limbs indue
With milk-white stocking and the well-black'd shoe,
And court that mirror for a final grace
With dazzling ribbons nodding round their face.
Behold our Bridget tripping to the fair;
Her shawl is splendid, but her feet are bare;
Till, quick the little bundle here untied,
The shoes come forth, the skirts are shaken wide,
And Biddy enters Lisnamoy in pride.

Four Ducks on a Pond

FOUR ducks on a pond,
A grass-bank beyond,
A blue sky of spring,
White clouds on the wing;
What a little thing
To remember for years—
To remember with tears!

The Maids of Elfin-Mere

WHEN the spinning-room was here,
Came Three Damsels, clothed in white,
With their spindles every night;
One and two and three fair Maidens,
Spinning to a pulsing cadence,
Spinning songs of Elfin-Mere;
Till the eleventh hour was toll'd,
Then departed through the wold.
Years ago, and years ago;
And the tall reeds sigh as the wind doth blow.

Three white Lilies, calm and clear,
And they were loved by every one;
Most of all, the Pastor's Son,
Listening to their gentle singing,
Felt his heart go from him, clinging
To these Maids of Elfin-Mere;
Sued each night to make them stay,
Sadden'd when they went away.
Years ago, and years ago;
And the tall reeds sigh as the wind doth blow.

Hands that shook with love and fear
Dared put back the village clock,—
Flew the spindle, turn'd the rock,
Flow'd the song with subtle rounding,
Till the false 'eleven' was sounding;
Then these Maids of Elfin-Mere
Swiftly, softly left the room,
Like three doves on snowy plume.
Years ago, and years ago;
And the tall reeds sigh as the wind doth blow.

One that night who wander'd near,
Heard lamentings by the shore,
Saw at dawn three stains of gore
In the waters fade and dwindle.
Never more with song and spindle
Saw we Maids of Elfin-Mere.
The Pastor's Son did pine and die;
Because true love should never lie.
Years ago, and years ago;
And the tall reeds sigh as the wind doth blow.

JEREMIAH JOSEPH CALLANAN
1795–1829

JEREMIAH JOSEPH CALLANAN
1795–1829

CALLANAN, about whose names there has been some confusion since he seems to have been baptized James, was born at Cork in 1795. Little is known of his childhood. He was educated locally until at about twenty, being intended for the Roman Catholic priesthood, he entered Maynooth College. Here, though he was a studious and sincere pupil, he came to the conclusion that he had no vocation for the Church. He therefore transferred to Dublin University where he vacillated between Medicine and the Law, and where he twice won the Vice-Chancellor's prize for verse.

All his brief life Callanan seems to have been dogged by a spirit of topographical inconstancy. He left Dublin after two years without taking a degree. He returned to Cork where he was unable to settle down and where he enlisted in the 18th Royal Irish Regiment then under orders for Malta. Like other poets—Dermody or Coleridge—he soon found that a soldier's life was unlikely ever to suit him and, at the last moment before he was due to go overseas, he prevailed on friends to buy him off.

For two years after leaving the army Callanan was private tutor in a family near Killarney. But evidently two years was the very limit to his endurance of any one place, and in 1822 he was back in Cork city doing nothing in particular. Next year, however, he got a job as a master in the school run by William Maginn, father of the famous wit.

This was one of Callanan's few fortunate moves;

for Maginn, recognizing his talent, not only encouraged him to write poems but got six of his translations from the Irish published in *Blackwood's Magazine*. Yet even regular work in such comparatively congenial conditions could not hold him for long. He abandoned schoolmastering and went to live by himself on the Island of Inchidony. He also wandered much about the countryside collecting Irish poems and legends from the peasantry. His vagrant but not dissolute life at last caused a breakdown in his health which by 1829 had become so serious that he again accepted a post as private tutor—this time to an Irish family in Lisbon.

At Lisbon he spent a few unhappy months, ill in body and desperately homesick. In September 1829 he set out once more for Cork, but he died in Portugal before his journey was well begun, and there he is buried.

Callanan wrote little and, during his lifetime published less. A thin volume of his *Collected Poems* was printed at Cork after his death. This book went through several editions but has long been out of print. In spite of the handicap of small output and publication in an Irish provincial town, Callanan's reputation has stood and stands extraordinarily high, not only in his own country but also in America and England. His longest and most ambitious work, *The Recluse of Inchidony*, is a respectable, rather Byronic poem in Spenserian stanzas. It contains some good landscape passages in the contemporary style. His other long poem *The Revenge of Donal Comm*, is no better and no worse than many a forgotten romance of the period dominated by Byron and Scott.

It is not on these long poems, but on his lyrics and particularly on his translations from the Irish that Callanan's reputation has always rested. Here he showed originality and genius. He was by no means the first to turn Gaelic poetry into English verse—Swift had attempted it, and towards the end of the eighteenth century the thing had been done on a large scale by Charlotte Brooke—but Callanan was the first to transmute not only the verbal meaning but also the rhythms, something of the emotional charge, and the alien spirit of the poems into English. By this very considerable achievement, in which he has never been surpassed, he shares with Tom Moore the credit of having started an independent Anglo-Irish literature. Swift and Goldsmith, Cunningham and Sheridan, were poets and Irishmen, but it is only our extreme poverty in Ireland that makes us claim them as Irish poets. Moore and Callanan, on the contrary, were the founders of a new tradition which, since their time, has never quite lost its first flavour or been entirely absorbed in the traditions of England.

J. J. CALLANAN

BIBLIOGRAPHY

Recluse of Inchidony, 1830.
Poems, 1861.

Written to A Young Lady

On entering a Convent

'Tis the rose of the desert,
So lovely so wild,
In the lap of the desert
It's infancy smiled;
In the languish of beauty
It droops o'er the thorn,
And its leaves are all wet
With the bright tears of morn.

Yet 'tis better thou fair one,
To dwell all alone,
Than recline on a bosom
Less pure than thine own;
Thy form is too lovely
To be torn from its stem,
And thy breath is too sweet
For the children of men.

Bloom on thus in secret,
Sweet child of the waste,
Where no lips of profaner,
Thy fragrance shall taste;
Bloom on where no footstep
Unhallowed hath trod,
And give all thy blushes
And sweets to thy God.

Pure is the Dewy Gem

Pure is the dewy gem that sleeps
Within the roses fragrant bed,

And dear the heart-warm drop that steeps
The turf where all we loved is laid;
But far more dear, more pure than they,
The tear that washes guilt away.

Sweet is the morning's balmy breath,
Along the valley's flowery side,
And lovely on the Moon-lit heath,
The lute's soft tone complaining wide;
But still more lovely, sweeter still,
The sigh that wails a life of ill.

Bright is the morning's roseate gleam
Upon the Mountains of the East,
And soft the Moonlight silvery beam,
Above the billow's placid rest;
But O!—what ray ere shone from Heaven
Like God's first smile on a soul forgiven.

Note.—This trifle was composed before the author read Moore's *Paradise and the Peri*.

To * * * * *

LADY—the lyre thou bid'st me take,
No more can breathe the minstrel strain;
The cold and trembling notes I wake,
Fall on the ear like plashing rain;
For days of suffering and of pain,
And nights that lull'd no care for me,
Have tamed my spirit—then in vain
Thou bid'st me wake my harp for thee.

But could I sweep my ocean lyre,
As once this feeble hand could sweep,

Or catch once more the thought of fire,
  That lit the Mizen's stormy steep,
Or bid the fancy cease to sleep,
  That once could soar on pinion free,
And dream I was not born to weep;
  O then I'd wake my harp for thee.

And now 'tis only friendship's call,
  That bids my slumbering lyre awake,
It long hath slept in sorrow's hall,
  Again that slumber it must seek;
Not even the light of beauty's cheek,
  Or blue eye beaming kind and free,
Can bid its mournful numbers speak;
  Then lady, ask no lay from me.

Yet if on Desmond's mountain wild,
  By glens I love, or ocean cave,
Nature once more should own her child,
  And give the strength that once she gave;
If he who lights my path should save
  And what I was I yet may be;
Then lady, by green Erin's wave,
  I'll gladly wake my harp for thee.

from

Serenade

i

THE blue waves are sleeping;
  The breezes are still;
The light dews are weeping
  Soft tears on the hill;

The moon in mild beauty,
   Looks bright from above;
Then come to the casement,
   Oh MARY, my love.

Not a sound, or a motion
   Is over the lake,
But the whisper of ripples,
   As shoreward they break;
My skiff wakes no ruffle
   The waters among,
Then listen, dear maid,
   To thy true lover's song.

ii

From the storms of this world
   How gladly I'd fly,
To the calm of that breast,
   To the heaven of that eye!
How deeply I love thee
   'Twere useless to tell;
Farewell, then, my dear one,
   My MARY, farewell.

When each Bright Star is Clouded

WHEN each bright star is clouded that illumin'd our
   way,
And darkly through the bleak night of life we stray,
What joy then is left us, but alone to weep
O'er the cold dreary pillow where loved ones sleep?

This world has no pleasure that is half so dear,
That can soothe the widow'd bosom like memory's
tear.
'Tis the desert rose drooping in moon's soft dew
In those pure drops looks saddest, but softest too.

Oh, if ever death should sever fond hearts from me,
And I linger like the last leaf on Autumn's tree,
While pining o'er the dead mates all sear'd below,
How welcome will the last blast be that lays me low.

Song

Awake thee, my Bessy, the morning is fair,
The breath of young roses is fresh on the air,
The sun has long glanced over mountain and lake,
Then awake from thy slumbers, my Bessy, awake.

Oh come whilst the flowers are still wet with the dew,
I'll gather the fairest, my Bessy, for you,
The lark poureth forth his sweet strain for thy sake,
Then awake from thy slumbers, my Bessy, awake.

The hare from her soft bed of heather hath gone,
The coote to the water already hath flown—
There is life on the mountain and joy on the lake,
Then awake from thy slumbers, my Bessy, awake.

Dirge of O'Sullivan Bear

THE sun upon Ivera
No longer shines brightly;
The voice of her music
No longer is sprightly;
No more to her maidens
The light dance is dear,
Since the death of our darling,
O'SULLIVAN Bear.

SCULLY! thou false one,
You basely betray'd him;
In his strong hour of need
When thy right hand should aid him;
He fed thee;—he clad thee;—
You had all could delight thee;
You left him;—you sold him;—
May Heaven requite thee!

SCULLY! may all kinds
Of evil attend thee;
On thy dark road of life
May no kind one befriend thee;
May fevers long burn thee,
And agues long freeze thee;
May the strong hand of God
In his red anger seize thee.

Had he died calmly,
I would not deplore him,
Or if the wild strife
Of the sea-war closed o'er him;
But with ropes round his white limbs,
Through ocean to trail him,

Like a fish after slaughter!—
'Tis therefore I wail him.

Long may the curse
Of his people pursue them;
SCULLY that sold him,
And soldier that slew him,
One glimpse of Heaven's light
May they see never;
May the hearth-stone of hell
Be their best bed for ever!

In the hole which the vile hands
Of soldier's had made thee,
Unhonoured, unshrouded,
And headless they laid thee;
No sigh to regret thee,
No eye to rain o'er thee,
No dirge to lament thee,
No friend to deplore thee.

Dear head of my darling,
How gory and pale,
These aged eyes saw thee
High spiked on their gaol;
That cheek in the summer sun
Ne'er shall grow warm,
Nor that eye e'er catch light,
But the flash of the storm.

A curse, blessed ocean,
Is on thy green water,
From the haven of Cork
To Ivera of slaughter,
Since the billows were dyed
With the red wounds of fear,

Of Muiertach Oge,
Our O'SULLIVAN Bear.

The Girl I Love

THE girl I love is comely, straight and tall,
Down her white neck her auburn tresses fall,
Her dress is neat, her carriage light and free—
Here's a health to that charming maid whoe'er she be!

The rose's blush but fades beside her cheek,
Her eyes are blue, her forehead pale and meek,
Her lips like cherries on a summer tree—
Here's a health to the charming maid who'er she be!

When I go to the field no youth can lighter bound,
And I freely pay when the cheerful jug goes round;
The barrel is full, but its heart we soon shall see—
Come here's to that charming maid whoe'er she be!

Had I the wealth that props the Saxon's reign,
Or the diamond crown that decks the King of Spain,
I'd yield them all if she kindly smiled on me—
Here's a health to the maid I love whoe'er she be!

Five pounds of gold for each lock of her hair I'd pay,
And five times five, for my love one hour each day;
Her voice is more sweet than the thrush on its own
green tree—
Then my dear may I drink a fond deep health to thee!

The Convict of Clonmel

How hard is my fortune
  And vain my repining;
The strong rope of fate
  For this young neck is twining!
My strength is departed,
  My cheeks sunk and sallow,
While I languish in chains
  In the gaol of Clonmala.

No boy of the village
  Was ever yet milder;
I'd play with a child
  And my sport would be wilder;
I'd dance without tiring
  From morning 'till even,
And the goal-ball I'd strike
  To the light'ning of Heaven.

At my bed foot decaying
  My hurl-bat is lying;
Through the boys of the village
  My goal-ball is flying;
My horse 'mong the neighbours
  Neglected may fallow,
While I pine in my chains
  In the gaol of Clonmala.

Next Sunday the patron[1]
  At home will be keeping,
And the young active hurlers
  The field will be sweeping;

[1] Patron,—Irish *Patruin,*—a festive gathering of the people on tented ground.

With the dance of fair maidens
  The evening they'll hallow,
While this heart once so gay
  Shall be cold in Clonmala.

The Outlaw of Loch Lene

O MANY a day have I made good ale in the glen,
That came not of stream, or malt, like the brewing of
  men.
My bed was the ground, my roof, the greenwood
  above,
And the wealth that I sought—one far kind glance
  from my love.

Alas! on that night when the horses I drove from
  the field,
That I was not near from terror my angel to shield.
She stretched forth her arms,—her mantle she flung to
  the wind,
And swam o'er Loch Lene, her outlawed lover to find.

O would that a freezing sleet-winged tempest did
  sweep,
And I and my love were alone far off on the deep!
I'd ask not a ship, or a bark, or pinnace to save,—
With her hand round my waist, I'd fear not the wind
  or the wave.

'Tis down by the lake where the wild tree fringes its
  sides,
The maid of my heart, the fair one of Heaven resides—
I think as at eve she wanders its mazes along,
The birds go to sleep by the sweet wild twist of her
  song.

AUBREY DE VERE
1814–1902

AUBREY DE VERE

1814–1902

Aubrey De Vere is one of those poets who, having been famous, for one reason or another, in their own day, continue to enjoy —if that is the right word—an academic reputation in ours. In any case, neither De Vere's life nor his poetry has ever been quite neglected. The facts of his life are indeed fairly well known from the number and eminence of his friends. He was born at Curragh Chase, County Limerick, in 1814; and he died there in his eighty-ninth year in 1902. During that long life he was the friend of Samuel Rodgers, Wordsworth, and Landor, of Tennyson and Newman, of Edmund Gosse and Von Hügel, and of almost every other poet or man of letters. He was a patriotic Irishman, devoted to his country, rejecting or at least mildly refusing to notice Landor's savage injunction—

Aubrey de Vere! Fling far aside all heed
Of that hyaena race whose growls and smiles
Alternate, and which neither blows nor food,
Nor stern nor gentle brow, domesticate.
Await some Cromwell, who alone hath strength
Of heart to dash down its wild wantonness,
And fasten its fierce grin with steady gaze . . .

During the great famine he worked indefatigably to alleviate its horrors, not only in his own district, but throughout Ireland. In middle life he became a Roman Catholic. He remained unmarried which, considering the insipidity of his love poems, is not surprising.

Edmund Gosse has left some record of him as he was at the age of eighty-four:

'He entered the room swiftly and gracefully, the front of his body thrown a little forward. His countenance bore a singular resemblance to the portraits of Wordsworth, although the type was softer and less vigorous . . . I never knew a more persistent speaker. The progress of a meal would be interrupted and delayed from the very first by his talk, which was softly, gently unbroken, like a fountain falling on mosses. On one occasion Mr. de Vere talked with no other interruption than brief pauses for reflection, for three hours . . . He possessed a maidenly vivacious brightness.'

Gosse's manners, not always of the best, seem to have stood the strain very fairly; and if there is a hint of acidity in his account, it should be forgiven.

As a poet, De Vere was prolific—far too prolific. He paradoxically admired, and even preferred, the duller areas of Wordsworth; and for sheer dullness he could easily outstrip his master. But he was not always being Wordsworthian. In his early books there is much charming poetry in the manner of Landor—an *Idyll* that would not be out of place among the *Hellenics*, and many poems that remind one of Landor and his Ianthe:

Psyche, I said, when thou art nigh,
Transpicuous grow the mists of years;
I cannot ever wholly die
If on my grave should drop thy tears . . .

delightful as a copy of verses, but hardly overwhelming, perhaps not even very exhilarating to the girl he was walking out with. Some of his early sonnets also are Wordsworthian in the best sense. But there can be no doubt that De Vere's best poetry is, for the most part, contained in his *Inisfail, A Lyrical Chronicle of Ireland*, published by Duffy of Dublin in 1862. This book is a kind of history of Ireland from legendary times down to De Vere's own day, each poem dealing with some episode, more or less well known, or with some imaginative reconstruction of a probable scene. Irish history being what it is, many of the poems are inevitably *Dirges*—a species of poetry for which there is no English model, and which therefore strikes on English ears with an original impact.

It is not, however, his Landorian, his Wordsworthian, nor his Irish poems that have proved the most popular. De Vere was a distinguished convert to the Roman Church—this fact is the central theme of his official biography by Wilfrid Ward—and after it he devoted, like Faber and Newman, a good deal of his time to the writing of hymns. These hymns have been much pushed forward by his admiring co-religionists and have done his reputation no good—though he has not suffered so badly as that remarkable poet F. W. Faber, who has been almost obliterated by the title 'hymnologist.' Actually, the chief fault of De Vere's religious poems is similar to that of his love poetry—it is difficult to believe that there was any very urgent emotion behind it. There is one exception, the *Dei Genitrix*, which will be found in the following selection.

It seems probable that Aubrey de Vere has a permanent if rather crepuscular place in virtue of his careful good-craftsmanship, his high seriousness, and his always unforced, unrhetorical utterance. There will always be a standard reference to him in textbooks. There will always be a poem or two by him in any representative anthology. But there seems no reason why the same three poems should always be printed—one can reasonably hope better for him than that, without at all demanding a collected edition of his works.

AUBREY DE VERE

BIBLIOGRAPHY

The Waldenses, 1842.
The Search after Proserpine, 1843.
Poems, 1855.
May Carols, 1857.
Inisfail, 1862.
The Infant Bridal, 1864.
St. Thomas of Canterbury, 1867.
The Legends of St. Patrick, 1872.
Alexander the Great, 1874.
Antar and Zara, 1877.
Legends of the Saxon Saints, 1879.
The Foray of Queen Maeve, 1882.
Legends and Records of the Church and the Empire, 1887.
St. Peter's Chains, 1888.
Mediaeval Records and Sonnets, 1893.
English Misrule and Irish Misdeeds (prose), 1848.
Picturesque Sketches of Greece and Turkey (prose), 1850.

Aubrey De Vere, A Memoir, by Wilfrid Ward, 1904.

The Wedding of the Clans

A Girl's Babble

I GO to knit two clans together;
  Our clan and this clan unseen of yore:—
Our clan fears nought! but I go, O whither?
  This day I go from my mother's door.

Thou redbreast sing'st the old song over,
  Though many a time thou hast sung it before;
They never sent thee to some strange new lover:—
  I sing a new song by my mother's door.

I stepp'd from my little room down by the ladder,
  The ladder that never so shook before;
I was sad last night; to-day I am sadder,
  Because I go from my mother's door.

The last snow melts upon bush and bramble;
  The gold bars shine on the forest's floor;
Shake not, thou leaf! it is I must tremble
  Because I go from my mother's door.

From a Spanish sailor a dagger I bought me;
  I trail'd a rose-tree our grey bawn o'er;
The creed and my letters our old bard taught me;
  My days were sweet by my mother's door.

My little white goat that with raised feet huggest
  The oak stock, thy horns in the ivies frore,
Could I wrestle like thee—how the wreaths thou
    tuggest!—
  I never would move from my mother's door.

Oh weep no longer, my nurse and mother!
My foster-sister, weep not so sore!
You cannot come with me, Ir, my brother—
Alone I go from my mother's door.

Farewell, my wolf-hound, that slew Mac Owing
As he caught me and far through the thickets bore:
My heifer, Alb, in the green vale lowing,
My cygnet's nest upon Lorna's shore!

He has kill'd ten chiefs, this chief that plights me;
His hand is like that of the giant Balor:
But I fear his kiss; and his beard affrights me,
And the great stone dragon above his door.

Had I daughters nine with me they should tarry;
They should sing old songs; they should dance at my door;
They should grind at the quern;—no need to marry;
Oh when will this marriage-day be o'er?

Had I buried, like Moirin, three mates already
I might say, 'Three husbands! then why not four?'
But my hand is cold and my foot unsteady
Because I never was married before!

Epilogue

AT my casement I sat by night, while the wind remote in dark valleys
Voluminous gather'd and grew, and waxing swell'd to a gale:

An hour I heard it or more ere yet it sobb'd on my lattice:
Far off, 'twas a People's moan; hard by, but a widow's wail.

To God there is fragment none: nothing single; no isolation:
The ages to Him are one; round Him the woe, and the wrong
Roll like a spiritual star, and the cry of the desolate Nation:
The Souls that are under the Altar respond in music 'how long?'

By the casement I sat alone till sign after sign had descended:
The Hyads rejoin'd their sea, and the Pleiads by fate were down borne:
And then with that distant dirge a tenderer anthem was blended,
And, glad to behold her young, the bird gave thanks to the morn.

Florence MacCarthy's Farewell to his English Love

We seem to tread the self-same street,
To pace the self-same courts or grass;
Parting, our hands appear to meet:
O vanitatum vanitas!

Distant as earth from heaven or hell
From thee the things to me most dear:

Ghost-throng'd Cocytus and thy will
  Between us rush. We might be near.

Thy world is fair: my thoughts refuse
  To dance its dance or drink its wine;
Nor canst thou hear the reeds and yews
  That sigh to me from lands not thine.

The Dirge of Kildare

A.D. 1595

THE North wind clanged on the sharp hill-side:
The mountain muttered: the cloud replied;
'There is one rides up through thy woods, Tyrone!
That shall ride on a bier of the pine branch down.'

The flood roars over Danara's bed:
'Twas green at morning: to-night 'tis red:
What whispers the raven to oak and cave?
'Make ready the bier and make ready the grave.'

Kildare, Kildare! Thou hast left the bound
Of hawk and heron, of hart and hound;
With the hunters art come to the Lion's lair:
He is mighty of limb and old. Beware!

Beware, for on thee that eye is set
Which looked upon Norreys at Clontibret:
And that hand is lifted, from horse to heath
Which hurled the giant they mourn in Meath!

Kildare, Kildare! There are twain this hour
With brows turned north from Maynooth's grey
  tower:
The mother sees nought: the bride shall see
The Herald and Death-flag far off—not thee.

The Sea-Watcher

I

The crags lay dark in strange eclipse:
  From waves late flushed the glow was gone:
The topsails of the far-off ships
  Alone in lessening radiance shone:
Against a stranded boat a maid
  Stood leaning, gunnel to her breast,
As though some pain that pressure stayed:
  Her large eyes rested on the west.

II

'Beyond the sea! beyond the sea!
  The weeks, the months, the years go by!
Ah! when will some one say of me
  "Beyond the sky! beyond the sky!"
And yet I would not have thee here
  To look upon thy country's shame:
For me the tear: for me the bier:
  Free hearth for thee, and honest fame.'

The Friendly Blight

I

A March-wind sang in a frosty wood,
'Twas in Oriel's land on a mountain brown,
While the woodsman stared at the hard black bud,
And the sun through mist went down:
'Not always,' it sang, 'shall triumph the wrong,
For God is stronger than man, they say:'
(Let no man tell of the March-wind's song
Till comes the appointed day.)

II

'Sheaf after sheaf upon Moira's plain,
And snow upon snow on the hills of Mourne!
Full many a harvest-moon must wane,
Full many a Spring return!
The right shall triumph at last o'er wrong:
Yet none knows how, and none the day:'—
The March-wind sang; and bit 'mid the song
The little black bud away.

III

'Blow south-wind on through my vineyard blow!'
So pray'd that land of the palm and vine;
O Eire, 'tis the north-wind and wintry snow
That strengthen thine oak and pine!
The storm breaks oft upon Uladh's hills;
Oft falls the wave on the stones by Saul;
In God's time cometh the thing God wills,
For God is the Lord of all!

Dirge of Rory O'More

A.D. 1642

UP the sea-sadden'd valley at evening's decline
A heifer walks lowing; 'the silk of the kine';[1]
From the deep to the mountain she roams, and again
From the mountains' green urn to the purple-rimm'd
  main.

Whom seek'st thou, sad Mother! Thine own is not
  thine!
He dropp'd from the headland; he sank in the brine!
'Twas a dream! but in dream at thy foot did he follow
Through the meadow-sweet on by the marish and
  mallow!

Was he thine? Have they slain him? Thou seek'st him,
  not knowing
Thyself too art theirs, thy sweet breath and sad lowing!
Thy gold horn is theirs; thy dark eye, and thy silk!
And that which torments thee, thy milk, is their milk!

'Twas no dream, Mother Land! 'Twas no dream,
  Inisfail!
Hope dreams, but grief dreams not—the grief of the
  Gael!
From Leix and Ikerren to Donegal's shore
Rolls the dirge of thy last and thy bravest—O'More!

[1]One of the mystical names for Ireland used by the bards.

Dirge

A.D. 1652

I

WHOSE were they those voices? What footsteps came near me?
  Can the dead to the living draw nigh and be heard?
I wept in my sleep; but ere morning to cheer me
  Came a breeze from the woodland, a song from the bird.
O sons of my heart! the long-hair'd the strong-handed!
  Your phantoms rush by me with war-cry and wail:—
Ye too for your Faith and your Country late banded,
  My sons by adoption, mail'd knights of the Pale!

II

Is there sorrow, O ye that pass by, like my sorrow?
  Of the kings I brought forth there remaineth not one!
Each day is dishonour'd; disastrous each morrow:—
  In the yew-wood I couch till the day-light is done.
At midnight I lean from the cliff o'er the waters,
  And hear, as the thunder comes up from the sea,
Your moanings, my sons, and your wailings, my daughters:
  With the sea-dirge they mix not: they clamour to me!

In Ruin Reconciled

I HEARD a woman's voice that wailed
  Between the sandhills and the sea:
The famished sea-bird past me sailed
  Into the dim infinity.

I stood on boundless, rainy moors:
  Far off I saw a great Rock loom;
The grey dawn smote its iron doors;
  And then I knew it was a Tomb.

Two queenly shapes before the grate
  Watched, couchant on the barren ground;
Two regal shades in ruined state,
  One Gael, one Norman; both discrowned.

Parvuli Ejus

IN the night, in the night, O my Country, the stream calls out from afar:
  So swells thy voice through the ages, sonorous and vast:
In the night, in the night, O my Country, clear flashes the star:
  So flashes on me thy face through the gloom of the past.

I sleep not; I watch: in blows the wind ice-wing'd, and ice-finger'd:
  My forehead it cools and slakes the fire in my breast;

Though it sighs o'er the plains where oft thine exiles look'd back, and long linger'd,
And the graves where thy famish'd lie dumb and thine outcasts find rest.

For up from those vales wherein thy brave and thy beautiful moulder,
And on through the homesteads waste and the temples defiled,
A voice goes forth on that wind, as old as the Islands and older,
'God reigns: at His feet earth's Destiny sleeps like a child.'

Religio Novissima

THERE is an Order by a northern sea,
Far in the West, of rule and life more strict
Than that which Basil rear'd in Galilee,
In Egypt Paul, in Umbria Benedict.

Discalced it walks; a stony land of tombs,
A strange Petræa of late days, it treads!
Within its court no high-tossed censer fumes;
The night-rain beats its cells, the wind its beds.

Before its eyes no brass-bound, blazon'd tome
Reflects the splendour of a lamp high-hung:
Knowledge is banish'd from her earliest home
Like wealth: it whispers psalms that once it sung.

It is not bound by the vow celibate,
Lest, through its ceasing, anguish too might cease;

In sorrow it brings forth; and Death and Fate
  Watch at Life's gate, and tithe the unripe increase.

It wears not the Franciscan's sheltering gown;
  The cord that binds it is the Stranger's chain:
Scarce seen for scorn, in fields of old renown
  It breaks the clod; another reaps the grain.

Year after year it fasts; each third or fourth
  So fasts that common fasts to it are feast;
Then of its brethren many in the earth
  Are laid unrequiem'd like the mountain beast.

Where are its cloisters? Where the felon sleeps!
  Where its novitiate? Where the last wolf died!
From sea to sea its vigil long it keeps—
  Stern Foundress! is its Rule not mortified?

Thou that hast laid so many an Order waste,
  A Nation is thine Order! It was thine
Wide as a realm that Order's seed to cast,
  And undispensed sustain its discipline!

Song

THE little Black Rose shall be red at last!
  What made it black but the East wind dry,
And the tear of the widow that fell on it fast?
  It shall redden the hills when June is nigh!

The Silk of the Kine shall rest at last!
  What drave her forth but the dragon-fly?
In the golden vale she shall feed full fast
  With her mild gold horn, and her slow dark eye.

The wounded wood-dove lies dead at last:
The pine long-bleeding, it shall not die!
—This song is secret. Mine ear it pass'd
In a wind o'er the stone plain of Athenry.

The Year of Sorrow

IRELAND—1849

SPRING

ONCE more, through God's high will and grace
Of hours that each its task fulfils,
Heart-healing Spring resumes its place;—
The valley throngs and scales the hills,

In vain. From earth's deep heart o'ercharged,
The exulting life runs o'er in flowers;—
The slave unfed is unenlarged:
In darkness sleep a Nation's powers.

Who knows not Spring? Who doubts, when blows
Her breath, that Spring is come indeed?
The swallow doubts not; nor the rose
That stirs, but wakes not; nor the weed.

I feel her near, but see her not;
For these with pain uplifted eyes
Fall back repulsed; and vapours blot
The vision of the earth and skies.

I see her not—I feel her near,
As, charioted in mildest airs,
She sails through yon empyreal sphere,
And in her arms and bosom bears

That urn of flowers and lustral dews,
  Whose sacred balm, o'er all things shed,
Revives the weak, the old renews,
  And crowns with votive wreaths the dead.

Once more the cuckoo's call I hear;
  I know in many a glen profound
The earliest violets of the year
  Rise up like water from the ground.

The thorn I know once more is white;
  And far down many a forest dale
The anemones in dubious light
  Are trembling like a bridal veil.

By streams released that singing flow
  From craggy shelf, through sylvan glades,
The pale narcissus, well I know,
  Smiles hour by hour on greener shades.

The honeyed cowslip tufts once more
  The golden slopes; with gradual ray
The primrose stars the rock, and o'er
  The wood-path strews its milky way.

From ruined huts and holes come forth
  Old men, and look on yonder sky!
The Power Divine is on the earth:
  Give thanks to God before ye die!

And ye, O children worn and weak,
  Who care no more with flowers to play,
Lean on the grass your cold, thin cheek,
  And those slight hands, and whispering, say,

'Stern mother of a race unblest,
In promise kindly, cold in deed!—
Take back, O Earth, into thy breast,
The children whom thou wilt not feed.'

WINTER

FALL, snow, and cease not! Flake by flake
The decent winding-sheet compose;
Thy task is just and pious; make
An end of blasphemies and woes.

Fall flake by flake! by thee alone,
Last friend, the sleeping draught is given;
Kind nurse, by thee the couch is strown—
The couch whose covering is from heaven.

Descend and clasp the mountain's crest;
Inherit plain and valley deep:
This night, in thy maternal breast.
A vanquished nation dies in sleep.

Lo! from the starry Temple gates
Death rides, and bears the flag of peace;
The combatants he separates;
He bids the wrath of ages cease.

Descend, benignant Power! But O,
Ye torrents, shake no more the vale;
Dark streams, in silence seaward flow;
Thou rising storm, remit thy wail.

Shake not, to-night, the cliffs of Moher,
  Nor Brandon's base, rough sea! Thou Isle,
The rite proceeds! From shore to shore,
  Hold in thy gathered breath the while.

Fall, snow! in stillness fall, like dew,
  On temple's roof and cedar's fan;
And mould thyself on pine and yew,
  And on the awful face of man.

Without a sound, without a stir,
  In streets and wolds, on rock and mound,
O omnipresent Comforter,
  By thee, this night, the lost are found!

On quaking moor, and mountain moss,
  With eyes upstaring at the sky,
And arms extended like a cross,
  The long-expectant sufferers lie.

Bend o'er them, white-robed Acolyte!
  Put forth thine hand from cloud and mist,
And minister the last sad rite,
  Where altar there is none, nor priest.

Touch thou the gates of soul and sense;
  Touch darkening eyes and dying ears;
Touch stiffening hands and feet, and thence
  Remove the trace of sin and tears:

And ere thou seal those filmed eyes,
  Into God's urn thy fingers dip,
And lay, 'mid eucharistic sighs,
  The sacred wafer on the lip.

This night the Absolver issues forth:
This night the Eternal Victim bleeds:
O winds and woods—O heaven and earth!
Be still this night. The rite proceeds!

Urania

URANIA! Voice of Heaven, sidereal Muse!
Lo, through the dark vault issuing from afar,
She comes, reclining on a lucid star.
Her large eyes, trembling through celestial dews,
The glory of high thoughts far off diffuse;
While the bright surges of her refluent hair
Stream back, upraised upon sustaining air
Which lifts that scarf deep dyed in midnight hues
To a wide arch above her hung like heaven.
—I closed my eyes. Athwart me, like a blast,
Music as though of jubilant gods was driven.
Once more I gazed. That form divine had passed
Earth's dark confine. The ocean's utmost rim
Burned yet a moment: then the world grew dim.

Spring Song

HOLD on, hold on, while yet ye can,
Old oak-leaves red and sere;
Hold on, and clasp in narrow span
The sunset of last year!

Your boast is just; yet, ancient friends,
Forgive me if at times

On that green beech my glance descends.
On that white thorn my rhymes.

The rookery from the wintry woods
Clanged like a cataract's roar:
Each eve our closed eyes saw great floods
O'er rocky barriers pour;

But now the linnet or the thrush
So shakes with treble clear
Yon apple bloom—that alder bush,
No meaner sound we hear!

'Tis true when Winter's furrowed brow
Through snow-drifts lowered, we praised
Those hollies, grim and threatening now,
And dark though sunshine-glazed.

But constant who to such could be,
And this young Spring resist,
Who flings her arms round every tree,
Nor leaves a bud unkissed?

Dusk cedar drest in rusty vest
Through every season worn,
Thou stand'st the Mayday's wedding guest,
Yet treat'st the bride with scorn.

Thy part I take:—yet be not vexed
If, here and there, I throw
A random glance to see where next
Yon butterfly will go!

Glauce

I LOVE you, pretty maid, for you are young:
I love you, pretty maid, for you are fair:
I love you, pretty maid, for you love me.

They tell me that, a babe, smiling you gazed
Upon the stars, with open, asking eyes,
And tremulous lips apart. Erelong, self-taught,
You found for every star and every flower
Legends and names and fables sweet and new.
I, since I loved you, am grown half immortal.

O that when far away I still might see thee!
How oft when wearied with the din of life
On thee mine eyes would rest, thy Latmian heavens
Brightening that orbèd brow and those white shoulders!
Hesper should shine upon thee—lamp of Love,
Beneath whose radiance thou wert born.—O Hesper!
Thee will I love and reverence evermore.—
Bind up that shining hair into a knot,
And let me see that polished neck of thine
Uprising from the bed snow-soft snow-white
In which it rests so gracefully! What God
Hath drawn upon thy forehead's ivory plane
Those two clear streaks of sweet and glistening black
Lifted in earnest mirth or lovely awe?
Open those Pleiad eyes, liquid and tender,
And let me lose myself among their depths!
Caress me with thine infant hands, and tell me
Old tales divine that love makes ever new
Of Gods and men entoiled in flowery nets,
Of heroes sighing all their youth away,
And which the fairest flower of Venus' isle.
  Come forth, dear maid, the day is calm and cool,

And bright though sunless. Like a long green scarf,
The tall Pines crowning yon gray promontory
In distant ether hang, and cut the sea.
But lovers better love the dell, for there
Each is the other's world.—How indolently
The tops of those pale poplars bending sway
Over the violet-braided river brim!
Whence comes their motion, for no wind is heard,
And the long grasses move not, nor the reeds?
Here we will sit, and watch the rushes lean
Like locks, along the leaden-coloured stream
Far off; and thou, O child, shalt talk to me
Of Naiads and their loves. A blissful life
They lead, who live beneath the flowing waters:
They cherish calm, and think the sea-weeds fair;
They love to sleek their tresses in the sun;
They love each other's beauty; love to stand
Among the lillies, holding back their tresses
And listening, with their gentle cheek reclined
Upon the flood, to some sweet melody
Of Pan or shepherd piping in lone woods,
Until the unconscious tears run down their face.
Mild are their loves, nor burdensome their thoughts—
And would that such a life were mine and thine!

Ione

IONE, fifteen years have o'er you passed,
And, taking nothing from you in their flight,
Have given you much. You look like one for whom
The day has morning only, time but Spring.
Your eyes are large and calm, your lips serene,
As if no Winter with your dreams commingled,
You that dream always, or that never dream.

Dear maid, you should have been a shepherdess—
But no: ill tended then your flocks had strayed.
Young fawns you should have led; such fawns as once
The quivered Queen had spared to startle! Then
Within your hand a willow wand, your brow
Wreathed with red roses dabbled in warm rains,
How sweetly, with half-serious countenance,
Through the green alleys had you ta'en your way!
And they, your spotted train, how happily
Would they have gambolled by you—happiest she
The milk-white creature in the silver chain!

Ione, lay the tapestry down: come forth—
No golden ringlet shall you add this morn
To bright Apollo: and poor Daphne there!
Without her verdant branches she must rest
Another day—a cruel tale, sweet girl!
You will not? Then farewell our loves for ever!
We are too far unlike: not Cyclops more
Unlike that Galatea whom he courted.
I love the loud-resounding sea divine;
I love the wintry sunset, and the stress
Inexorable of wide-wasting storms;
I love the waste of foam-washed promontories,
Thunder, and all portentous change that makes
The mind of mortals like to suns eclipsed
Waning in icy terrors. These to you
Are nothing. On the ivied banks you lie
In deep green valleys where the noontide dew
Chills the dusk ground, and twilight ever reigns.
There bathe your feet in bubbling springs—your
 hands
Playing with the moist pansies near your face.

These bowers are musical with nightingales
Morning and noon and night. Among these rocks

A lovely life is that you lead; but I
Will make it lovelier with some pretty gift
If you are constant to me. A boat I'll make,
Scooped from a pine; yourself shall learn to row it
Swifter than winds or sounds can fleet; or else
Your scarf shall be the sail, and you shall glide,
While the stars drop their light upon the bay,
On like a bird between the double heaven.
Are these but trivial joys? Ah me! fresh leaves
Gladden the forests, but no second life
Invests our branches; feathers new make bright
The birds, but when our affluent locks desert us
No Spring restores them; dried-up streams once more
The laughing Nymphs replenish, but man's life,
By fate drawn down and smothered in the sands,
Never looks up. Alas, my sweet Ione,
Alcæus also loved; but in his arms
No longer now reclines the Lesbian maid:
The indignant hand attesting Gods and men
Achilles lifts no more; to dust is turned
His harp that glittered through the wild sea spray,
Though the black wave falls yet on Ilion's shore.
All things must die—the Songs themselves, except
The devout hymn of grateful love; or hers,
The wild swan's, chanting her death melody.

Song

I

Softly, O midnight Hours!
Move softly o'er the bowers
Where lies in happy sleep a girl so fair!
For ye have power, men say,

Our hearts in sleep to sway,
And cage cold fancies in a moonlight snare.
Round ivory neck and arm
Enclasp a separate charm:
Hang o'er her poised; but breathe nor sigh nor prayer.
Silently ye may smile,
But hold your breath the while,
And let the wind sweep back your cloudy hair!

2

Bend down your glittering urns
(Ere yet the dawn returns)
And star with dew the lawn her feet shall tread;
Upon the air rain balm;
Bid all the woods be calm;
Ambrosial dreams with healthful slumbers wed.
That so the Maiden may
With smiles your care repay
When from her couch she lifts her golden head;
Waking with earliest birds,
Ere yet the misty herds
Leave warm 'mid the gray grass their dusky bed.

Song

He found me sitting among flowers,
My Mother's, and my own;
Whiling away too happy hours
With songs of doleful tone.

My Sister came, and laid her book
Upon my lap; and he,
He too into the page would look,
And asked no leave of me.

The little frightened creature laid
  Her face upon my knee—
'Deftly thou teachest, pretty maid;
  And I would fain teach thee.'

He taught me Joy more blest, more brief
  Than that mild vernal weather:
He taught me Love; he taught me Grief:
  He taught me both together.

Give me a sun-warmed nook to cry in,
  And a wall-flower's perfume;
A nook to cry in, and to die in,
  'Mid the Ruin's gloom.

Lines

You drop a tear for those that die:
To me, yet living, grant a sigh.
Surely they rest: no rest have I.

The sighing wind dies on the tree.
I cannot sigh: sigh thou for me.
The broken heart is sadly free.

You bid me say what I would have,
Will one flower serve? or do I crave
A wreath—to decorate a grave?

Fling poppies on the grave of Youth:
Fling pansies on the tomb of Truth;—
On mine to-morrow morn fling both.

All day I sat below your gate,
My spirit calmed by its own weight;
Then Sorrow grew importunate.

I rose, and on the steps I writ
These fragments of a wildered wit;—
To be erased beneath your feet.

Erase them, haughty feet—I live!
I wished, not hoped that you might grieve.
You can forget: ah then, forgive!

Incompatibility

FORGIVE me that I love you as I do,
Friend patient long; too patient to reprove
The inconvenience of superfluous love.
You feel that it molests you, and 'tis true.
In a light bark you sit, with a full crew.
Your life full orbed, compelled strange love to
  meet,
Becomes, by such addition, incomplete:—
Because I love I leave you. O adieu!
Perhaps when I am gone the thought of me
May sometimes be your acceptable guest.
Indeed you love me: but my company
Old time makes tedious; and to part is best.
Not without Nature's will are natures wed:—
O gentle Death, how dear thou makest the dead!

Troilus and Cressida

HAD I been worthy of the love you gave,
That love withdrawn had left me sad but strong;
My heart had been as silent as my tongue,
My bed had been unfevered as my grave;
I had not striven for what I could not save;
Back, back to heaven my great hopes I had flung;
To have much suffered, having done no wrong,
Had seemed to me that noble part the brave
Account it ever. What this hour I am
Affirms the unworthiness that in me lurked:
Some sapping poison through my substance worked,
Some sin not trivial, though it lacked a name,
Which ratifies the deed that you have done
With plain approval. Other plea seek none.

Flowers I would bring

FLOWERS I would bring if flowers could make thee
fairer,
And music if the Muse were dear to thee,
(For loving these would make thee love the bearer);
But sweetest songs forget their melody,
And loveliest flowers would but conceal the wearer:
A rose I marked, and might have plucked; but she
Blushed as she bent, imploring me to spare her,
Nor spoil her beauty by such rivalry.
Alas! and with what gifts shall I pursue thee,
What offerings bring, what treasures lay before thee,
When earth with all her floral train doth woo thee,
And all old poets and old songs adore thee,

And love to thee is naught; from passionate mood
Secured by joy's complacent plenitude.

The Mighty Mountain Plains

THE mighty mountain plains have we two trod
Both in the glow of sunset and sunrise;
And lighted by the moon of southern skies
The snow-white torrent of the thundering flood
We two have watched together: In the wood
We two have felt the warm tears dim our eyes
While zephyrs softer than an infant's sighs
Ruffled the light air of our solitude.
O Earth, maternal Earth, and thou O Heaven,
And Night first born, who now, e'en now, dost waken
The host of stars, thy constellated train,
Tell me if those can ever be forgiven,
Those abject, who together have partaken
These Sacraments of Nature—and in vain?

May Carols

I

WHO feels not, when the Spring once more,
  Stepping o'er Winter's grave forlorn
With winged feet retreads the shore
  Of widowed Earth, his bosom burn?

As ordered flower succeeds to flower,
  And May the ladder of her sweets

Ascends, advancing hour by hour
  From scale to scale, what heart but beats?

Some Presence veiled, in fields and groves,
  That mingles rapture with remorse,
Some buried joy beside us moves,
  And thrills the soul with such discourse

As they, perchance, that wondering pair
  Who to Emmaus bent their way,
Hearing, heard not: like them our prayer
  We make—'The night is near us . . Stay!'

With Paschal chants the churches ring,
  Their echoes strike along the tombs;
The birds their Hallelujahs sing;
  Each flower with floral incense fumes.

Our long-lost Eden seems restored;
  As on we move with tearful eyes
We feel through all the illumined sward
  Some upward-working Paradise.

VI

The night through yonder cloudy cleft,
  With many a lingering last regard,
Withdraws—but slowly—and hath left
  Her mantle on the dewy sward.

The lawns with silver dews are strown;
  The winds lie hushed in cave and tree;
Nor stirs a flower, save one alone
  That bends beneath the earliest bee.

Peace over all the garden broods;
  Pathetic sweets the thickets throng;
Like breath the vapour o'er the woods
  Ascends—dim woods without a song—

Or hangs, a shining fleecelike mass
  O'er half yon lake that winds afar
Among the forests, still as glass,
  The mirror of that Morning Star.

Which, half way wandering from the sky,
  Amid the crimson East delays
And (large and less alternately)
  Bends down a lustrous, tearful gaze.

Fair Planet! Home of spirits blest!
  Bright gate of Heaven and golden bower!
Thy best of blessings, love and rest,
  Depart not till on earth thou shower!

Festum Nativitatis

PRIMEVAL night had repossessed
  Her empire in the fields of space;
Calm lay the kine on earth's dark breast;
  The earth lay calm in heaven's embrace.

That hour, where shepherds kept their flocks,
  From God a glory sudden fell:
The splendour smote the trees and rocks,
  And lay, like dew, along the dell.

God's angel close beside them stood:
  'Fear nought,' that angel said, and then,

'Behold, I bring you tidings good:
  The Saviour Christ is born to men.'

And straightway round him myriads sang
  Again that anthem, and again,
Till all the hollow valley rang,
  'Glory to God, and peace to men.'

Thus in the violet-scented grove,
  The May breeze murmuring softly by them,
The children sang. Who Mary love
  The long year through have Christmas nigh them!

Dei Genitrix

I SEE Him: on thy lap He lies
  'Mid that Judean stable's gloom:
O sweet, O awful Sacrifice!
  He smiles in sleep, yet knows the doom.

Thou gav'st Him life! But was not this
  That life which knows no parting breath?
Unmeasured life? unwaning bliss?
  Dread priestess, lo! thou gav'st Him death!

Beneath the Tree thy Mother stood;
  Beneath the Cross thou too shalt stand:
O Tree of Life! O bleeding Rood!
  Thy shadow stretches far its hand.

That God who made the sun and moon
  In swaddling bands lies dumb and bound!
Love's Captive! darker prison soon
  Awaits Thee in the garden ground.

He wakens, Paradise looks forth
   Beyond the portals of the grave.
Life, life thou gavest! life to earth,
   Not Him. Thine Infant dies to save.

SIR SAMUEL FERGUSON
1810–1886

SIR SAMUEL FERGUSON

1810–1886

Of all poets, except perhaps Browning, Samuel Ferguson was the most inconspicuously normal. He was born of upper middle-class parents at Belfast in 1810. He was educated at the Belfast Academical Institution and at Trinity College, Dublin, where he read Law—being called to the Irish Bar in 1838. For the next thirty years or so he practised as a successful Counsel and then retired to become Deputy Keeper at the Dublin Record Office—a job which thoroughly suited him. At intervals he published books of poems and books on antiquarian and historical subjects. He married well and happily, was elected President of the Royal Irish Academy ('he possesses in an eminent degree the graces appropriate to such a dignity', wrote Sir Robert Ball the astronomer), received various honorary degrees and, in 1878, the crowning honour of Knighthood. 'I think it will be a pleasure to you to know', he says in a letter to Allingham, 'that I have received the honour of Knighthood, and that the distinction is given as well on literary as on official grounds.'

However that may be, Allingham entered in his Diary when Ferguson died in 1886 that among the obituary notices there was 'not one word or hint of his poetry or other writings . . . no London paper speaks of Ferguson as a man of letters'. To which Mrs. Allingham adds a note doubting 'whether his work is better known in England in 1911 than it was in 1886'. And what was true in 1911 is probably true still. He is not included in Ward's 'English Poets', though he gets thirteen pages in that mausoleum of mediocrity, *The Oxford Book of Victorian Verse.* His poems, in common with those of almost every Irish poet since Goldsmith, have never been collected—nor in his case is there the smallest reason why they should be.

All the same, Ferguson, though neglected in England and America, is certainly not negligible and has always had the ear of his own countrymen. He deliberately chose to publish in Ireland, even in Belfast, to encourage the Irish book trade, when he might quite well have found publishers in London; and in other ways too he seems to have been careless of his literary reputation. Indeed, it is probable that most often he preferred to think of himself as an antiquary rather than as a poet.

Ferguson's poetry, so far as its mode and mood go, holds a middle place as a kind of connecting link between Mangan, Callanan, and the 'Celtic note' school on the one side, and the more anglicized verse of Allingham and De Vere on the other. He almost always chose Irish themes and he was a successful translator from the Irish; but even most of his translations, apart from occasional Gaelic refrains, could take a place in any English anthology without calling attention to themselves—a thing that very few poems by Mangan could do.

This 'protective colouration' has proved of poor survival value to Ferguson. He is less well known than Mangan not because his poetry is less good but because to the English ear it is less unusual. He was a more ambitious poet than Mangan in that he several times attempted the long poem—never quite successfully. Of these narrative poems *The Welshmen of Tirawley* is the best. The story is well and economically told: it is by its insecure metrics and ill-chosen stanza form that the poem fails. The Welshmen of

Tirawley in Connaught were offered the choice of castration or blinding and they chose blinding—

> *For 'tis neither in eye nor eyesight that a man*
> *Bears the fortunes of himself and his clan,*
> *But in the manly mind.*
> And in loins with vengeance lined,
> *That your needles could never find*
>   *Though they ran*
>   *Through my heart-strings!*
> *Sing the vengeance of the Welshmen of Tirawley.*

It was a tricky theme for those days and Ferguson managed it with such delicacy that he changed the line in roman to the botched inversion of *These darkened orbs behind*. Again, his long epic, *Congal*, would have been more readable and more read if he had written it in the heroic blank verse of which one is tempted to say that it cannot go wrong.

Ferguson is, then, no exception to the rule that Irish poets must stand upon their short poems. Of these he left a sufficient number. They have always an honesty and frequently a felicity which will commend them in any Victorian revival.

SIR SAMUEL FERGUSON

BIBLIOGRAPHY

The Cromlech on Howth, 1864.
Lays of the Western Gael, 1865.
Congal, 1872.
Poems, 1880.
Deirdre, 1880.
The Forging of the Anchor, 1883.
The Remains of St. Patrick, 1888.

Lays of the Red Branch, 1897.
Poems, edited by A. P. Graves, 1918.

Ogham Inscriptions in Ireland, Wales, and Scotland (prose), 1887.
Sir Samuel Ferguson, by Lady Ferguson, 1896.

The Burial of King Cormac

'Crom Cruach and his sub-gods twelve,'
Said Cormac, 'are but carven treene;
The axe that made them, haft or helve,
Had worthier of our worship been.

'But He who made the tree to grow,
And hid in earth the iron-stone,
And made the man with mind to know
The axe's use, is God alone.'

Anon to priests of Crom was brought—
Where, girded in their service dread,
They minister'd on red Moy Slaught—
Word of the words King Cormac said.

They loosed their curse against the king;
They cursed him in his flesh and bones;
And daily in their mystic ring
They turn'd the maledictive stones,

Till, where at meat the monarch sate,
Amid the revel and the wine,
He choked upon the food he ate,
At Sletty, southward of the Boyne.

High vaunted then the priestly throng,
And far and wide they noised abroad
With trump and loud liturgic song
The praise of their avenging God.

But ere the voice was wholly spent
That priest and prince should still obey,

To awed attendants o'er him bent
  Great Cormac gather'd breath to say,—

'Spread not the beds of Brugh for me
  When restless death-bed's use is done:
But bury me at Rossnaree
  And face me to the rising sun.

'For all the kings who lie in Brugh
  Put trust in gods of wood and stone;
And 'twas at Ross that first I knew
  One, Unseen, who is God alone.

'His glory lightens from the east;
  His message soon shall reach our shore;
And idol-god, and cursing priest
  Shall plague us from Moy Slaught no more.

Dead Cormac on his bier they laid:—
  'He reign'd a king for forty years,
And shame it were,' his captains said,
  'He lay not with his royal peers.

'His grandsire, Hundred-Battle, sleeps
  Serene in Brugh: and, all around,
Dead kings in stone sepulchral keeps
  Protect the sacred burial ground.

'What though a dying man should rave
  Of changes o'er the eastern sea?
In Brugh of Boyne shall be his grave,
  And not in noteless Rossnaree.'

Then northward forth they bore the bier,
  And down from Sletty side they drew,

With horsemen and with charioteer,
  To cross the fords of Boyne to Brugh.

There came a breath of finer air
  That touch'd the Boyne with ruffling wings,
It stirr'd him in his sedgy lair
  And in his mossy moorland springs.

And as the burial train came down
  With dirge and savage dolorous shows,
Across their pathway, broad and brown
  The deep, full-hearted river rose;

From bank to bank through all his fords,
  'Neath blackening squalls he swell'd and boil'd;
And thrice the wondering gentile lords
  Essay'd to cross, and thrice recoil'd.

Then forth stepp'd grey-hair'd warriors four;
  They said, 'Through angrier floods than these,
On link'd shields once our king we bore
  From Dread-Spear and the hosts of Deece.

'And long as loyal will holds good,
  And limbs respond with helpful thews,
Nor flood, nor fiend within the flood,
  Shall bar him of his burial dues.'

With slanted necks they stoop'd to lift;
  They heaved him up to neck and chin;
And, pair and pair, with footsteps swift,
  Lock'd arm and shoulder, bore him in.

'Twas brave to see them leave the shore:
  To mark the deep'ning surges rise,

And fall subdued in foam before
  The tension of their striding thighs.

'Twas brave, when now a spear-cast out,
  Breast-high the battling surges ran;
For weight was great, and limbs were stout,
  And loyal man put trust in man.

But ere they reach'd the middle deep,
  Nor steadying weight of clay they bore,
Nor strain of sinewy limbs could keep
  Their feet beneath the swerving four.

And now they slide, and now they swim,
  And now, amid the blackening squall,
Grey locks afloat, with clutching grim,
  They plunge around the floating pall.

While, as a youth with practised spear
  Through justling crowds bears off the ring,
Boyne from their shoulders caught the bier
  And proudly bore away the king.

At morning, on the grassy marge
  Of Rossnaree, the corpse was found,
And shepherds at their early charge
  Entomb'd it in the peaceful ground.

A tranquil spot: a hopeful sound
  Comes from the ever youthful stream,
And still on daisied mead and mound
  The dawn delays with tenderer beam.

Round Cormac Spring renews her buds:
  In march perpetual by his side,

Down come the earth-fresh April floods,
And up the sea-fresh salmon glide;

And life and time rejoicing run
From age to age their wonted way;
But still he waits the risen Sun,
For still 'tis only dawning Day.

The Death of Dermid

FINN on the mountain found the mangled man,
The slain boar by him. 'Dermid,' said the king,
'It likes me well at last to see thee thus.
This only grieves me, that the womankind
Of Erin are not also looking on:
Such sight were wholesome for the wanton eyes
So oft enamour'd of that specious form:
Beauty to foulness, strength to weakness turn'd.'
'Yet in thy power, if only in thy will,
Lies it, oh Finn, even yet to heal me.'

'How?'

'Feign not the show of ignorance, nor deem
I know not of the virtues which thy hand
Drew from that fairy's half-discover'd hall,
Who bore her silver tankard from the fount,
So closely follow'd, that ere yet the door
Could close upon her steps, one arm was in;
Wherewith, though seeing nought, yet touching all,
Thou grasped'st half the spiritual world;
Withdrawing a heap'd handful of its gifts,—
Healing, and sight prophetic, and the power
Divine of poesy: but healing most

Abides within its hollow:—virtue such
That but so much of water as might wet
These lips, in that hand brought, would make me
whole.
Finn, from the fountain fetch me in thy palms
A draught of water, and I yet shall live.'

'How at these hands canst thou demand thy life,
Who took'st my joy of life?'

'She loved thee not:
Me she did love and doth; and were she here
She would so plead with thee, that, for her sake,
Thou wouldst forgive us both, and bid me live.'

'I was a man had spent my prime of years
In war and council, little bless'd with love;
Though poesy was mine, and, in my hour,
The seer's burthen not desirable;
And now at last had thought to have a man's share
Of marriage blessings; and the King supreme,
Cormac, had pledged his only daughter mine;
When thou, with those pernicious beauty-gifts,
The flashing white tusk there hath somewhat spoil'd,
Didst win her to desert her father's house,
And roam the wilds with thee.'

'It was herself,
Grania, the Princess, put me in the bonds
Of holy chivalry to share her flight.
"Behold," she said, "he is an aged man,
(And so thou art, for years will come to all;)
And I, so young; and at the Beltane games,
When Carbry Liffacher did play the men
Of Brea, I, unseen, saw thee snatch a hurl,

And thrice on Tara's champions win the goal;
And gave thee love that day, and still will give."
So she herself avow'd. Resolve me, Finn,
For thou art just, could youthful warrior, sworn
To maiden's service, have done else than I?
No: hate me not—restore me—give me drink.'

'I will not.'

'Nay, but, Finn, thou hadst not said
"I will not," though I'd ask'd a greater boon,
That night we supp'd in Breendacoga's lodge.
Remember: we were faint and hunger-starved
From three day's flight; and even as on the board
They placed the viands, and my hand went forth
To raise the wine-cup, thou, more quick of ear,
O'erheardst the stealthy leaguer set without;
And yet should'st eat or perish. Then 'twas I,
Fasting, that made the sally; and 'twas I,
Fasting, that made the circuit of the court;
Three times I cours'd it, darkling, round and round;
From whence returning, when I brought thee in
The three lopp'd heads of them that lurk'd without—
Thou hadst not then, refresh'd and grateful, said
"I will not," had I ask'd thee, "Give me drink." '

'There springs no water on this summit bald.'

'Nine paces from the spot thou standest on,
The well-eye—well thou knowest it—bubbles clear.'

Abash'd, reluctant, to the bubbling well
Went Finn, and scoop'd the water in his palms;
Wherewith returning, half-way, came the thought
Of Grania, and he let the water spill.

'Ah me,' said Dermid, 'hast thou then forgot
Thy warrior-art that oft, when helms were split,
And buckler-bosses shatter'd by the spear,
Has satisfied the thirst of wounded men?
Ah, Finn, these hands of thine were not so slack
That night, when, captured by the king of Thule,
Thou sayest in bonds within the temple gate
Waiting for morning, till the observant king
Should to his sun-god make thee sacrifice.
Close-pack'd thy fingers then, thong-drawn and
squeezed,
The blood-drops oozing under every nail,
When, like a shadow, through the sleeping priests
Came I, and loos'd thee: and the hierophant
At day-dawn coming, on the altar-step,
Instead of victim straighten'd to his knife,
Two warriors found, erect, for battle arm'd.'

Again abash'd, reluctant to the well
Went Finn, and scoop'd the water in his palms,
Wherewith returning, half-way, came the thought
That wrench'd him; and the shaken water spill'd.

'False one, thou didst it purposely! I swear
I saw thee, though mine eyes do fast grow dim.
Ah me, how much imperfect still is man!
Yet such were not the act of Him, whom once
On this same mountain, as we sat at eve—
Thou yet mayst see the knoll that was our couch,
A stone's throw from the spot where now I lie—
Thou showedst me, shuddering, when the seer's fit,
Sudden and cold as hail, assail'd thy soul
In vision of that Just One crucified
For all men's pardoning, which, once again,
Thou sawest, with Cormac, struck in Rossnaree.'

Finn trembled; and a third time to the well
Went straight, and scoop'd the water in his palms;
Wherewith in haste half-way return'd, he saw
A smile on Dermid's face relax'd in death.

Pastheen Finn

Irish Rustic Song

OH, my fair Pastheen is my heart's delight,
Her gay heart laughs in her blue eye bright,
Like the apple blossom her bosom white,
And her neck like the swan's, on a March morn bright!
Then, Oro, come with me! come with me! come[1]
with me!
Oro, come with me! brown girl, sweet!
And, oh! I would go through snow and sleet,
If you would come with me, brown girl, sweet!

Love of my heart, my fair Pastheen!
Her cheeks are red as the rose's sheen,
But my lips have tasted no more, I ween,
Than the glass I drank to the health of my queen!
Then, Oro, come with me! come with me! come
with me!
Oro, come with me! brown girl, sweet!
And, oh! I would go through snow and sleet,
If you would come with me, brown girl, sweet!

Were I in the town, where's mirth and glee,
Or 'twixt two barrels of barley bree,
With my fair Pastheen upon my knee,
'Tis I would drink to her pleasantly!

[1] The emphasis is on 'come'.

Then, Oro, come with me! come with me! come
with me!
Oro, come with me! brown girl, sweet!
And oh! I would go through snow and sleet,
If you would come with me, brown girl, sweet!

Nine nights I lay in longing and pain,
Betwixt two bushes, beneath the rain,
Thinking to see you, love, once again;
But whistle and call were all in vain!
Then, Oro, come with me! come with me! come
with me!
Oro, come with me! brown girl, sweet!
And, oh! I would go through snow and sleet,
If you would come with me, brown girl, sweet!

I'll leave my people, both friend and foe;
From all the girls in the world I'll go;
But from you, sweetheart, oh, never! oh, no!
Till I lie in the coffin, stretch'd cold and low!
Then, Oro, come with me! come with me! come
with me!
Oro, come with me! brown girl, sweet!
And oh! I would go through snow and sleet,
If you would come with me, brown girl, sweet!

Molly Asthore

Irish Song

OH, Mary, dear, oh, Mary, fair,
Oh, branch of generous stem,
White blossom of the banks of Nair,
Though lilies grow on them!

You've left me sick at heart for love,
So faint I cannot see,
The candle swims the board above,
I'm drunk for love of thee!
Oh, stately stem of maiden pride,
My woe it is, and pain,
That I, thus sever'd from thy side,
The long night must remain!

Through all the towns of Inisfail
I've wander'd far and wide;
But from Downpatrick to Kinsale,
From Carlow to Kilbride,
'Mong lords and dames of high degree,
Where'er my feet have gone,
My Mary, one to equal thee
I've never look'd upon;
I live in darkness and in doubt
Whene'er my love's away,
But, were the blessed sun put out,
Her shadow would make day!

'Tis she indeed, young bud of bliss,
And gentle as she's fair,
Though lily-white her bosom is,
And sunny-bright her hair,
And dewy-azure her blue eye,
And rosy-red her cheek,—
Yet brighter she in modesty,
More beautifully meek!
The world's wise men from north to south
Can never cure my pain;
But one kiss from her honey mouth
Would make me whole again!

Cashel of Munster

Irish Rustic Ballad

I'D wed you without herds, without money, or rich array,
And I'd wed you on a dewy morning at day-dawn grey;
My bitter woe it is, love, that we are not far away
In Cashel town, though the bare deal board were our marriage-bed this day!

Oh, fair maid, remember the green hill side,
Remember how I hunted about the valleys wide;
Time now has worn me; my locks are turn'd to grey,
The year is scarce and I am poor, but send me not, love, away!

Oh, deem not my blood is of base strain, my girl,
Oh, deem not my birth was as the birth of the churl;
Marry me, and prove me, and say soon you will,
That noble blood is written on my right side still!

My purse holds no red gold, no coin of the silver white,
No herds are mine to drive through the long twilight!
But the pretty girl that would take me, all bare though I be and lone,
Oh, I'd take her with me kindly to the county Tyrone.

Oh, my girl, I can see 'tis in trouble you are,
And, oh, my girl, I see 'tis your people's reproach you bear:
'I am a girl in trouble for his sake with whom I fly,
And, oh, may no other maiden know such reproach as I!'

Ceann Dubh Deelish [1]

Irish Song

PUT your head, darling, darling, darling,
  Your darling black head my heart above;
Oh, mouth of honey, with the thyme for fragrance,
  Who, with heart in breast, could deny you love?
Oh, many and many a young girl for me is pining
  Letting her locks of gold to the cold wind free,
For me, the foremost of our gay young fellows;
  But I'd leave a hundred, pure love, for thee!
Then put your head, darling, darling, darling,
  Your darling black head my heart above;
Oh, mouth of honey, with the thyme for fragrance,
  Who, with heart in breast, could deny you love?

The Lapful of Nuts

From the Irish

WHENE'ER I see soft hazel eyes
  And nut-brown curls,
I think of those bright days I spent
  Among the Limerick girls;
When up through Cratla woods I went,
  Nutting with thee;
And we pluck'd the glossy clustering fruit
  From many a bending tree.

Beneath the hazel boughs we sat,
  Thou, love, and I,
And the gather'd nuts lay in thy lap,
  Beneath thy downcast eye:

[1] Pronounced *cawn dhu deelish*, i.e. dear black head.

But little we thought of the store we'd won,
  I, love, or thou;
For our hearts were full, and we dare not own
  The love that's spoken now.

Oh, there's wars for willing hearts in Spain,
  And high Germanie!
And I'll come back, ere long, again,
  With knightly fame and fee:
And I'll come back, if I ever come back,
  Faithful to thee,
That sat with thy white lap full of nuts
  Beneath the hazel tree.

Hopeless Love

From the Irish

SINCE hopeless of thy love I go,
Some little mark of pity show;
And only one kind parting look bestow.

One parting look of pity mild
On him, through starless tempest wild,
Who lonely hence to-night must go, exiled.

But even rejected love can warm
The heart through night and storm:
And unrelenting though they be,
Thine eyes beam life on me.

And I will bear that look benign
Within this darkly-troubled breast to shine,
Though never, never can thyself, ah me, be mine!

SIR SAMUEL FERGUSON

The Fair Hills of Ireland

Old Irish Song

A PLENTEOUS place is Ireland for hospitable cheer,
Uileacan dubh O!
Where the wholesome fruit is bursting from the yellow barley ear;
Uileacan dubh O!
There is honey in the trees where her misty vales expand,
And her forest paths, in summer, are by falling waters fann'd,
There is dew at high noontide there, and springs i'the yellow sand,
On the fair hills of holy Ireland.

Curl'd he is and ringletted, and plaited to the knee,
Uileacan dubh O!
Each captain who comes sailing across the Irish sea;
Uileacan dubh O!
And I will make my journey, if life and health but stand,
Unto that pleasant country, that fresh and fragrant strand,
And leave your boasted braveries, your wealth and high command,
For the fair hills of holy Ireland.

Large and profitable are the stacks upon the ground,
Uileacan dubh O!
The butter and the cream do wondrously abound,
Uileacan dubh O!
The cresses on the water and the sorrels are at hand,
And the cuckoo's calling daily his note of mimic bland,

And the bold thrush sings so bravely his song i'the
forests grand,
On the fair hills of holy Ireland.

The Forging of the Anchor

COME, see the Dolphin's anchor forged—'tis at a white
heat now:
The bellows ceased, the flames decreased though on the
forge's brow
The little flames still fitfully play through the sable
mound,
And fitfully you still may see the grim smiths ranking
round,
All clad in leathern panoply, their broad hands only
bare:
Some rest upon their sledges here, some work the
windlass there.

The windlass strains the tackle chains, the black
mound heaves below,
And red and deep a hundred veins burst out at every
throe:
It rises, roars, rends all outright—O, Vulcan, what a
glow!
'Tis blinding white, 'tis blasting bright—the high sun
shines not so!
The high sun sees not, on the earth, such fiery fearful
show,
The roof-ribs swarth, the candent hearth, the ruddy
lurid row
Of smiths that stand, an ardent band, like men before
the foe,

As, quivering through his fleece of flame, the sailing monster, slow
Sinks on the anvil:—all about the faces fiery grow;
'Hurrah!' they shout, 'leap out—leap out;' bang, bang the sledges go:
Hurrah! the jetted lightnings are hissing high and low—
A hailing fount of fire is struck at every squashing blow;
The leathern mail rebounds the hail, the rattling cinders strow
The ground around; at every bound the sweltering fountains flow,
And thick and loud the swinking crowd at every stroke pant 'ho!'
Leap out, leap out, my masters; leap out and lay on load!
Let's forge a goodly anchor—a bower thick and broad;
For a heart of oak is hanging on every blow, I bode;
I see the good ship riding all in a perilous road—
The low reef roaring on her lee—the roll of ocean pour'd
From stem to stern, sea after sea, the mainmast by the board,
The bulwarks down, the rudder gone, the boats stove at the chains!
But courage still, brave mariners—the bower yet remains,
And not an inch to flinch he deigns, save when ye pitch sky high;
Then moves his head, as though he said, 'Fear nothing—here am I.'
Swing in your strokes in order, let foot and hand keep time;
Your blows make music sweeter far than any steeple's chime:

But, while you sling your sledges, sing—and let the burthen be,
The anchor is the anvil-king, and royal craftsmen we!
Strike in, strike in—the sparks begin to dull their rustling red;
Our hammers ring with sharper din, our work will soon be sped.
Our anchor soon must change his bed of fiery rich array,
For a hammock at the roaring bows, or an oozy couch of clay;
Our anchor soon must change the lay of merry craftsmen here,
For the yeo-heave-o', and the heave-away, and the sighing seaman's cheer;
When, weighing slow, at eve they go—far, far from love and home;
And sobbing sweethearts, in a row, wail o'er the ocean foam.

In livid and obdurate gloom he darkens down at last:
A shapely one he is, and strong, as e'er from cat was cast:
O trusted and trustworthy guard, if thou hadst life like me,
What pleasures would thy toils reward beneath the deep green sea!
O deep-Sea-diver, who might then behold such sights as thou?
The hoary monster's palaces! methinks what joy 'twere now
To go plumb plunging down amid the assembly of the whales,
And feel the churn'd sea round me boil beneath their scourging tails!

Then deep in tangle-woods to fight the fierce sea unicorn,
And send him foil'd and bellowing back, for all his ivory horn:
To leave the subtle sworder-fish of bony blade forlorn;
And for the ghastly-grinning shark, to laugh his jaws to scorn:
To leap down on the kraken's back, where 'mid Norwegian isles,
He lies, a lubber anchorage for sudden shallow'd miles;
Till snorting, like an under-sea volcano, off he rolls;
Meanwhile to swing, a-buffeting the far astonished shoals
Of his back-browsing ocean-calves; or, haply, in a cove,
Shell-strown, and consecrate of old to some Undiné's love,
To find the long-hair'd mermaidens; or, hard by icy lands,
To wrestle with the Sea-serpent, upon cerulean sands.

O broad-arm'd Fisher of the deep, whose sports can equal thine?
The Dolphin weighs a thousand tons, that tugs thy cable line;
And night by night, 'tis thy delight, thy glory day by day,
Through sable sea and breaker white the giant game to play—
But shamer of our little sports! forgive the name I gave—
A fisher's joy is to destroy—thine office is to save.
O lodger in the sea-kings' halls, couldst thou but understand

Whose be the white bones by thy side, or whose that
 dripping band,
Slow swaying in the heaving waves, that round about
 thee bend,
With sounds like breakers in a dream blessing their
 ancient friend—
Oh, couldst thou know what heroes glide with larger
 steps round thee,
Thine iron side would swell with pride; thou'dst leap
 within the sea!
Give honour to their memories who left the pleasant
 strand,
To shed their blood so freely for the love of Father-
 land—
Who left their chance of quiet age and grassy church-
 yard grave,
So freely, for a restless bed amid the tossing wave—
Oh, though our anchor may not be all I have fondly
 sung,
Honour him for their memory, whose bones he goes
 among!

from

Bird and Brook

BIRD that pipest on the bough,
Would that I could sing as thou;
Runnel gurgling on beneath,
Would I owned thy liquid breath;
I would make a lovely lay
Worthy of the pure-bright day—

Worthy of the freshness spread
Round my path and o'er my head;
Of the unseen airs that rise
Incensing the morning skies
As from opening buds they spring
In the dew's evanishing—

Brighter yet, and even more clear
Than that blue encasing sphere,
Worthy of the gentle eyes
Opening on this paradise,
With their inner heavens as deep,
Fresh from youth's enchanted sleep—

Worthy of the voices sweet
That my daily risings greet,
And, to even-song addressed,
Ere we lay us down to rest,
Lift my spirit's laggard weight
Half-way to the heavenly gate—

I would make it with a dance
Of the rhythmic utterance,
With a gambit and retreat
Of the counter-trilling feet
And a frolic of the tone
To the song-bird only known.

With a soft transfusing fall
Would I make my madrigal,
Full as rills that, as they pass,
Shake the springing spikes of grass,
And that ample under-speech
Only running waters reach.

I would sing it loud and well,
Till the spirits of Amabel,
And of Ethel, from their nests,
Caught with new delicious zests
Of the soul's life out-of-door,
Forth should peep, and crave for more.

But, because I own not these,
Oh, ye mountains and ye trees,
Oh, ye tracts of heavenly air,
Voices sweet, and sweet eyes fair
Of my darlings, ye must rest
In my rhyme but half-expressed.

Paul Veronese: Three Sonnets

I

PAUL, let thy faces from the canvas look
  Haply less clearly than Pietro's can,
  Less lively than in tints of Titian,
Or him who both the bay-wreath-chaplets took:
Yet shalt thou therefore have no harsh rebuke
  Of me whom, while with eager eye I scan
  O'er painted pomps of Brera and Vatican,
The first delight thou gavest ne'er forsook.
For in thy own Verona, long ago,
  Before one masterpiece of cool arcades,
    I made a friend; and such a friend was rare.—
For him, I love thy velvet's glorious show,
  Thy sheens of silk 'twixt marble balustrades,
    Thy breathing-space and full translucent air.

II

Loved for themselves, too. Oft as I behold,
  Adown the curtain'd gallery's sumptuous gloom,
  A separate daylight shining in the room,
There find I still thy groupings manifold
Of holy clerks, of nobles grave and bold,
  Swart slaves, brave gallants, maidens in their
    bloom,
  With what of Persian and Ligurian loom
May best consort with marble dome and gold:
There find thy dog, whose teeth Time's teeth defy
  To raze the name from less enduring leaves
    Of loved Canossa: there, in cynic ease,
Thy monkey: and beneath the pearly sky
  See lovely ladies wave their handkerchiefs,
    And lend sweet looks from airy balconies.

III

They err who say this long-withdrawing line
  Of palace-fronts Palladian, this brocade
  From looms of Genoa, this gold-inlaid
Resplendent plate of Milan, that combine
To spread soft lustre through the grand design,
  Show but in fond factitious masquerade
  The actual feast by leper Simon made
For that great Guest, of old, in Palestine.
Christ walks amongst us still; at liberal table
  Scorns not to sit: no sorrowing Magdalene
    But of these dear feet kindly gets her kiss
Now, even as then; and thou, be honorable,
  Who, by the might of thy majestic scene,
    Bringest down that age and minglest it with this.

from

Deirdre

DEIRDRE

GIVE me my harp, and let me sing a song;
And, nurse, undo the fastenings of my hair;
For I would mingle tresses with the wind
From Etive side, where happy days were mine.

I

Harp, take my bosom's burthen on thy string,
And, turning it to sad, sweet melody,
Waste and disperse it on the careless air.

II

Air, take the harp-string's burthen on thy breast,
And, softly thrilling soulward through the sense
Bring my love's heart again in tune with mine.

III

Bless'd were the hours when, heart in tune with heart.
My love and I desired no happier home
Than Etive's airy glades and lonely shore.

IV

Alba, farewell! Farewell, fair Etive bank!
Sun kiss thee; moon caress thee; dewy stars
Refresh thee long, dear scene of quiet days!

Deirdre's Farewell to Alba

From the Irish

FAREWELL to fair Alba, high house of the Sun,
Farewell to the mountain, the cliff, and the Dun;
Dun Sweeny adieu! for my Love cannot stay,
And tarry I may not when love cries: 'Away!'

Glen Vashan! Glen Vashan! where roebucks run free,
Where my Love used to feast on the red deer with me,
Where rock'd on thy waters while stormy winds blew,
My Love used to slumber, Glen Vashan, adieu!

Glendaro! Glendaro! where birchen boughs weep
Honey dew at high noon o'er the nightingale's sleep,
Where my Love used to lead me to hear the cuckoo,
'Mong the high hazel bushes, Glendaro, adieu!

Glen Urchy! Glen Urchy! where loudly and long
My Love used to wake up the woods with his song,
While the Son of the Rock[1] from the depths of his dell
Laugh'd sweetly in answer, Glen Urchy, farewell!

Glen Etive! Glen Etive! where dappled does roam,
Where I leave the green sheeling I first call'd a home;
Where with me my true Love delighted to dwell,
And the Sun made his mansion. Glen Etive, farewell!

Farewell to Inch Draynach, adieu to the roar
Of the blue billow bursting in light on the shore;
Dun Fiagh, farewell! for my Love cannot stay,
And tarry I may not when love cries: 'Away!'

[1] Mac an Alla, i.e. Echo.

Deirdre's Lament for the Sons of Usnach

From the Irish

THE lions of the hill are gone,
And I am left alone—alone—
Dig the grave both wide and deep,
For I am sick, and fain would sleep!

The falcons of the wood are flown,
And I am left alone—alone—
Dig the grave both deep and wide,
And let us slumber side by side.

The dragons of the rock are sleeping,
Sleep that wakes not for our weeping:
Dig the grave and make it ready;
Lay me on my true Love's body.

Lay their spears and bucklers bright
By the warriors' sides aright;
Many a day the Three before me
On their linked bucklers bore me.

Lay upon the low grave floor,
'Neath each head, the blue claymore;
Many a time the noble Three
Redden'd those blue blades for me.

Lay the collars, as is meet,
Of their greyhounds at their feet;
Many a time for me have they
Brought the tall red deer to bay.

Oh! to hear my true Love singing,
Sweet as sound of trumpets ringing:

Like the sway of ocean swelling
Roll'd his deep voice round our dwelling.

Oh! to hear the echoes pealing
Round our green and fairy sheeling,
When the Three, with soaring chorus,
Pass'd the silent skylark o'er us.

Echo now, sleep, morn and even—
Lark alone enchant the heaven!—
Ardan's lips are scant of breath,—
Neesa's tongue is cold in death.

Stag, exult on glen and mountain—
Salmon, leap from loch to fountain
Heron, in the free air warm ye—
Usnach's Sons no more will harm ye!

Erin's stay no more you are,
Rulers of the ridge of war;
Never more 'twill be your fate
To keep the beam of battle straight.

Woe is me! by fraud and wrong—
Traitors false and tyrants strong—
Fell Clan Usnach, bought and sold,
For Barach's feast and Conor's gold!

Woe to Eman, roof and wall!—
Woe to Red Branch, hearth and hall!—
Tenfold woe and black dishonour
To the false and foul Clan Conor!

Dig the grave both wide and deep,
Sick I am, and fain would sleep!
Dig the grave and make it ready,
Lay me on my true Love's body.

Lament for the Death of Thomas Davis

I WALKED through Ballinderry in the springtime,
When the bud was on the tree,
And I said, in every fresh-ploughed field beholding
The sowers striding free,
Scattering broadcast for the corn in golden plenty,
On the quick, seed-clasping soil,
Even such this day among the fresh-stirred hearts of Erin
Thomas Davis, is thy toil!

I sat by Ballyshannon in the summer,
And saw the salmon leap,
And I said, as I beheld the gallant creatures
Spring glittering from the deep,
Through the spray and through the prone heaps striving onward
To the calm, clear streams above,
So seekest thou thy native founts of freedom, Thomas Davis,
In thy brightness of strength and love!

I stood on Derrybawn in the autumn,
I heard the eagle call,
With a clangorous cry of wrath and lamentation
That filled the wide mountain hall,
O'er the bare, deserted place of his plundered eyrie,
And I said, as he screamed and soared,
So callest thou, thou wrathful-soaring Thomas Davis,
For a nation's rights restored.

Young husbandman of Erin's fruitful seed-time,
In the fresh track of danger's plough!
Who will walk the heavy, toilsome, perilous furrow,

Girt with freedom's seed-sheets now?
Who will banish with the wholesome crop of knowledge
The flaunting weed and the bitter thorn,
Now that thou thyself art but a seed for hopeful planting
Against the resurrection morn?

Young salmon of the flood-time of freedom
That swells round Erin's shore,
Thou wilt leap against their loud, oppressive torrents
Of bigotry and hate no more!
Drawn downward by their prone material instinct,
Let them thunder on their rocks, and foam;
Thou hast leaped, aspiring soul, to founts beyond their raging,
Where troubled waters never come.

But I grieve not, eagle of the empty eyrie,
That thy wrathful cry is still,
And that the songs alone of peaceful mourners
Are heard to-day on Erin's hill.
Better far if brothers' wars are destined for us—
God avert that horrid day, I pray!—
That ere our hands be stained with slaughter fratricidal,
Thy warm heart should be cold in clay.

But my trust is strong in God who made us brothers,
That He will not suffer these right hands,
Which thou hast joined in holier rites than wedlock,
To draw opposing brands.
O many a tuneful tongue that thou madest vocal,
Would lie cold and silent then,

And songless long once more should often-widowed
Erin
Mourn the loss of her brave young men.

O brave young men, my love, my pride, my promise,
'Tis on you my hopes are set,
In manliness, in kindliness, in justice,
To make Erin a nation yet;
Self-respecting, self-relying, self-advancing,
In union or in severance, free and strong,
And if God grant this, then, under God, to Thomas
Davis
Let the greater praise belong!

from

Congal

'THE LAND IS OURS'

i

Look forth and say, 'Lo, on the left, from where
tumultuous Moyle
Heaves at Benmore's foot-fettering rocks with cease-
less surging toil,
And, half escaping from the clasp of that stark chain
of stone,
The soaring Foreland, poised aloft, as eagle newly
flown,
Hangs awful on the morning's brow, or rouses
armed Cantyre,
Red kindling 'neath the star of eve the Dalriad's warn-
ing fire;
South to the salt, sheep-fattening marsh and long-
resounding bay

Where young Cuchullin camped his last on dread
  Muirthevne's day;
And southward still to where the weird De Danaan
  kings lie hid,
High over Boyne, in cavern'd cairn and mountain
  pyramid;
And on the right hand from the rocks where Balor's
  bellowing caves
Up through the funnelled sea-cliffs shoot forth the
  exploding waves
South to where lone Gweebarra laves the sifted sands
  that strow
Dark Boylagh's banks; and southward still to where
  abrupt Eas-Roe
In many a tawny heap and whirl, by glancing salmon
  track't,
Casts down to ocean's oozy gulfs the great sea-
  cataract,
The land is ours!—from earth to sea, from hell to
  heaven above,
It and its increase, and the crown and dignity thereof!'

SIMILE

ii

No longer soiled with stain of earth, what seemed
  his mantle shone
Rich with innumerable hues refulgent, such as one
Beholds, and thankful-hearted he, who casts abroad
  his gaze
O'er some rich tillage-country-side, when mellow
  Autumn days
Gild all the sheafy foodful stooks; and broad before
  him spread,—
He looking landward from the brow of some great sea-
  cape's head,

Bray or Ben-Edar—sees beneath, in silent pageant grand,
Slow fields of sunshine spread o'er fields of rich, corn-bearing land;
Red glebe and meadow-margin green commingling to the view
With yellow stubble, browning woods, and upland tracts of blue;—
Then, sated with the pomp of fields, turns, seaward, to the verge
Where, mingling with the murmuring wash made by the far-down surge,
Comes up the clangorous song of birds unseen, that, low beneath,
Poised off the rock, ply underfoot; and, 'mid the blossoming heath,
And mint-sweet herb that loves the ledge rare-air'd, at ease reclined,
Surveys the wide pale-heaving floor crisped by a curling wind;
With all its shifting, shadowy belts, and chasing scopes of green,
Sun-strown, foam-freckled, sail-embossed, and blackening squalls between,
And slant, cerulean-skirted showers that with a drowsy sound,
Heard inward, of ebullient waves, stalk all the horizon round;
And haply, being a citizen just 'scaped from some disease
That long has held him sick indoors, now, in the brine-fresh breeze,
Health-salted, bathes; and says, the while he breathes reviving bliss,
'I am not good enough, oh God, nor pure enough for this!'—

THOMAS CAULFIELD IRWIN
1823–1892

THOMAS CAULFIELD IRWIN
1823–1892

THOMAS CAUFIELD IRWIN was born at Warrenpoint, Co. Down, in 1823. His father was a comparatively wealthy physician who was able to send his son travelling in Europe with a private tutor. The family fortune seems somehow to have been lost in 1848, and from then on T. C. Irwin had to earn his living by his pen. Though I have met people, still living, who knew him in his old age, it has been difficult to glean much about his life. From his writings one can deduce that he was married and had a son who died in childhood, that he was a classical scholar, a vegetarian, a pacifist, and that he travelled, not only in Europe, but also in Syria and North Africa. In his later life he became suspicious, acrimonious, squalid, and more than a little mad. He was fond of cats, and on June 16th, 1872, he issued the following advertisement:

'Robbery! One Pound Reward. Stolen from the back drawing-room at No. 1 Portland Street, North Circular Road, Dublin, between the hours of one and three o'clock of Saturday, 15th June, 1872, A Large Dark Grey and Black Male Cat, the property of Mr. Thomas C. Irwin. This poor animal, who answers to the name of Ton, and is lame in the left forepaw and weak in the left eye, can be of no value to anyone but Mr. Irwin, who had him for five years before he lost him through the cruel and desperate act of a miscreant. One Pound will be given by me to whoever restores the animal uninjured, and at once, to above address, or who affords authentic information as to the party who entered Mr. Irwin's room and committed the robbery.'

Nine years later he was advertising, rather less provocatively, for the return of 'Two grey brindled striped Cats, male and female' which, he said, had been 'stolen' from No. 41 Stephens Green.

The only other glimpse of him is in a letter from John O'Donovan, the antiquary, to Sir Samuel Ferguson—

'I understand', writes O'Donovan, 'that the mad poet who is my next-door neighbour claims acquaintance with you. He says I am his enemy, and watch him through the thickness of the wall which divides our houses. He threatens in consequence to shoot me. One of us must leave. I have a houseful of books and children; he has an umbrella and a revolver. If, under the circumstances, you could use your influence and persuade *him* to remove to other quarters, you would confer a great favour on, yours sincerely, John O'Donovan.'

He died in the Dublin suburb of Rathmines in the spring of 1892.

During his life Irwin produced at least seven volumes of poetry and one of prose. With one exception these were all published in Dublin. The one exception is his only book of distinctively Irish verse, for which he found a publisher in Glasgow. His bibliography is confused, most of his books are badly printed, and they all contain formidable and incomplete lists of Errata. Many of his poems are still uncollected in obscure Irish magazines to which he contributed.

Like most of the minor poets of his time Irwin was strongly influenced by Tennyson. This does not mean that he imitated Tennyson as, a few years earlier, many smaller poets had imitated Byron. The Byronic accent had then been in the air and such writers as Felicia Hemans had used it unnaturally. In the sixties a Tennysonian accent was about, and it happened to fit Irwin's mind like a glove. He is, perhaps, the only Irish Tennysonian—at least the only one with some true originality of his own, that makes his neglected poetry worth re-reading. The difference in stature between the two poets can be measured by their noses—noses which are so rare in poetry that I do not remember any beside these: Irwin's Ethel had a 'Tiny delicate-nostrilled nose'—which is good. But Tennyson's Lynette had a nose 'Tip-tilted like the petal of a flower'—which is perfect.

Irwin seldom approaches perfection. Generally speaking, he cannot or will not concentrate. His mind and his muse wander undisciplined, picking up odd rhymes and odd syntax to suit his metrical schemes, and leaving the sense to follow as best it may. His poems frequently go out of focus. In a rather desultory poem describing a barge coming down a canal he suddenly, as it were, whips out his pocket-lens and shows us how

Around the stalk of the hollyhock
The yellow, long, thin-waisted wasp,
Emitting sounds, now like a lisp
In the dry glare, now like a rasp,
Climbed slowlily with stealthy clasp,
And vicious, intermittent hum;
Nosed awhile each sickly bloom
Withered round the edges crisp—
Then headlong vanishing grew dumb . . .

There is no point at all in that wasp—except that it happened to occur as, when, and where the poet describes it. The same kind of thing—as though he were putting on and taking off his spectacles—happens in poems of a less visual character, and will be found disconcerting by some readers.

Yet, again and again there are passages which one can only call inspired; passages and, occasionally, whole poems which only a man of genius could have written. Sometimes they are mere phrases imbedded in an undistinguished matrix—

Her laugh is low, like some sweet well
Bubbling through blossoms in a dell,
Or pleasure's pulse, by some wild spell
Of radiant lips made audible . . .

As some rare swan in sunset's calm
Sailing the lakelet's marge of balm,
Watching herself, delighted goes
Amid the shadow of her snows . . .

These and many other equal passages will not be found in the following selections simply because they gleam in otherwise dull or feeble poems.

He is fairly prodigal, too, of neologisms—*honeyly*, *lengths* used as a verb, *splendours* also as a verb, *conquerless*, and a coinage from the Greek—*sithurysmal*—Kisses, and sithurysmal murmurs sweet—which may not be a new word, but which is new and charming to me.

The most disappointing of all Irwin's books is unfortunately the one devoted to Irish National Poems. As he says in the preface, it 'contains nearly six thousand lines of Original Poetry for sixpence', and, barring one poem, that is really the best that can be said of it. The exception, however, which makes the book worth while, is the fine description of Swift's ride on his last visit to Vanessa. This poem alone ought to have kept his memory alive among his compatriots. But it has not done so, and the obscurities of publication are enough to account for his being hitherto unknown in England. I hope that an English public will be glad to have at least as much of his poetry as is included in the present volume.

T. C. IRWIN

BIBLIOGRAPHY

Versicles, 1856.
Poems, 1862.
Irish Poems and Legends, 1869.
Songs and Romances, 1878.
Pictures and Songs, 1880.
Sonnets on the Poetry and Problem of Life, 1881.
Poems, Sketches and Songs, 1889.
Winter and Summer Stories and Slides from Fancy's Lantern (prose), 1879.

from

Elizabethan Days

I

'TIS pleasant, stretched on grassy lawn,
  Or ocean summit grand and grey,
    To watch the change of sun and sky,
    The shadowy shapes that voyage by—
Rich golden fleets along the dawn,
  Proud pageants in the western day,—

II

Lone clouds that move, at set of sun,
  Like pilgrims to some sacred star;
    Long moonlit hosts that seem to bear
    White banners through the waste of air;
Like steeled crusaders marching on
  Through deserts to some field of war.

III

But sweeter still to ponder o'er
  The wonders of the visioned vast;
    In History's argosy to sail
    The seas of time, in fancy's gale,
Along some bay, or fruitful shore,
  Or noble headland of the Past.

IV

In trancéd muse to charm the hour
  From dawn till summer dark, and gaze
    On pictures wrought in gold and gloom,

The fleets of Tyre, the wars of Rome,
The pomp of old Venetian power,
The brightness of Britannic days:—

V

Bright days, like golden bells that rang
A pæan o'er each sun's decline;
When Shakespeare shaped his world of dreams,
When Bacon moulded mighty themes
To rule the future; Spenser sang,
And gallant Raleigh sailed the brine!

. . . . . .

VII

Come, let us choose from soldier, sage,
And poet spirits bright and ripe
Who moved along the ample ways
Of rich Elizabethan days,
The tall Sir Walter; he, the type
And blossom of th' Adventurous Age.

VIII

But not while fortune's splendour pours
Around him, shall we hover nigh;
But while within his prison gloom
He hears the muttering tongue of doom;—
When life drifts on to sullen shores
Black with the wrath of destiny:—

. . . . . .

X

He sees the grey ancestral hall
In thickest girth of woods withdrawn;
The leafy shadows round the door,

The seats of stone that stretch before—
The dim old mirrors on the wall,
The moon-lit deer upon the lawn.

XI

Sweet days that make his pulses beat,
Rise in the calm. Once more he gives
A blue ring to a lady fair,
His best beloved, his only dear,
As under sycamore boughs they meet
In moonlight by the thymey hives.

XII

Old scenes of voyage and of strife
Shape in the shadows of the room;
And while the mournful winds enfold
His midnight turret, dark and old,
The gloried pictures of his life
In drifting pageants fire the gloom:—

XIII

Where bugled troops of gallant men
A hunting went with dawning's light,
Or prancing back through sunset trees
Beheld the ladies' balconies
Alive with smiles; and feasting then,
With masks and dances closed the night.

XIV

'Tis now an eve of moonlit March,
When issuing through the portal broad,
Girt by a train of captains, he
Rides from his mansion toward the sea,

Between old rows of oak and larch,
  Along the well-remembered road.

. . . . . .

XVI

And fast away through foam and breeze
  His galleon cleaves the ocean's breast,
    Toward regions of a mightier mould,
    Thick fruited woods and lands of gold;
Passing through tempests on the seas
  To combats in the crimson west.

XVII

The vision melts along the gloom,
  And forms another; swift beside
    The summer-shining river's flow
    His comrades of the tournay go;
While brassy harness, spur and plume
  Fall mirrored on the glittering tide.

XVIII

Now groups of maids and gallants gay
  Come trooping down each avenue:
    Minglings of armour, scarf and blade
    Flash through the moving cavalcade;
The glossy chestnut coursers neigh
  The silver clarions storm the blue.

. . . . . .

XX

But hush! the Queen draws near the while;
The jewels spark each yellow tress;
    As 'mid the bowing courtiers there
    She moves with cold grey eye of care,

And slender lips with settled smile
  Of vanity and stateliness;

XXI

Or girt by trains of page and maid
  All homage-hushed, erect she stands;
    Chats with the knights, laughs loud and long,
    Or through th' ambassadorial throng
Airs with a peacock-like parade
  Her language store of foreign lands.

. . . . . .

XXIII

But now the knights have sprung to horse,
  The tournay and the feast are o'er,
    And brightly sword and stirrup gleams
    As townward by the moonlit Thames,
In misty gallop, glade and gorse
  Sweep past them, holding by the shore.

XXIV

And fast away through gloom and gleam,
  By proud domain, and peasant's door,
    'Till by the stretch of forest brown,
    They spy the towers of London town;
The snowy sails upon the stream,
  The flitting lights along the shore.

XXV

And now beneath a gateway bends
  His plume, and from the drowsy throng
    A varlet leaps, and takes the rein;
    Aground he springs, and off again

Along the silent city wends,
   Trolling a jocund Spanish song.

. . . . . .

XXXI

Fade, pictured memories, fade! The light
   Is sinking, and the room is dim:
      He hears the grey and testy rain
      Fretting against the window pane,
And rising, looks across the night
   Upon a world that fades for him.

XXXII

For through the stillness long and loud
   Grey Paul's has tolled the hour, and toward
      The east, a glimmer red as blood,
      Severs the darkness from the flood;
And slanting o'er an ebon cloud
   Falls night's last moon-beam like a sword!

from

Antique Glimpses

I

GREY-FACED Spirit! let us sit—
   Sit and muse an hour with thee,
      While before our visioned eyes
      Something of the past may rise;
Rise, and live again, and flit
   As through a sphere of alchemy:

II

Come, then, jocund firstling, come,
Mounted on thy milky goat;
Dusky form, with Indian brow,
We can hear thy piping now,
Cheerful as the cricket's hum,
Along the sunny silence float.

III

Beside thy path a ruddy shape
Chants snatches of old song divine;
While slyest lights amid his hair
Are sliding, as in thickets there,
With head thrown back upon a vine,
He lips the purple drooping grape.

IV

And who art thou, and who art thou,
With viny ringlets down thy neck?
We know thee too, thou rosy, coy,
Low-lisping, lithe Idalian boy;
No marvel that thy beauties' beck
Should draw the nymphs to kiss thy brow.

V

Who follows next? The winged girl
Who loved thee, roving by thy side
In balsam breathings through the May
Of many a lonely amber day,
When she would wreathe thy locks, and hide
Her blushes in some golden curl.

VI

Come, Nayad, draped in woven weeds,
And dripping lilies of the stream;
Sweet image! on thy wat'ry cheek
The sunlight plays in touches meek,
And, slanting o'er the level meads
Crowns thy cold forehead with its beam.

VII

Hark! from yon temple nigh the shore,
Piled high with many a marble shaft,
There comes a rush of wings, and lo!
A shape mercurial, white as snow,
Winks at the towns he hurries o'er,
From close-capp'd brow of wit and craft.

VIII

See, by yon Autumn river's drift,
Slow curving round the fields of corn,
Its red-faced god, with rushes crowned,
Sits by the windless bank, embrowned
With fallen leaves, and seems to lift
And faintly blow his wreathed horn.

IX

But who is this that seems to pass
Like music from the noon-white sky?
What form of beauty, grace, and bloom,
From yonder bower of myrtle gloom,
Comes floating o'er the sun-warm grass,
In soft Olympian majesty?

X

Ah! who could miss thy name, though screened
  In golden clouds thou movest thus,
    With blossomed mouth, and breath of musk,
    And eyes as sweet as summer dusk,
And breast with tremulous azure veined,
  Like vase of white convolvulus?

. . . . . .

XII

But, while we muse, the wintry god
  Who moves the winds, and floods the springs
    With saddened face, grey as the thaw
    And beard of icicle and snow,
Above the distant lonely road
  Sails silently on wat'ry wings.

Winter Life and Scenery

BARE Winter owns the earth at last;
  The white sun rises late and slow,
With scatter'd fires, and breathes the blast
  Bitterly from the hills of snow:
The world is dumb, the stream is dead,
  The dim shrubs shiver by the pane,
  And sounds, as from some aged brain,
Swoon from the poplar overhead.
  Yet, though chill clouds of morning grey
Around our lonely roof are rolled,
  From wintry day we'll turn away,
Nor heed, by yonder hearth, the cold.

Come, Mary, close beside me rest,
  While flames the cheery crackling hearth;
The while our pleasant morning guest
  Shall gossip stories of the earth:
Here shall we read of mighty wars
  That tyrants glory to renew—
  Great struggles of the good and true—
Wild voyages under foreign stars;
  The world has still its faery tale;
Still new Aladins search for gold;—
  Hark! it is but the wandering gale,
Tapping the pane with fingers cold.

A walk?—yes, through the clear-aired day,
  Still facing southward let us go,
Where spreads the quiet sky away
  In slips, like blue lakes in the snow.
The land is dark, the forests sigh—
  See yonder branch, all ledged with sleet,
  The numb bird clasps with tiny feet,
And chirps a little shivering cry.
  Ah! bleakly breathes the bitter air;
Come, Mary, by the woods we'll hold;
  The woods shall yield, though grey and bare,
A kindly shelter from the cold.

All day beneath the sullen sky
  Some mighty Presence labours round;
The sunlight glimmers dolefully;
  The leaves are starched along the ground:
Blank sounds the gunshot through the air
  In frosted fields and fens beyond,
  And, dumb beside the harden'd pond,
The cattle stand with piteous stare:—
  But though the season, wild and bleak,
Swathes earth in many a snowy fold,

Yet, Mary sweet, your chilly cheek
It only rosies o'er with cold.

Hark! now from yonder bosky mounds
Echoes the clear hilarious horn!
In circles yelp the spotted hounds
In empty fields all stubble-shorn:
The jocund huntsmen gallop forth
'Mid slanting drifts of pelting hail,
And, bending, breast the icy gale
Set in with noon from the blue north:—
Press closer, closer to my side;
In muffling mist the sun has rolled,
The frost-ghost wanders far and wide,
The sky is dark, the world is cold.

Yet oft we paced o'er this old walk,
With summer moss beneath our feet,
When o'er the moor the shepherd's flock
Drowsed in the heavy evening heat;
And drifted past the cottage eaves,
As crimson dusk crept o'er the flood,
From the red bonfire in the wood,
The sweet faint scent of burning leaves:
Oft then, as through the quiet trees
The sunset streamed in shafts of gold,
We sighed for one sweet temperate breeze
To freshen earth with norland cold.

from

To a Skull

DUMB are the heavens: sphere controlling sphere
  Chariot the void through their allotted span;
And man acts out his little drama here
  As though the only Deity were man.

Cold Fate, who sways creation's boundless tides,
  Instinct with masterdom's eternal breath,
Sits in the void invisible, and guides
  The huge machinery of life and death;

Now strewing seeds of fresh immortal bands
  Through drifts of universes deepening down;
Now moulding forth with giant spectral hands
  The fire of suns colossal for his crown;

Too prescient for feeling, still enfolds
  The stars in death and life, in night and day,
And, clothed in equanimity, beholds
  A blossom wither or a world decay;

Sleepless, eternal, labouring without pause,
  Still girds with life his infinite abode,
And moulds from matter by developed laws
  With equal ease the insect or the God!

Poor human skull, perchance some mighty race,
  The giant birth of never-ceasing change,
Winging the world, may pause awhile to trace
  Thy shell in some re-oreant Alpine range;

Perchance the fire of some angelic brow
  May glow above thy ruin in the sun,
And higher shapes reflect, as we do now,
  Upon the structure of the Mastodon.

Imogen—in Wales

I

At noon she left her cavern cell,
  And stood beneath its rushy shed,
Where from the wide gray willow fell
  The pining leaves; and overhead
The scattered cloud and scarfing haze
  Blew drily. By the yellow road
Floated the sifting Autumn rays
  In slumb'rous stillness toward the flood:
But not a vessel marked the sea,
  But not a single sail was there
  To cômfort those sad eyes of care
That southward strainèd tearfully;
Then dumbly moving in the blast
  That shook the thickets by the shore,
  She sate her down, and pondered o'er
Her old love life, her vanished past;
    But through the day of light and grey,
      As the heart of the wanderer sadly pined,
    The bee hummed over the withering flowers,
      And the thistle-down went on the wind.

II

From morn till noon the silent sky
  Had shown a huff'd and hazy look;
The low hills brooded rain; anigh

In the wet wind the sand-grass shook:
Across the doleful moorland brown
The solitary river flowed
In glimmering curves; the lonely road
Wound bleakly toward the inland town;
And from the forest twilight came
The woodman's song and hatchet stroke,
At times upon the air that broke
In vague dry gleams of passing flame;
Then warming in the brooding heat,
The seering foliage wavered bright,
The distance smiled from height to height,
And sang the blue stream faint and sweet:
But all the day as hope made play
With fancy in her silent mind,
The bee hummed over the withering flowers,
And the thistle-down went on the wind.

III

Onward, as in a vacant dream,
She sought the river bank anigh:
The pale noon sun looked from the stream,—
A blot of white flame to the eye;
And past the low wind idly crept
Through seering reed and turban'd rush,
And whitening through each willow bush
In melancholy dirges swept
The inland, where the crane was heard
Clanging his marshy call, and where
The scattering crowflock swarmed the air;
The restless swallow crossed and skirred:
But as in heart-thought lonelily
She wandered, humming memory drowned
With voices dear all other sound
Save of the dim cold spacing sea.

Still through the day of light and grey,
As the breast of the wanderer sadly pined,
The bee hummed over the withering flowers,
And the thistle-down went on the wind.

IV

Asouth, beneath the ashen sky
The sullen wind seemed brooding wrath
For storm; the bleak sea marge anigh
Lay slubbered over with shivering froth.
Anon, the clouds broke overhead,
And sunlight poured around her there,
And passed from peak to peak, and spread
Warm silence through the wide grey air:
Anon, a mist crept o'er the flood,
And blurred the flying mountain beam;
The weedy scent of the rank wet wood
Breathed down the coldly flowing stream:
And stone-still lay the grey inland;
And nought was heard on the dismal shore,
Save the wash of the waves on the foggy strand
And the scream of the curlew flying o'er.
Still, as throughout the desolate hours
Her empty soul with sorrow pined,
The bee hummed over the withering flowers,
And the thistle-down went on the wind.

V

But when the evening fell, there came
A dewy lustre from the west;
And as she clasped her palms and blessed
In mournful prayer her lover's name,
Across the clear gold ocean's flow
Whereon the land wind faintly stirred,
Remotest thunder grand and low
Beyond the purple clouds was heard;

The while, upon the air of night,
  Odours, as from the thymey drought
  Of terraced gardens in the South,
Came breathing from the fading light;
And as she prayed—upon the rim
  Of moonlit waters faint and pale
  A little speck,—a silent sail
Glimmered a space, and all was dim:
    Thus through the day as hope made play
      With fancy in her lonely mind,
    The bee hummed over the withering flowers,
      And the thistle-down went on the wind.

Nature's Key-Notes

I

WHEN on the level summer seas
  The air scarce puffs the pinnace sheet,
And breathless droop the full-leaved trees
  By shores and fields of rough green wheat;
When cottiers earth their rows of peas,
  And in the turf-land spade the peat,
And drowsy hum the honeyed bees
  O'er heather-stretches hazed in heat:—
Tchu-chu—tchu-chu—the bright day long
The gay Grasshopper shapes his song.

II

When barnward roll the yellow loads,
  And lads in haggarts pile the sheaves,
And rivers swell with mountain floods,
  And whitely crisp the frost-cloud heaves;
When drear the scattered sunset bodes

O'er empty fields where twilight grieves,
And folk pace by October roads
To evening fires, 'mid falling leaves:—
Chi-chirp—chi-chirp—beside the hearth
The Cricket cheers the dusk with mirth.

Autumn

I

Lo! from the woodland skirting the old town,
The nymph of Autumn, through the freckled morn
Broadening o'er haze and vapour, wanders down
By orchard thickets and wide breadths of corn.
Along the stream, that sings amid the grass,
Falls the rich image of her blooming face;
And moving o'er the wold
That brownly lengths along the tranquil flood,
The dry herb pressured by her foot returns
A perfume on the wind; and if she pace
The forest skirt, the leaf she touches burns
With colour red as blood,
And in the level sunset hangs in gold.

II

At noon she wanders o'er the blossomed ground
Of gardens by the sea—a shape as fair
As fruitful; scattering mists of odour round
From aureate censer burning in the air:
Or wading waist-deep through the fields of grain,
Startles the plover feeding silently
Beneath the sultry stems in alleys dim:
Now pausing, sunny-smiled, to catch the song
The dwindling sky-lark showers from on high;

Now moving with a mellow grace along
The yellow shores of the rich harvest main,
Where fluttering poppy-blossoms lightly swim,
Like crimson bubbles on a golden sea.

III

But when the August evening sunset floods
The hamlet elm-row, high in rich mid air
She views the harvest carts, by rural roads
Come winding through green arches homeward there:
By meadow hedges, thick with crimson haws,
The milkmaids sing; the heavy oxened team
Awhile is seen to pause,
And drink beneath the sycamore-shadow'd stream.
And night falls drowsily, while one great star
Watches o'er vacancy till rise of morn;
And naught is heard, save on the wind afar
The sultry whisper of the dry-eared corn.

from

Swift

I

Two women loved him, shapes of Heaven,
Radiant as aught beneath the sky.
One gentle as the summer moon,
One ardent as the golden noon;
And to the first his heart was given,
And to the last his vanity.

II

Equal in love, alike in doom—
Content to yield in proud desire
Their souls for shelter in that breast,
Palsied with passion-long unrest,
Content to worship and expire
Silent within its upas gloom.

. . . . . .

VIII

For what to him were loves of earth,
That light the humblest soul below?
His planet flamed in wider skies,
And moved for mightier destinies
Than circle round a homely hearth,
Or centre in its narrow glow.

IX

What! should the spirit which had soared
Ambition's eyrie as a King,
And wielded with a giant's power
The mighty movers of the hour,
Be cozened by some passion-bird,
And twitted with a feeble wing?

X

A truce with mockeries—the weak
Are greatest tyrants when they dare.
Too long, too long had he forborne
To check, in mere reserve of scorn,
This puppet play of changing cheek—
This fulsome puling of despair.

XI

It was a dim October day,
When clouds hung low on roof and spire,
He dashed his horse, to gallop pressed,
Along the old road leading west,
Where Liffey's waters shimmering lay
Beneath the noonlight's struggling fire.

XII

Aleft, the slopes of tillage spread;
And further, higher to the south,
The sloping slate-grey mountains rose,
Sun-pencill'd in the noon's repose,
And by his path the river bed,
Deep sanded with the summer drought.

XIII

The city sunk in smoke behind,
Before, the air rose blue and lone.
At times, from ivied hedge and wall,
Faint shrilled the robin's crystal call;
And, from the west, the careless wind
Was blowing in a monotone.

XIV

He marked not, as he swept along,
The golden woodland's glimmering domes;
He heard not as he trampled by,
The foliage whispering to the sky,
The laugh of children, or the song
Of mothers in their rustic homes.

XV

Unheeded all to eye and ear,
  The world's old genial beauty past;
    Nor reck'd he in that hour of wrath,
    Aught save the victim in his path,
Though pity, justice hovered near—
  Though God was watching from the vast.

XVI

At length, beneath its woody gloom,
  Old Marley's cloister ends his way.
    He lights—he knocks. The pigeon's plaint
    Swoons fitfully above and faint;
And glimmers through the garden's bloom
  The river's sheet of glassy grey.

XVII

Lo! from her memoried laurel bower,
  Where oft she sat alone, to hear
    His coming, she is hastening now,
    To meet him with a joyous brow,
Though saddened by th' impending hour,
  And shuddering with an unknown fear.

XVIII

She enters—springs to meet him. God!
  Can passion demonize a brow
    Of spirit-splendour! In a breath
    The letter's thrown; and he, like death,
Is gone, Hark! Ringing from the road
  His horse's trampling echoes now.

XIX

In terrored trance she burst the seal.
Ah, piteous aspect—shape forlorn!
Doom darkness o'er her, and she falls—
Dead as the shadow on the walls—
Dead, holding in her heart the steel—
Brain-blasted by his silent scorn.

XX

Ah, well! a purer, tenderer light
Still smiles upon his barren years.
Like a sweet planet glimmering o'er
Some silent waste of vanished war,
Sweet Stella charms life's falling night
With eyes whose love outlives their tears.

XXI

Yes; thou art true, though love has wreathed
Thy brow with cypress. Though the pall
Encircles life, thy voice, no less,
Is toned to soothe his loneliness,
Like melancholy music breathed
Through some funereal banquet hall.

XXII

Star of fidelity! Thy light
Soon set beneath the eternal wave,
And from thy place of cold repose,
Retributive remorse arose—
The fury of the deepening night,
And heaven darkened o'er thy grave.

XXIII

As twilight's leaden shadows fall,
He sits within the casement lone.
Bright letters from bright comrades lie
Unheeded round him; and anigh
One empty chair beside the wall:—
The world has vanished—she is gone.

XXIV

He muses—not in scorn or mirth,
And fondly clasps one raven tress;
Still flames the spirit vision through
Those deep-browed eyes of angry blue,
Too mighty for the mean of earth
Too critic clear for happiness.

XXV

Now hums the past its ceaseless song,
And through the chambers of his brain
The tender light of parted days,
Bright cordial smiles—old winning ways,
Remembered tones unheeded long,
Rise from the silent years again.

XXVI

Till, slowly deepens o'er his face
A mournful light, rare and divine,
Like Death's last smile; as silently,
And with a sad simplicity,
His aged hand essays to trace
That relic with one trembling line.

XXVII

'Only a woman's hair!' No more.
The golden dreams of pride are gone;
And nought remains save this poor prize,
Instinct with anguished memories;
Life's tree is leafless now, and roar
The bleak winds through its skeleton.

XXVIII

The dusk cathedral glooms the while—
The bell tolls in the upper air;
And silvering down the mouldered walls,
The winter moonlight coldly falls
Through one old window in the aisle,
On one memorial tablet there.

XXIX

Ah, what were fame's great trumpet breath,
The proud applause of mightiest men,
The storm, the struggle, and the crown,
The world, that darkened in his frown—
The love that he had scorned to death,
Were dearer than an empire then.

XXX

Oh, wisdom, manhood, where were ye
Thus in caprice of power to move—
To play with hearts whose truth you tried.
To watch, poor puppet of your pride,
How long sweet, earnest constancy
Would live with unrequited love.

XXXI

Vain requiem o'er a ruined life—
  Vain sorrow for the vanished bloom
    Of love's sweet blossom. Still with eyes
    Turned to its God, affection dies
With curses cankering from the strife
  Ambition epitaphs its tomb.

XXXII

Alone, long, dreary years alone,
  His days went down the darkened sky,
    Racked with the heart's revenging war;
    A Saturn on his icy star,
God-like upon a ruined throne,
  Friendless in his supremacy.

XXXIII

Till, last, by that grey brow there came
  Some angel pitying his distress;
    And tamed the soul that burned within,
    Sin-like revenging upon sin,
And quenched that hell of clearest flame,
    In ashes of forgetfulness.

XXXIV

His spirit lives within his page:
  Dissective subtlety of glance;
    Keen Truth, to make the merriest mourn,
    Fierce wit, that brightens but to burn,
Are there; and cold, ironic rage,
  Withering a world it views askance.

. . . . . .

XXXVI

And when we pace along the shrine
That coldly closed on his despair,
View, from his angered life apart,
The passioned tremble of the heart
That ripples in the little line—
'Only a woman's hair.'

The Ghost's Promenade

THERE was a long, old road anear the town
Skirted with trees;
One end joined a great highway, one led down
To open shore and seas;
There was no house upon it, saving one,
Built years ago;
Dark foliage thickly blinded from the sun
Its casements low;
And through the upper, broken and decayed,
The wind and rain
Entered its vacant chambers, dim and frayed
With time and stain.
Long, ivy trailers round the door had grown;
The ruined gate,
That swayed of windy nights with rusty moan,
Tall, desolate,
Seemed murmuring for the happy years long gone
To sullen fate;
And each the other seemed to watch alone,
Like love or hate,
Or, for some action sometime to be done,
Silent to wait.

Even in summer the long walk that led
Between them drear,
For all its leaves seemed whispering of the dead,
And full of fear;
At twilight, as you passed, a ghostly breath
Seemed swooning near;
Life had forgot this house, and even death,
Since the last bier
Shadowed its path, for people long grown old
Were infants then:
Forlorn it stood, deserted, distant, cold,
And strange to men.

Of evenings, when the moon, mingling with day
Slanted among
The summer foliage of this olden way,
Folk, old and young,
Came from the town awhile to breathe the air
Of fields and seas;
Lovers beneath its shadows whispered there,
Couched by the trees;
And others, who had made it their resort—
As I, who write—
For exercise, or after labour sport,
Were used at night
To see a tall and a solitary man,
Vague to the sight,
Walk in the shadows, gloomy-garbed, and wan,
And weighed with care;
And when the middle hour of dark drew near,
And few were there,
'Twas said within the gate would disappear,
As though he were
A shadow of the place, silent and drear,
Or breath of air.

One cloudy autumn night, when it was late,
And lone the road,
As I was passing by that gloomy gate
Awhile I stood,
And as I gazed on the deserted place
Felt a strange hand
Touch me; and turning, saw the strange man's face,
Mournful and grand,
Smiling upon me with a spectral grace,
Cold, pale, and still:
"'Tis late,' he said, 'and you may enter here,
Friend, if you will.'
So courteous was his look it banished fear;
So after him,
Without a word, I passed along the drear
Avenue dim;
Entered the dumb door, which stood wide, and soon,
Mounting the stair,
Found myself in a chamber, where the moon
Beamed cold and fair
Through the chill, broken casement's glassless sash,
Free to the air,
Which murmured 'mid the boughs of elm and ash,
And through which there
Long, glossy ivies, blent with rose, had grown
The walls around,
And o'er the mantelpiece, in shadow thrown,
Gleamily wound.

At first I thought that we two were alone;
But soon I found
Two other Shadows there: one young, yet gray
Was he, in sooth;
And one, a maiden, blue-eyed as a day
In April's youth.

As with them and the high, clear moon I stood,
I knew right well
That all were phantoms without flesh and blood,
Under some spell:
Yet, so familiar was this house, whose brown
Chimneys appeared
From my high study chamber in the town,
I nothing feared;
Nor had I cause, for kindly were the looks
Of all the three,
As those of clouds, or stars, or olden books
In my library.
At length the spectral host, faint-voiced, said:
'This house is ours;
We hold it still, albeit we are dead,
From the unseen Powers,
And shall, until the secret of our doom
Is known, as soon
It will; we three once perished in this room
Under yon moon,
Which looked upon us seventy years gone by.
My brother there
Then loved and loves our Eva, even as I.
Love cannot share
The heart it treasures: so we fought and fell—
One night like this;
And she, maddened by deed so horrible,
After one kiss
Given her dead cousins, whom she loved like well,
All loneily,
Knowing her life henceforward worthless, fired
A weapon we
Had left, into her bosom, and expired.'
Thus saying, he
Pointed unto the bullet marks which traced
The dim wall o'er,

And to the stains of blood not yet effaced
Upon the floor.
Then she, who hovered by the casement in
The silvered light,
'Mid rose and ivy, lifting slow her thin,
Faint finger white,
Advanced in the slanting moonbeams, said:
'For many years,
For our dark fate, that wrought in deeds so dread,
Fell our dark tears;
But, as even had we lived, we had been dead
Long ere this hour,
As we still loved, long since has sorrow shed
Its useless shower;
And on this very night 'tis ordered,
Before this rose
With dawn shall ope its leaves, that we depart
To the repose
Of spirits; happy that still, heart to heart,
To us 'tis given
In a fair phantom region to dwell,
Bordering on heaven,
And, as our fate was Love's, remote from hell.'

She smiled, and touched me with her hand serene.
Like drop of dew,
Chill, timid, tender, was that touch, I ween,
And gracious too,
With gentle sympathies which hers had been
In life passed through;
When the first sound of city clock that tolled
'Twelve' sounded afar,
And when it ceased I felt the dawn draught cold,
And saw one star

Shine through the dark trees, happy as her eyes;
And then, 'twas gone,
As they were—a long gust swept through the skies—
I was alone.

When I awoke—for this was but a dream—
So strong oft times,
Impressions of the things which only seem
Vibrate like rhymes,
That forwith hastened I to the old road;
And as I gazed
Through the dim gate on that once drear abode,
Stood much amazed;
For workmen were at work within, without,
Who with the o'ergrowth
Of herbage and of trees had made rude route.
The antique youth
Of the once foliage-hidden walls was cleft
Ruthlessly down,
And not a trace of rose or ivy left
The door to crown.
As, entering, I trod the stairs so late
Trodden by me,
And sought in that void chamber, marked by fate,
Its company,
But found instead two labourers, one of whom
Wrought at the floor,
And one tore from the window the sweet gloom
Of leaves it bore.

The place was still the same as I beheld
Some hours gone by;
But though unspectred, still I stood enspelled
With phantasy,
Awhile, till it resigned its influence
To visual truth;

Yet, although thoroughly assured to sense
        Ne'erless in sooth,
Perplexed, I was about to quit the place
        Where I had seen
Those friendly ghosts and her sweet phantom face
        Smile in the green
Light of the moonlit leaves with mournful grace;
        When glancing on
The hand that she had touched, I saw a trace,
        Slight, bluely wan,
Such as the lightning leaves upon a leaf,
        Or, oft upon
The mourner's temple has been stamped by grief:
        And though have shone
Suns many since the night of that so brief
        Communion
With those three spectre friends, and my belief
        In them is gone;
Ne'erless this phantom signet thus impressed—
        'Twas possibly the effect of phantasy—
Will still remain till I have reached my rest.

Song

I

My dreams were doleful and drear;
  And I wake with the sound of the sea
    Murmuring desolately.
  Winging athwart the morning red
      In the sombre glare
      Of troublous air,
  A passing crow shadows my bed:
    And closing weary eyes

Against the early skies,
The fitful lapse and rouse,
Of the autumnal boughs
Around the lonely house,
Tire me to rest again with withered lullabies.

II

The east wind, arid and frore,
Has been blowing from levels of gray.
All through the dismal day
Vacant and sad was the garden's light:
Around the wild shore
Beats evermore
The surge;—and again it is night:
And I hear the sullen boom
Of the billows through the gloom;
The universal stir,
And distant dim demur
Of the tempest's harbinger,—
While darkness settles heavy o'er the roof, like doom.

III

The hearth flamed long in a glow—
Then, redder and dimmer grew;
Funnelled the wind in the flue;
And I heard the old doors swing,
Open, and creak to-and-fro,
In the ghostly rooms below—
Then cease. And with the morning's birth,
A happy calm is on the earth,
As of a latter Spring:
The blue waves scarcely sigh,
The crows soar calm on high,
The seas shine, and anigh
Flashes above the sunny reef some snowy wing.

With the Dawn

Husband

WHY have you risen, to stand with naked feet
And thin robe stirring in the airs of night,
Looking from the casement?

Wife

It is sweet
To view upon the broad sea, glimmering white,
Sails, in the low moonlight.

Husband

I dream'd that you were lost to me afar,
And I had just recovered you once more.
Why linger you?—

Wife

To watch that last large star
Sparkle our cradled child's calm slumber o'er.
Soft as the little wave that sweet and frore
Rises and sinks upon the sandy shore,—
He breathes; and on his face there comes a smile,
Just as the dawn's pale gold has touched, the while,
Yon faint cloud cradled on the distant deep.
The calm sea-level turns from white to rose;
And, as the space a richer glory grows,
The earliest bird sings faintly far away
Upon the poplar by the ocean steep.

Husband

Awake him not, oh, dear one, till 'tis day ;
To be alive, and suffer not, is sleep.

A May Sunday

SUMMER vapours, soft and white,
  Sleep round the airy sunny Sabbath sky,
O'er full-leaved orchards, blithe with dewy light,
  And the blue sea anigh.

The fresh, new smell of grass
  Is blown from the long meadows inland, where,
From stile to stile, the quiet figures pass
  In twos and threes from prayer.

At times the wind brings down
  The breath of blossomed woodlands on the ridge,
Whose ruined turret looms with heroic frown
  In the long, red light mirrored by the bridge;

When crows are winging home;
  The shadows deepen, and one solemn star
Flames through the pale space west; and in gray gloom
  The wind begins to sound along the bar.

The Suire [1]

ONCE I had passed the shortened autumn day
  Upon a lonely river; now with oar
Speeding my boat along its levels gray,
  Now resting in the nooks along its shore,
Where the rathe grasses made a pillow sweet
With faint, dry odours, stored by the late heat,
  And withering height of interlacing bowers

[1] The Suires were the Naiads, or Water-spirits, of Celtic mythology.

Roofed in the silence of the cloudy hours:
The while I listened from each dim retreat
To the smooth, languid waters lisping slow
Anear, and broad and earnest onward flow
With ruffled rapid's gurgle in mid-stream,
Dappled with foam; or watched some sifting beam
Fan from the sleeping mists athwart the bank
O'er stem of hemlock or wild celery dank,
Or sparkling bubble passing or remote
O'er the gray mountains;—till once more afloat
I sauntered whitherway the waters went,
By rock, or grassy steep, or sycamore bent
Above its image in a glassy dream,—
All through the noon, until the sunset's flame
Levelled through horizontal vapours came
In blinding shafts from the low, wooded West
Upon the wat'ry evening scene of rest—
Warning me of the dark. On which I turned
My comrade boat, whose prow in fancied mood
I'd crowned with wreath of berried ivies black
And woven blossoms wild; and oaring back
Along the shadowy water-way that burned
Awhile with spots of sombre fire like blood,
Smote the sleek levels into foam. Soon night
Fell awsome round the land; large drops of rain
Sparse showered at first, soon thickening down the height,
Heralded deluge from the distant main;
And lurid grew the void: no more I heard
From beechen brakes amid whose stems the last
Thin streaks of sundown glimmered pale and ghast,
The twilight warble of the unseen bird;
But, from the rising tumult of deep gloom
The crepitating thunder, and its peal
And long, resounding, hoarse, cavernous boom,
As though a world were falling on a world;

And saw the cleaving lightnings blue as steel
  Flash from the clouds in pomp of terror curled.
Then in a moment as the air grew blind,
The torrent rain came driving on a wind
That bowed the trees along the river ridge;
When, happily, I reached an olden bridge,
And near the gloom of its impending span,
Moored me aloof from where the current ran.
Familiar was the place: oft from this arch
I'd watched on bleak, blue days of gusty March,
The swallow hither and thither skirring low
After the flies along the river's flow;
Above me heard the wagon lumbering slow,
And from the tillaged fields the squawking crow;
Here oft, when sheltering from the July heat,
The trout plump by the bank of rushy peat,
And thronging, chirping sparrows in the wheat
The while the trailers from the mouldering stone
Swayed in the wandering warm wind passing lone:
Here watched the slow, revealing lights, whence slid
Shapes and profiles fantastical that hid
In shade before, and felt the dim arch ache
With weary age, above the foamy flake
That round the buttress slid in stuttering swirls,
And drifted past its gloom in lessening whirls.
But now all dreary was the scene and dread:
The ceaseless thunder rattled overhead,
Shaking the earth that seemed a-light from hell,
With each cloud-opening burst of flame that fell
Along the foaming river, teeming trees
And distance flashing in the swamping seas
Of fire poured down from the infinities.
Close to the forlorn bridge's shaken wall
Massed with thick ivy, had I nigh an hour,
Sought shelter from the straight descending shower,
When methought something plunged into the tide,

And rose remote a sound, like a sweet moan:
But soon the repetitive thunder's tone
Swallowed all other sounds up in its own;
And when it died, the fancied voice had flown.

At length there came a lull, and more and more
Remote the tempest swept, and ceased to pour
The clouds through which the clear, pale crescent shed
Athwart the flying drifts, its lustre dead.
Upon the cool, refreshing, airy calm
Rose from exhaling herbage, gusts of balm;
And I was putting forth again, when, lo!
Anear me floated something white as snow.
At first I deemed it but a swath of foam,
But, as the moon shone from its azure dome.
I saw a form—a face serene and pure
As evening when the eastern stars allure
All eyes to leave the earth to gaze on them;
And on her brow a dripping diadem
Of silken grass and lilies of the deep
Smoothed to her hair, which floated soft as sleep
And as I gazed upon the twilight blue
Of her sweet, humid, innocent eyes, I knew
That this must be a Spirit of the stream—
Or else some happy-mooded visiting dream,
  Born of my long day's reverie, among
The silent nooks, and whispering leaves and grass,
And beam and bubble, that had seemed to pass
  Floating unto the river's moody song—
Risen for a moment, as I thought, to bless
My lonely worship of earth's loveliness.

Yet, surely ne'er took fancy such a form
As this pure, gentle Vision after storm;
Though I had read, in old poetic books,
Of nymphs a-many of the hills and brooks—

Shapes female fair, with faces simple-sweet,
As flower or orb in the cool wave's retreat:
Brows oval as a shell, eyes pure and meek,
And hair weed-woven, on each wat'ry cheek;
And others of the summer, zoned with rose,
Or autumn-crowned, whom fancy saw repose
Couched in the mellow West beside their star,
Sparkling o'er ledged hills of shimmering spar,
  Or golden forests' solitude, where swoons
In everlasting evening, near and far,
From recluse valleys full of yellow light,
Or lone recesses on the skirt of night,
  By fountains gleaming through the leaves, like
    moons,
Aerial harmonies of all delight.
But like a child in spirit and in grace,
  Though of eternal elements composed,
Seemed this fair dweller of the wave, whose face
  Was like a raindrop; though her cheek grew rosed
With unaccustomed fancies, thus to meet
  A human life beneath the hush of night,
When but winds wander, and the meteor glides,
  And stars slant down the earth's dark edge from
    sight,
  Or commune silent in the azure height:
  And, strange it seemed to her to speak by sign
A little space, nooked from the river tides
By the long sedges with me, who adored,
As some strange darling image of the brain,
The glimmering beauty of her neck, and feet,
  And forehead, like a wat'ry beam divine.
And while, in coy amaze, to stay she was fain,
  Smoothed down her dewy hair; yet spoke no word,
But, parting, signalled hope to meet again:
  On which she dipped her sweet brow in her hands,
And then gazed sadly upward, while she held

Toward me a little flower, purple bell'd.
This, tenderly I took and kissed, and gave
A leaf from my boat's crown, the which she took,
  While, with a low, wild laugh, most like the moan
Of some sad brook, her fitful image shook—
  Or sigh of wind through twilight tree-tops blown,
  Which haunts the memory with its monotone—
And, holding still the token, sunk to the sands
  Of the deep river, and I breathed alone.

Minnie

I

O CRYSTAL Well,
  Play daintly on golden sands,
    When she comes at morning lonely,
    Followed by her shadow only,
  To bathe those little dainty hands,
      All aweary gathering
      Seeds to make her blue bird sing,
O crystal Well.

II

O Forest brown,
  Breathe thy richest twilight balm,
    As she wanders pulling willow
    Leaflets for her fragrant pillow,
  Which with snowy cheek of calm
      She shall press with half-closed eyes
      While the great stars o'er thee rise,
O Forest brown.

III

O Lady Moon,
Light her as she mounts the stair
To her little sacred chamber
Like a mother; and remember,
While she slumbers full of prayer,
Sweetly then to fill her heart
With dreams of heaven where thou art,
O Lady Moon.

Glints of the Year—from a Window

I

On the floor of the low, white-clouded seas
Long lustres dazzle. O'erhead in the gray
The soft wet wind through the full-leaved trees
Sultrily swoons, and passes away.
The lark is a speck in the mists of the morn;
At night the great clusters watch o'er the green corn.

II

'Tis now an eve of softest shadow,
A clear sky west, sparked with one star;
Through clouds the moon flits; in the meadow
A corncrake singing;—list! afar—
Creek—creek,—creek—creek—in the grasses,
Where the dew falls—the shade passes.

III

Through chestnut blooms the bees are humming,
The gold streak grows on the apple's rind;

Dry hazes of fluctuant perfume are coming
  From ranunculus beds in rich sunlight and wind;
    And from the orchard's south brick walling
    You hear the peach in the hot hush falling.

IV

The azure lake spreads southward shimmering.
  O'ercrossed with misty, moulting rays,
As soft and stilly as the glimmering
  Last of slumb'rous autumn's days.
    And the swallows skirr o'er the purple heather
    In zig-zag flights through the evening weather.

V

Now ripest heaps of harvest mellow
  Bounteously shelter the olden house;
The gleam of the setting sun flames yellow
  Through the windy, withering autumn boughs;
    Then a ghostly air through the darkening sky
    Swoons off to the sea, with troublous sigh.

VI

The northern lights, like a drifting dawn,
  Rain fitful splendours over the sea,
Where great Orion's arm withdrawn,
  Sparkles wan and distantly:
    And the fly hums round with 'wildered hymn,
    Where the long-snuffed taper is burning dim.

VII

Now winter round the bare-browed mountain
  Lives in the dumb, gray air, and shrouds
The pastures; frozen is the fountain;
  Aloft the curlew wings the clouds;

The crane forlorn by the marsh marge chilly
In the dismal cold is guttling shrilly.

VIII

And as evening thickens, the rain storm, driven
  In gusts, moans over the desolate lands;
Then lulls at twelve: from the wide, dark heaven
  Pale meteors fall on the stretching sands,
    Where the sombrous red moon sets afar
    Past the booming line of the surging bar.

from

Winter Noon in the Woods

WITH witchlike branches, barren, bleak, and drear,
The woods in these cold wintry days appear;
Leaves frost-bitten and withered through their rifts
Shiver, or at their dumb feet lie in drifts:
  In icy sleep the little streamlet lies;
  The rustic bridge is ledged with snow, and flies
  Now and then from the sad branches brown
  Some airy faint flake down.

    Upon the road the snow lies hard and dry,
    And dreary is the sky
Through which the sterile east-wind grayly blows.
  Remote, the white hills spread
  Into the sea which shows
  Its bleak space dull as lead.
  Barrenly shake and sigh
  In the bitter breeze,
  That swooning vague and torpidly
  Sways their branches brown,

The forlorn trees.
Few ships are on the seas,
And few abroad upon the wintry ways,
So bitter keen the sky
These dark December days.

The Objects of the Summer Scene

I

THE objects of the summer scene entone
Or image present peace or dear regrets;
Something that life to be content must own,
Smiles near, though restless grief remotely frets;
Green sycamores brooding in the quiet sun;
And on gray hills beyond the golden sheaves,
Lone poplars, sisters of fallen Phaeton,
Quivering innumerate inconsolable leaves.

II

In wintry evening walks I turn where rest
Within one tomb affection's first, and last;
As in a wind, of some dead wind in quest,
I homeward pace companioned by the past.
For earth's great grave far ocean seems to moan;
And the sad mind but marks anear, afar,
The tinkle of the dead leaf by the lone
Sea road, the sad look of the setting star.

Hours I remember lonely and lovely to Me

HOURS I remember lonely and lovely to me
Living a life as simple as sunlight or tree,
When with some beautiful white cloud in love I would
  be,
  Or blossomed lime in warm hollow, or fresh little
    blue-browed billow
Playfully nearer and nearer washing the red weed to
  shore,
Innocent undulant under its clear ridge passing o'er,
Or grasses amiably waving in the warm wind of the sea.

Lovely and lonely days in the wide air and light,
When the moods of the woods on level or height,
One were with mine in their silence, dream and delight:
  When from far islanded seas came bright book
    memories,
    Fragment fancies, and lines that rippled about the
      wind-wooed ear,
    And others of ampler modern days, more earnest,
      and more dear,
  Sweet moods of minds that sang to their sun, or sea
    star low in the night.

Leaving Troy

GLOOMY with wind and driving cloud, the night
Spreads blankly down from Ida's wooded height,
Over the plain of Troy—where late had rung
The thunder of armisonous acclaim,
The cry of death and louder roar of fame,
O'er the green rushing seas and wastes of sand

And desolate levels of the long, black land:
As oaring through the sullen waves that flung
Their far-off surge on Tenedos, a band
Of heroes, Greece-ward bound, saddened in soul,
Strained through the darkness off the Sigean mole,
Where, as the sea-night deepened, and the wind
Drear gusting, drove the swelling waves behind
The long, black, high-pooped, wave-worn ships, and
burned
A transient lightning o'er the waters—one
A warrior, brazen armed, who by the mast
Stood gazing shoreward through the rising blast,
Pointed unto the promontory where
The tumulus that Ajax's bones inurned,
Loomed dim through watery haze and stormy air:
At which—the while a blaze bright as the sun
Sheened round the shore—all saw, looking that way,
A Spectre dark, taller than mortal, rise
Upon the grave-mound, under the rolling skies,
And gaze from under plumed brows upon
His living comrades, saddened at the sight,
One long, last time:—its phantom arm of might
Folded a minute o'er the countenance
Of shadow, waved a mournful last farewell—
And yet another—from the sinking shore,
And still stood gazing through the water's roar,
Long as the ships appeared. Then, as from trance
The voyagers wakened, knowing the mighty Ghost
Was that of Ajax—heroic tears burst forth,
Remembering him the leader of their host,
Now lessened to themselves. Then from the North
The tempest smote them, and clouds drearily
Closed o'er the fleet upon the starless sea.

THOMAS CAULFIELD IRWIN

L'Angelo

I

I SIT at eve within the curtain's fold,
  Where shone thy gentle face in the full moon
  So many an eve, and sing some antique tune
We sung together oftentimes of old:
In that dear nook the lonely moon-beams fall,
  And touch thy empty chair with mournful light:
Thy picture gazes on me from the wall;
  I hear thy footsteps in old rooms at night.

II

On lonely roads beneath the darksome dawn,
  When broods upon the broad dead land the wind,
  I wander sadly, looking oft behind,
Maychance that I may see thy spectre wan;
For still I deem thou followest me, and still
  Believe that love departs not with the clay:
Thy face looks on me from the morning hill,
  Thy smile comes sadly from the close of day.

III

Oft, oft, by sandy ridges o'er the sea,
  Or over distant famished fields at night,
  Where sheds some low pale star its slenderest light,
I seek in earth's dim solitudes for thee:
Proud of the everlasting love I bear,
  Still mix with nature, drawing thence relief;
While, o'er the space of sunset's fading air,
  The stars look on the glory of my grief.

Sonnets

I

THE rough green wealth of wheaten fields that sway
In the low wind of midsummer all day;
The morning valley's warm perfumed breeze
Floating from southern sycamore shadowed rills,
The singing forest on the dawn-topped hills,
The living depth of azure spacing seas:
Still, brooding shadows upon mossy walls,
Aërial vapours crumbling down the heights,
Silence of woods amid green mellow lights,
And sighs of distant drizzling waterfalls:
The sweet faint breath of the short moonlit nights
From misty meadows where the quaint crake calls;
Rare pageants in the western day withdrawn,
And fleets of rich light-laden clouds at dawn.

II

THE rainbow o'er the sea of afternoon
Whence comes the fresh sound of the distant wave;
The mirrored lights that roof the lonely cave,
Where roll the waters from the rising moon;
The airs that stir the grasses on the grave,
And whisper spirit-like to one beneath,
That love in Summer grieves no more for death:
The first sweet secret touch of lips grown dear
In happy twilight woods when none are near;
Sweet fancies just awaked at morn, when still
The level red cloud lies beyond the hill:—
Such are the thoughts and objects that appear,
To lap in sacred sadness, or inspire
Thy strings to Beauty's moods, oh, Summer lyre.

III

Regions of soft clear air, of cold green leaves,
Heaths, grasses, solitary as a sea:
Vistas of gold and violet radiancy,
Isles where the surge and the lone wave-bird grieves;
White-citied plains, hill-cinctured, whence there flow
Eurotean rivulets pellucidly
'Mid laurels, reeds, blue lilies;—in the glow
A cape, with sheep, and ruins like ripe sheaves;
Fallen columns smooth as aged ivory:
Some citadel remote or rocky pyre
The sunset turns to purple and to fire;
Gardens of thyme and groves of olives brown
Along the slopes Olympian vapours crown,
Like gods in commune, formless, divine and dire.

IV

Remote from smoky cities, aged and grey,
I pass the long-drawn Summer sea-side day:
Now reading in the garden arbour where
In light and silence comes the freckled morn
When dews are on the leaf, and cool the air;
The faint wave wash is heard the beach along,
Whence a warm wind waves languidly the corn;
And poised in haze the lark shakes out her song;
Now hearing in deep grass the sweeping scythe,
And, in the sultry stillness voices blythe,
'Till day is done. Blue coolness comes once more:
The reapers bind in twilight the last sheaf,
And the fresh spring-tide foams the sloaky reef
As floats the white moon up the lonely land.

V

INTO the wood at close of rainy day
I walk, dim cloud above, green leaves around;
Upon the humid air only the sound
Of drop on drop stirring the stillness grey:
Almost I hear the rose leaves fall away
Too heavily weighed with damp to cling o'er-blown
To their wet branches straggling o'er the copse;
Until the faint waved twilight airs entone
Tide-like along the blossom'd beech tree-tops;
And amid showers and flowers scattering, alone
Pass from the fresh dusk solitude among
Meadows in clouded moonlight, glimmeringly
Seen like the low blue hills; and hear the song
Of the last bird, and wash of the cool sea.

VI

AWAKENED, I behold through dewy leaves
Wavering in the air, the pale dawn's level glow;
And hear the sparrow's twitter on the eaves,
The engine's quick steam throb, the first cock's crow:
And soon a prayer-bell toll, remote and slow:
And then a-while with light-reclosed eyes
I float upon my pillow as a cloud,
Unto a land whose snowy ruins rise
Along a plain girt by blue mountains proud;
And under solitary Egerean skies,
Bright verdure and bright marbles, in a dell
Deserted, where within a recluse well,
Through leafy lights I see a nymph's face beam,
Which fades not when in daylight dies my dream.

VII

UPON an upland orchard's sunny side,
I pass the quiet blue September day:
There winds through tented fields they sometimes
hide,
Past woods and meadows green, the dusty way,
Down to the ship-speckled level of the bay,
And amber sands in crescent spreading wide.
Last night the winds were in the trees, and here
In golden moss a few red apples lie,
And from thc copsc a thrush flutes strong and clear,
And faintly humming flits the emerald fly:
All things autumnalised are rich and calm;
Steam-plumed argosies surge up the main,
And o'er the singing woodlands breathing balm,
One superb white cloud passes, dropping rain.

VIII

THE apples ripen under yellowing leaves,
And in the farm yards by the little bay
The shadows come and go amid the sheaves,
And on the long dry inland winding way:
Where, in the thinning boughs each air bereaves,
Faint sunlights golden, and the spider weaves.
Grey are the low-laid sleepy hills, and grey
The autumn solitude of the sea day,
Where from the deep 'mid-channel, less and less
You hear along the pale east afternoon
A sound, uncertain as the silence, swoon—
The tide's sad voice ebbing toward loneliness:
And past the sands and seas' blue level line,
Ceaseless, the faint far murmur of the brine.

IX

AN isle of trees full foliaged in a meadow,
  Along whose quiet grassy shores below
The white sheep bathe in level lengths of shadow,
  And sweet airs amiable as summer blow
Warmly and faint among the happy leaves,
  Loving each other in a green repose
Folded; or waking in the slumbrous glow
  Where the wind passing, indolently weaves
A net of lazy listless whisperings,
  Most like the liquid lullaby of springs
Pulsing demure and quaintly in some cool
  Dell of the woods; unseen save of some ray
Piercing the boughs, having somewhat to say
  To fairies couched on bubbles round the pool.

X

WHEN I had turned Catullus into rhyme,
And stars shone from the sea's blue southern zone,
Breathing in slumber tranquil as my own,
Above those pages of the antique time
Laid in a casement near me, where the vines
Trembled their shade: lo! on a sudden rose
Beautiful Venus naked amid glows
Of roseate cloud, and all the Lesbian lines
With her white finger touching as she smiled,
Stooped her, and kissed them, for a space beguiled,—
'Till with a sigh she vanished. Then above
The sheaf of song in darkness I beheld
Impassioned foreheads as of poet gods
Bend their gold curls, and o'er them muse enspelled;
And wild and epic music from their abodes,
Heard blend in the high night with those of love.

XI

YE two fair trees that I so long have known
And loved, as living over dust so dear;
Who silently have seen tear after tear
Rise from my heart, when to the engraved stone
I came to pray, and with true love alone
Live back old times, amid a world so drear
With cares and changes of a many a year,
And loss of most things I could love or own:—
Now 'mid the calm of this blue April noon
While the fresh wind breathes warm from the clear
 west,
Put fancy once more with thy leaves in tune
Green genial Muse of the grey grave:—for soon
By the dear dust it roofs, I too shall rest.

XII

A ROADSIDE inn this summer Saturday:—
The doors are open to the wide warm air,
The parlour, whose old window views the bay,
Garnished with cracked delph full of flowers fair
From the fields round, and whence you see the glare
Fall heavy on the hot slate roofs and o'er
The wall's tree shadows drooping in the sun.
Now rumbles slowly down the dusty street
The lazy drover's clattering cart; and crows
Fainter through afternoon the cock; with hoes
Tan-faced harvest folk trudge in the heat:
The neighbours at their shady doors swept clean,
Gossip, and with cool eve fresh scents of wheat,
Grasses and leaves, come from the meadows green.

XIII

I WALK of grey noons by the old canal
   Where rain-drops patter on the autumn leaves,
Now watching from some ivied orchard wall
   In slopes of stubble figures pile the sheaves;
Or under banks in shadow of their grass,
Blue water-flies by starts jettingly pass
'Mid large leaves level on the glassy cool;
   Or noiseless dizzy midges winking round
The yellow sallows of the meadow pool;
   While into cloudy silence ebbs each sound,
And sifts the moulting sunlight warm and mellow
O'er sandy beach remote, or slumberous flood,
Or rooky, red brick mansion by the wood,
   Mossed gate, or farmyard hay-stacks tanned and
      yellow.

XIV

NOW, winter's dolorous days are o'er, and through
March morning casements comes the sharp spring air,
And noises from the distant city, where
The steeples stand up keenly in the blue:
No more the clouds by crispy frost defined,
Pile the pale North, but float, dispersed shapes;
Though still around the cool grey twilight capes,
The sullen sea is dark with drifts of wind.
Like a forgotten fleck of snow still left,
The cascade gleams in the far mountain cleft;
Brown rushes by the river's brimming bank
Rustle, and matted sedges sway and sigh,
Where grasses in sleek shallows waver dank,
Or drift in windy ripples greyly by.

Spring

Blow, summer wind, from yonder ocean blow
Along the wild sea banks and grasses drear,
And loamy shores, where mosses brown and sere
And pale pinks in the sandy ridges grow;
Float round yon promontory in the brine,
Whose stretching arm in deepest azure lies,
Where quiet browse the heavy-uddered kine
By rock and shining shallow, grey and clear;
And fill, this listless hour, the dreamy ear
With thy scarce toned and wordless harmonies:
For here with Nature will I rest, and please
My heart with sweetest fancies all the noon,
Until the limpid crescent of the moon
Lights the blue east above the evening trees.

December

It is bleak December noon,
  Winter-wild and rainy grey:
By the old road thinly strewn
  Drifts of dead leaves skirts the way:
    Oh! the long canals are drear,
    And the floods o'erflow the weir,
    And the old deserted Year
Seems dying with the day.

By the banks the leafless larch
  Shakes its boughs in dismal plight;
The blank bridge's lonely arch
  Marks the sullen sky with white:
    Beyond the current flows

Through banks of misty snows,
And the wind the water blows
Here and there, a little bright.

From the dim and silent hill
Looks the moon with face of care
O'er the sad fields, frosty still,
And the icy brooklet there;
And nooked beside the way
The hamlet children play,
Whispering weirdly in the grey
Of the dumb cold evening air.

Iphione

WHERE in the summer-warm woodlands, with the sweet wind,
From yon blue ocean, solitarily smiling,
Wanderest thou, with tresses
Cinctureless, in wildernesses
Of whispering leaves and blown foam, like a fleet hind,
With virginal phantasies the hours beguiling?—
Now the cool, curved waves chasing,
Or, bosom-billowed, embracing
Cold passionless lovers of the eternal sea,
Throbbing with broken breathings innumerably:
Or, couched, with wet ear listening
To what some wreathed shell glistening
With dry salt sprays and rainbow colours is telling
Close to thy airy soul of its measureless dwelling—
Melodies of the sad brine,
Remote and lonely, dim, divine.

JAMES CLARENCE MANGAN
1803–1849

JAMES CLARENCE MANGAN

1803–1849

MANGAN is a problem both to the biographer and to the bibliographer—or he would be if the problem ever really arose. His poems have never been fully collected and his personal history has never been properly disentangled from his personal myth. But for ordinary purposes enough is probably known of both.

James Mangan, then, whose middle name was a romantic interpolation of his own, was born in Dublin on May Day, 1803. His father was a small grocer and wine-merchant of whom Mangan has left a curious and rather startling description:

'His nature was truly noble. He was of an ardent and forward-bounding disposition; and though deeply religious, he hated the restraints of social life, and seemed to think that all feelings with regard to family connections, and the obligations imposed by them, were beneath his notice. Me, my two brothers, and my sister, he treated habitually as a huntsman would treat refractory hounds. It was his boast, uttered in pure glee of heart, that we would run into a mouse-hole to shun him! While my mother lived, he made her miserable, he led my only sister such a life that she was obliged to leave our house; he kept up a continual succession of hostilities with my brothers; and if he spared me more than others, it was, perhaps, because I displayed a greater contempt of life and everything connected with it. May God assoil his great and mistaken soul, and grant him eternal peace and foregiveness! But I have an inward feeling that to him I owe all my misfortunes.'

One can hardly doubt that that passage throws more light on the son than it does upon the father. But it makes clear that Mangan looked back with not much pleasure at his childhood. And indeed, a father who managed to go bankrupt eight times was unlikely to provide a very good home for his family—and there is no question about the eight bankruptcies. So feckless was he that the children, whilst they were no more than children, were sent out to earn support for their parents. At least that was the children's story. It is known that Mangan himself at the age of fifteen was apprenticed to a scrivener where he worked long hours—from five in the morning, it is incredibly said, till eleven at night, summer and winter through—for seven years and small pay. From the scriveners he went to a solicitor's office. There he remained for an unknown number of years, variously estimated by his various biographers at three to eleven. He had been writing poems from at least the age of fifteen, and in about 1830 he began to earn something as a free-lance journalist. Translations were all the vogue at the time, and Mangan supplied 'translations', for the most part without any reference to real originals, which appeared copiously in the Dublin papers and magazines. In 1833 he fell in love with a young woman whom John Mitchell described as 'beautiful, spirituelle, and a coquette'. She, after at first encouraging Mangan, toyed with him, tired of him, and jilted him—thereby adding one more clause to his very genuine but, by himself, certainly exaggerated hard-luck story.

In 1838 the scholar and antiquary George Petrie got him a job in the historical branch of the Irish Ordnance Survey. He also had some sort of part-time employment in Trinity College Library. Here John Mitchell saw him:

'Being in the College Library, and having occasion for a book in that gloomy apartment called the Fagel Library, which is the innermost recess of the stately building, an acquaintance pointed out to me a man perched on the top of a ladder, with the whispered information that the figure was Clarence Mangan. It was an unearthly and ghostly figure, in a brown garment: the same garment, to all appearance, which lasted till the day of his death. The blanched hair was totally unkempt, the corpse-like features still as marble; a large book was in his arms, and all his soul was in the book.'

One can see that legendary accretions were bound to gather round such a character, and Mangan was amused and perhaps flattered by their growth, and certainly encouraged them.

Probably about this time he took to opium. The evidence for his being a drug-addict is very strong but, like everything else connected with him, not quite conclusive. It is hard to doubt that some of his poetry had this one factor in common with Crabbe's *World of Dreams* and *Sir Eustace Grey*. He himself wished it to be thought that his only anodyne was alcohol. In either case, he became unemployed and unemployable. He never lacked friends, and nothing could stop him writing poems. In June 1849, when cholera was epidemic in Dublin, he died smiling, happy in the last rites of his Church, and having written poetry practically up to the last minute, in the Meath Hospital where he had been taken by the Public Health authorities. His death, however, was not from cholera but from exposure and exhaustion.

Many people who knew or saw Mangan have left vivid descriptions of him. This is how he appeared to W. F. Wakeman, the historian, who worked in the Ordnance Survey with him—

'His teeth were an ill-fitting set. He used a large pair of green spectacles. He had narrow shoulders, so much so that for appearance sake the breast of his coat was thickly padded. His voice was low and sweet, but very tremulous. Sometimes, even in the most settled weather, he might be seen parading the streets with a very voluminous umbrella under each arm.'

Though his appearance must have been so unusual as to be freakish even in Dublin, his friends—Anster who translated Faust, or the priest Father Meehan—seem to have taken it in their stride; and for Mangan's own sake, not because he was a poet.

As a poet perhaps he is more disconcerting that he was as a person, for his poetry has this quality, that through long familiarity it is impossible to hold a constant, and difficult to strike a just, appreciation of its merits. Sometimes its force so arrests one that he must be almost a major poet—as Lionel Johnson seems to have held him. Though even Johnson's enthusiasm—the main cause of his own adoption of Irish nationality—was tempered by reservations. At other times his greatness is altogether illusive and Mangan becomes as meretricious as Poe, whom it is hard to believe he did not influence. A part explanation may be found in the fact that Mangan was a rhetorician and one is not always in the mood for rhetoric. And this more particularly because most of his readers, Irish no less than English, are accustomed to the English poetic tradition where obvious rhetoric has always seemed slightly ill-bred and beyond the pale. It is just condoned in Marlowe, it is not condoned in Macaulay, and all Mr. Eliot's casuistry has hardly made it acceptable in Kipling. But then, though Mangan wrote in English, he undoubtedly was from beyond the Pale. He too, like Callanan, wrote at his best in an un-English mode. In him what is recognisable as the 'Celtic note' was evident at its most strident. And Ireland was ever a land of orators where rhetoric was respected.

The difference between the two modes, the English and the Irish, can be seen by remembering some typically English poem, such as *When the lamp is shattered*, and then reading this comparable stanza from Mangan:

Weep, fairest and frailest!
Since bitter, though fruitless, regret
For the loss thou bewailest
Hath power to win tears from thee yet;
Weep, while from their fountain
Those drops of affliction can roll—
The snows on the mountain
Will soon be less cold than thy soul.

It is not only that Shelley is the better artist—perhaps stanza for stanza he is not—but that he never allows his poem to generate an emotion that he cannot perfectly subdue. Mangan, on the other hand, winds up his emotion to the frenzy of 'The snows on the mountain will soon be less cold than thy soul', which is very fine but, when the frenzy has settled, just a shade meaningless.

That tendency to excess is characteristic of his verse as a whole. So that after reading much of it one is spiritually deafened. But, taken a poem or two at a time, it has a verve and bravura which is urgently exciting. And in *My Dark Rosaleen* Mangan wrote one poem at least whose quality is unique and which approaches perfection.

J. C. MANGAN

BIBLIOGRAPHY

German Anthology, 1845.

Poets and Poetry of Munster, 1850.

Poems, edited with a memoir by John Mitchell, 1859

Poems of J. C. Mangan, edited by D. J. O'Donoghue, 1903.

Prose of J. C. Mangan, edited by D. J. O'Donoghue, 1903.

Life and Writings of J. C. Mangan, by J. D. O'Donoghue, 1898.

Mangan, by J. D. Sheridan, 1937.

Dark Rosaleen

O MY Dark Rosaleen,
  Do not sigh, do not weep!
The priests are on the ocean green,
  They march along the Deep.
There's wine . . . from the royal Pope
  Upon the ocean green;
And Spanish ale shall give you hope,
  My Dark Rosaleen!
  My own Rosaleen!
Shall glad your heart, shall give you hope,
Shall give you health, and help, and hope,
  My Dark Rosaleen.

Over hills and through dales
  Have I roamed for your sake;
All yesterday I sailed with sails
  On river and on lake.
The Erne . . . at its highest flood
    I dashed across unseen,
For there was lightning in my blood,
  My Dark Rosaleen!
  My own Rosaleen!
Oh! there was lightning in my blood,
Red lightning lightened through my blood,
  My Dark Rosaleen!

All day long in unrest
  To and fro do I move,
The very soul within my breast
  Is wasted for you, love!

The heart . . . in my bosom faints
  To think of you, my Queen,
My life of life, my saint of saints,
  My Dark Rosaleen!
  My own Rosaleen!
To hear your sweet and sad complaints,
My life, my love, my saint of saints,
  My Dark Rosaleen!

Woe and pain, pain and woe,
  Are my lot night and noon,
To see your bright face clouded so,
  Like to the mournful moon.
But yet . . . will I rear your throne
  Again in golden sheen;
'Tis you shall reign, shall reign alone,
  My Dark Rosaleen!
  My own Rosaleen!
'Tis you shall have the golden throne,
'Tis you shall reign, and reign alone,
  My Dark Rosaleen!

Over dews, over sands
  Will I fly for your weal;
Your holy delicate white hands
  Shall girdle me with steel.
At home . . . in your emerald bowers,
  From morning's dawn till e'en,
You'll pray for me, my flower of flowers,
  My Dark Rosaleen!
  My fond Rosaleen!
You'll think of me through Daylight's hours,
My virgin flower, my flower of flowers,
  My Dark Rosaleen!

I could scale the blue air,
  I could plough the high hills,
Oh, I could kneel all night in prayer,
  To heal your many ills!
And one . . . beamy smile from you
  Would float like light between
My toils and me, my own, my true,
  My Dark Rosaleen!
  My fond Rosaleen!
Would give me life and soul anew,
A second life, a soul anew,
  My Dark Rosaleen!

O! the Erne shall run red
  With redundance of blood,
The earth shall rock beneath our tread,
  And flames wrap hill and wood,
And gun-peal, and slogan cry,
  Wake many a glen serene,
Ere you shall fade, ere you shall die,
  My Dark Rosaleen!
  My own Rosaleen!
The Judgment Hour must first be nigh,
Ere you can fade, ere you can die,
  My Dark Rosaleen!

O'Hussey's Ode to the Maguire

From the Irish of O'Hussey

WHERE is my Chief, my Master, this bleak night, *mavrone!*
O, cold, cold, miserably cold is this bleak night for Hugh,

It's showery, arrowy, speary sleet pierceth one through and through,
Pierceth one to the very bone!

Rolls real thunder? Or was that red, livid light
Only a meteor? I scarce know; but through the midnight dim
The pitiless ice-wind streams. Except the hate that persecutes *him*
Nothing hath crueller venomy might.

An awful, a tremendous night is this, meseems!
The flood-gates of the rivers of heaven, I think, have been burst wide—
Down from the overcharged clouds, like unto headlong ocean's tide,
Descends grey rain in roaring streams.

Though he were even a wolf ranging the round green woods,
Though he were even a pleasant salmon in the unchainable sea,
Though he were a wild mountain eagle, he could scarce bear, he,
This sharp, sore sleet, these howling floods.

O, mournful is my soul this night for Hugh Maguire!
Darkly, as in a dream, he strays! Before him and behind
Triumphs the tyrannous anger of the wounding wind,
The wounding wind, that burns as fire!

It is my bitter grief—it cuts me to the heart—
That in the country of Clan Darry this should be his fate!

O, woe is me, where is he? Wandering, houseless, desolate,
Alone, without or guide or chart!

Medreams I see just now his face, the strawberry bright,
Uplifted to the blackened heavens, while the tempestuous winds
Blow fiercely over and round him, and the smiting sleet-shower blinds
The hero of Galang to-night!

Large, large affliction unto me and mine it is,
That one of his majestic bearing, his fair, stately form,
Should thus be tortured and o'erborne—that this unsparing storm
Should wreak its wrath on head like his!

That his great hand, so oft the avenger of the oppressed,
Should this chill, churlish night, perchance, be paralysed by frost—
While through some icicle-hung thicket—as one lorn and lost—
He walks and wanders without rest.

The tempest-driven torrent deluges the mead,
It overflows the low banks of the rivulets and ponds—
The lawns and pasture-grounds lie locked in icy bonds
So that the cattle cannot feed.

The pale bright margins of the streams are seen by none.
Rushes and sweeps along the untamable flood on every side—

It penetrates and fills the cottagers' dwellings far and
wide—
Water and land are blent in one.

Through some dark woods, 'mid bones of monsters,
Hugh now strays,
As he confronts the storm with anguished heart, but
manly brow—
O! what a sword-wound to that tender heart of his
were now
A backward glance at peaceful days.

But other thoughts are his—thoughts that can still
inspire
With joy and an onward-bounding hope the bosom of
Mac-Nee—
Thoughts of his warriors charging like bright billows
of the sea,
Borne on the wind's wings, flashing fire!

And though frost glaze to-night the clear dew of his
eyes,
And white ice-gauntlets glove his noble fine fair fingers
o'er,
A warm dress is to him that lightning-garb he ever
wore,
The lightning of the soul, not skies.

AVRAN[1]

Hugh marched forth to the fight—I grieved to see him
so depart;
And lo! to-night he wanders frozen, rain-drenched,
sad, betrayed—

[1] A concluding stanza, generally intended as a recapitulation of the entire poem.

But the memory of the lime-white mansions his right
  hand hath laid
In ashes warms the hero's heart!

A Lamentation

FOR THE DEATH OF SIR MAURICE FITZGERALD, KNIGHT OF KERRY

From the Irish of Pierce Ferriter

THERE was lifted up one voice of woe,
  One lament of more than mortal grief,
Through the wide South to and fro,
  For a fallen Chief.
In the dead of night that cry thrilled through me,
  I looked out upon the midnight air!
Mine own soul was all as gloomy,
  And I knelt in prayer.

O'er Loch Gur, that night, once—twice—yea, thrice—
  Passed a wail of anguish for the Brave
That half curdled into ice
  Its moon-mirroring wave.
Then uprose a many-toned wild hymn in
  Choral swell from Ogra's dark ravine,
And Mogeely's Phantom Women [1]
  Mourned the Geraldine!

Far on Carah Mona's emerald plains
  Shrieks and sighs were blended many hours,
And Fermoy in fitful strains
  Answered from her towers.
Youghal, Keenalmeaky, Eemokilly

[1] Banshees.

Mourned in concert, and their piercing *keen*
Woke to wondering life the stilly
Glens of Inchiqueen.

From Loughmoe to yellow Dunanore
There was fear; the traders of Tralee
Gathered up their golden store,
And prepared to flee;
For, in ship and hall from night till morning
Showed the first faint beamings of the sun,
All the foreigners heard the warning
Of the Dreaded One!

'This,' they spake, 'portendeth death to us,
If we fly not swiftly from our fate!'
Self-conceited idiots! thus
Ravingly to prate!
Not for base-born higgling Saxon trucksters
Ring laments like those by shore and sea!
Not for churls with souls of hucksters
Waileth our Banshee!

For the high Milesian race alone
Ever flows the music of her woe!
For slain heir to bygone throne,
And for Chief laid low!
Hark! . . . Again, methinks, I hear her weeping
Yonder! Is she near me now, as then?
Or was't but the night-wind sweeping
Down the hollow glen?

The Woman of Three Cows

From the Irish

O WOMAN of Three Cows, *agra!* don't let your tongue
thus rattle!
O, don't be saucy, don't be stiff, because you may have
cattle.
I have seen—and, here's my hand to you, I only say
what's true—
A many a one with twice your stock not half so proud
as you.

Good luck to you, don't scorn the poor, and don't be
their despiser,
For worldly wealth soon melts away, and cheats the
very miser,
And Death soon strips the proudest wreath from
haughty human brows;
Then don't be stiff, and don't be proud, good Woman
of Three Cows!

See where Momonia's heroes lie, proud Owen More's
descendants,
'Tis they that won the glorious name, and had the
grand attendants!
If *they* were forced to bow to Fate, as every mortal
bows,
Can *you* be proud, can *you* be stiff, my Woman of
Three Cows!

The brave sons of the Lord of Clare, they left the land
to mourning;
Mavrone! for they were banished, with no hope of their
returning—

Who knows in what abodes of want those youths were
driven to house?
Yet *you* can give yourself these airs, O Woman of
Three Cows!

O, think of Donnell of the Ships, the Chief whom
nothing daunted—
See how he fell in distant Spain, unchronicled,
unchanted!
He sleeps, the great O'Sullivan, where thunder cannot
rouse—
Then ask yourself, should *you* be proud, good Woman
of Three Cows!

O'Ruark, Maguire, those souls of fire, whose names
are shrined in story—
Think how their high achievements once made Erin's
highest glory—
Yet now their bones lie mouldering under weeds and
cypress boughs,
And so, for all your pride, will yours, O Woman of
Three Cows!

The O'Carrolls, also, famed when Fame was only for
the boldest,
Rest in forgotten sepulchres with Erin's best and
oldest;
Yet who so great as they of yore in battle or carouse?
Just think of that, and hide your head, good Woman
of Three Cows!

Your neighbour's poor, and you, it seems, are big with
vain ideas,
Because, *inagh!* you've got three cows—one more, I
see, than *she* has.

That tongue of yours wags more at times than Charity allows,
But if you're strong, be merciful, great Woman of Three Cows!

THE SUMMING UP

Now, there you go! You still, of course, keep up your scornful bearing,
And I'm too poor to hinder you; but, by the cloak I'm wearing,
If I had but *four* cows myself, even though you were my spouse,
I'd thwack you well to cure your pride, my Woman of Three Cows!

The Fair Hills of Eirè, O!

From the Irish of Donogh Mac-Con-Mara, or Macnamara

TAKE a blessing from my heart to the land of my birth
And the fair hills of Eirè, O!
And to all that yet survive of Eibhear's tribe on earth,
On the fair hills of Eirè, O!
In that land so delightful the wild thrush's lay
Seems to pour a lament forth for Eirè's decay.
Alas, alas! why pine I a thousand miles away
From the fair hills of Eirè, O!

The soil is rich and soft, the air is mild and bland,
On the fair hills of Eirè, O!
Her barest rock is greener to me than this rude land;
O, the fair hills of Eirè, O!
Her woods are tall and straight, grove rising over grove,

Trees flourish in her glens below and on her heights
above;
Ah! in heart and in soul I shall ever, ever love
The fair hills of Eirè, O!

A noble tribe, moreover, are the now hapless Gael,
On the fair hills of Eirè, O!
A tribe in battle's hour unused to shrink or fail,
On the fair hills of Eirè, O!
For this is my lament in bitterness outpoured
To see them slain or scattered by the Saxon sword;
O, woe of woes! to see a foreign spoiler horde
On the fair hills of Eirè, O!

Broad and tall rise the *cruachs* in the golden morning
glow
On the fair hills of Eirè, O!
O'er her smooth grass for ever sweet cream and honey
flow
On the fair hills of Eirè, O!
Oh, I long, I am pining, again to behold
The land that belongs to the brave Gael of old!
Far dearer to my heart than a gift of gems or gold
Are the fair hills of Eirè, O!

The dewdrops lie bright 'mid the grass and yellow corn
On the fair hills of Eirè, O!
The sweet-scented apples blush redly in the morn
On the fair hills of Eirè, O!
The water-cress and sorrel fill the vales below,
The streamlets are hushed till the evening breezes blow,
While the waves of the Suir, noble river! ever flow
'Neath the fair hills of Eirè, O!

A fruitful clime is Eirè, through valley, meadow, plain,
And the fair hills of Eirè, O!

The very bread of life is in the yellow grain
  On the fair hills of Eirè, O!
Far dearer unto me than the tones music yields
Is the lowing of the kine and the calves in her fields,
In the sunlight that shone long ago on the shields
  Of the Gaels, on the fair hills of Eirè, O!

from

The Geraldine's Daughter

From the Irish of Egan O'Rahilly

A BEAUTY all stainless, a pearl of a maiden,
  Has plunged me in trouble, and wounded my heart;
With sorrow and gloom is my soul overladen,
  An anguish is there that will never depart.
I would voyage to Egypt across the deep water,
  Nor care about bidding dear Eirè farewell,
So I only might gaze on the Geraldine's daughter,
  And sit by her side in some green, pleasant dell!

Her curling locks wave round her figure of lightness,
  All dazzling and long, like the purest of gold;
Her blue eyes resemble twin stars in their brightness,
  And her brow is like marble or wax to behold.
The radiance of heaven illumines her features
  Where the snows and the rose have erected their
    throne;
It would seem that the sun had forgotten all creatures,
  To shine on the Geraldine's daughter alone.

Her bosom is swan-white, her waist smooth and
    slender,
  Her speech is like music, so sweet and so free;

The feelings that glow in her noble heart lend her
  A mien and a majesty lovely to see.
Her lips, red as berries, but riper than any,
  Would kiss away even a sorrow like mine!
No wonder such heroes and noblemen many
  Should cross the blue ocean to kneel at her shrine.

Ellen Bawn

From the Irish

ELLEN BAWN, O Ellen Bawn, you darling, darling dear, you,
Sit awhile beside me here, I'll die unless I'm near you!
'Tis for you I'd swim the Suir and breast the Shannon's waters;
For, Ellen dear, you've not your peer in Galway's blooming daughters!

Had I Limerick's gems and gold at will to mete and measure,
Were Loughrea's abundance mine, and all Portumna's treasure,
These might lure me, might insure me many and many a new love,
But O! no bribe could pay your tribe for one like you, my true love!

Blessings be on Connaught! that's the place for sport and raking!
Blessing, too, my love, on you, a-sleeping and a-waking!

I'd have met you, dearest Ellen, when the sun went under,
But, woe! the flooding Shannon broke across my path in thunder!

Ellen! I'd give all the deer in Limerick's parks and arbours,
Ay, and all the ships that rode last year in Munster's harbours,
Could I blot from Time the hour I first became your lover,
For, O! you've given my heart a wound it never can recover!

Would to God that in the sod my corpse to-night were lying,
And the wild birds wheeling o'er it, and the winds a-sighing,
Since your cruel mother and your kindred choose to sever
Two hearts that Love would blend in one for ever and for ever!

Welcome to the Prince of Ossory

From the Irish of William Heffernan the Blind

I

LIFT . . . up the drooping head,
Meehal Dubh Mac-Giolla-Kierin!
Her blood yet boundeth red
Through the myriad veins of Erin.
No! no! she is not dead,
Meehal Dubh Mac-Giolla-Kierin!

Lo! she redeems
The lost years of bygone ages—
New glory beams
Henceforth on her History's pages!
Her long penitential Night of Sorrow
Yields at length before the reddening Morrow!

II

You . . . heard the thunder-shout,
Meehal Dubh Mac-Giolla-Kierin!
Saw lightning streaming out
O'er the purple hills of Erin!
And bide you yet in doubt,
Meehal Dubh Mac-Giolla-Kierin?
O! doubt no more!
Through Ulidia's voiceful valleys,
On . . . Shannon's shore,
Freedom's burning spirit rallies,
Earth and Heaven unite in sign and omen
Bodeful of the downfall of our foemen.

III

Thurot commands the North,
Meehal Dubh Mac-Giolla-Kierin!
Louth sends her heroes forth
To hew down the foes of Erin!
Swords gleam in field and gorth,
Up! up! my friend!
There's a glorious goal before us;
Here will we blend
Speech and soul in this grand chorus—
'By the Heaven that gives us one more token,
We will die, or see our shackles broken!'

IV

Charles leaves the Grampian hills,
Meehal Dubh Mac-Giolla-Kierin!
Charles, whose appeal yet thrills,
Like a clarion-blast, through Erin.
Charles, he whose image fills
Thy soul, too, Mac-Giolla-Kierin!
Ten . . . thousand strong,
His clans move in brilliant order,
Sure that e'er long
He will march them o'er the Border,
While the dark-haired daughters of the Highlands
Crown with wreaths the Monarch of three islands!

V

Fill, then, the ale-cup high,
Meehal Dubh Mac-Giolla-Kierin!
Fill!—the bright hour is nigh
That shall give her own to Erin!
Those who so sadly sigh,
Even as you, Mac-Giolla-Kierin,
Henceforth shall sing.
Hark!—O'er heathery hill and dell come
Shouts for the King!
Welcome, our Deliverer! Welcome!
Thousands this glad night, ere turning bedward,
Will, with us, drink 'Victory to Charles Edward!'

Night is Nearing

From the Persian

Allah Akbar![1]
All things vanish after brief careering;
Down one gulf Life's myriad barks are steering;
Headlong mortal! hast thou ears for hearing?
Pause! Be wise! The Night, thy Night, is nearing!
Night is nearing!

Allah Akbar!
Towards the Darkness whence no ray is peering,
Towards the Void from which no voice comes cheering,
Move the countless Doomed—none volunteering—
While the Winds rise and the Night is nearing!
Night is nearing!

Allah Akbar!
See the palace-dome its pride uprearing
One fleet hour, then darkly disappearing!
So must all of Lofty or Endearing
Fade, fail, fall;—to all the Night is nearing!
Night is nearing!

Allah Akbar!
Then, since nought abides, but all is veering,
Flee a world which Sin is hourly searing,
Only so mayest front thy fate unfearing
When Life wanes, and Death, like Night, is nearing!
Night is nearing!

[1] Great is God.

A Triplet on the Reign of the Great Sultan

BY NEDSCHATI

SUCH are the stillness and peace that prevail through the Sultan's dominions
That the dread Angel of Death, when he startles thy couch with his pinions,
Can bring thee no stillier peace than is found in the Sultan's dominions.

Three Proverbs

From the Ottoman

I

AN hour of Good, a day of Ill,
This is the lot of mourning Man,
Who leaves the world whene'er he will,
But goes to Heaven whene'er he—can.

II

The steed to the man who bestrides it newly,
The sabre to him who best can wield it,
The damsel to him who has wooed her truly,
And the province to him who refuses to yield it.

III

Nought, I hear thee say,
Can fill the greedy eye;
Yet a little clay
Will fill it by and by.

Gone in the Wind

SOLOMON! where is thy throne? It is gone in the wind.
Babylon! where is thy might? It is gone in the wind.
Like the swift shadows of Noon, like the dreams of the
Blind,
Vanish the glories and pomps of the earth in the wind.

Man! canst thou build upon aught in the pride of thy
mind?
Wisdom will teach thee that nothing can tarry behind;
Though there be thousand bright actions embalmed
and enshrined,
Myriads and millions of brighter are snow in the wind.

Solomon! where is thy throne? It is gone in the wind.
Babylon! where is thy might? It is gone in the wind.
All that the genius of Man hath achieved or designed
Waits but its hour to be dealt with as dust by the wind.

Say, what is Pleasure? A phantom, a mask undefined;
Science? An almond, whereof we can pierce but the
rind;
Honour and Affluence? Firmans that Fortune hath
signed
Only to glitter and pass on the wings of the wind.

Solomon! where is thy throne? It is gone in the wind.
Babylon! where is thy might? It is gone in the wind.
Who is the Fortunate? He who in anguish hath pined!
He shall rejoice when his relics are dust in the wind!

Mortal! be careful with what thy best hopes are
  entwined;
Woe to the miners for Truth—where the Lampless
  have mined!
Woe to the seekers on earth for—what none ever find!
They and their trust shall be scattered like leaves on the
  wind.

Solomon! where is thy throne? It is gone in the wind.
Babylon! where is thy might? It is gone in the wind.
Happy in death are they only whose hearts have con-
  signed
All Earth's affections and longings and cares to the
  wind.

Pity, thou, reader! the madness of poor Humankind,
Raving of Knowledge,—and Satan so busy to blind!
Raving of Glory,—like me,—for the garlands I bind
(Garlands of song) are but gathered, and—strewn in
  the wind!

Solomon! where is thy throne? It is gone in the wind.
Babylon! where is thy might? It is gone in the wind.
I, Abul-Namez, must rest; for my fire hath declined,
And I hear voices from Hades like bells on the wind.

And Then No More

I SAW her once, one little while, and then no more:
'Twas Eden's light on Earth awhile, and then no more.
Amid the throng she passed along the meadow-floor:
Spring seemed to smile on Earth awhile, and then no
  more;

But whence she came, which way she went, what garb
she wore
I noted not; I gazed awhile, and then no more!

I saw her once, one little while, and then no more:
'Twas Paradise on Earth awhile, and then no more.
Ah! what avail my vigils pale, my magic lore?
She shone before mine eyes awhile, and then no more.
The shallop of my peace is wrecked on Beauty's shore.
Near Hope's fair isle it rode awhile, and then no more!

I saw her once, one little while, and then no more:
Earth looked like Heaven a little while, and then no
more.
Her presence thrilled and lighted to its inner core
My desert breast a little while, and then no more.
So may, perchance, a meteor glance at midnight o'er
Some ruined pile a little while, and then no more!

I saw her once, one little while, and then no more:
The earth was Peri-land awhile, and then no more.
Oh, might I see but once again, as once before,
Through chance or wile, that shape awhile, and then
no more!
Death soon would heal my griefs! This heart, now sad
and sore,
Would beat anew a little while, and then no more.

Ichabod! Thy Glory has Departed

I RIDE through a dark, dark Land by night,
Where moon is none and no stars lend light,
And rueful winds are blowing;

Yet oft have I trodden this way ere now,
With summer zephyrs a-fanning my brow,
And the gold of the sunshine glowing.

I roam by a gloomy garden wall;
The death-stricken leaves around me fall;
And the night-blast wails its dolours;
How oft with my love I have hitherward strayed
When the roses flowered, and all I surveyed
Was radiant with Hope's own colours!

But the gold of the sunshine is shed and gone
And the once bright roses are dead and wan,
And my love in her low grave moulders,
And I ride through a dark, dark land by night
With never a star to bless me with light,
And the Mantle of Age on my shoulders.

Song

O, STREW the way with rosy flowers,
And dupe with smiles thy grief and gloom,
For tarnished wreaths and songless hours
Await thee in the tomb.
Lo! in the brilliant festal hall
How lightly Youth and Beauty tread!
Yet, gaze again—the grass is tall
Above their charnel bed!

In blaze of noon the jewelled bride
Before the altar plights her faith:
Ere weep the skies of eventide
Her eyes are dulled in death!

Then sigh no more—if life is brief
  So are its woes; and why repine?
Pavilioned by the linden leaf
  We'll quaff the chaliced wine.

Wild music from the nightingale
  Comes floating on the loaded breeze,
To mingle in the bowery vale
  With hum of summer bees:
Then taste the joys that God bestows,
  The beaded wine, the faithful kiss,
For while the tide of Pleasure flows,
  Death bares his black abyss.

In vain the Zephyr's breath perfumes
  The House of Death—in vain its tones
Shall mourn at midnight round the tombs
  Where sleep our blackening bones.
The star-bright bowl is broken there,
  The witchery of the lute is o'er,
And—wreck of wrecks!—there lie the Fair
  Whose beauty wins no more!

The Lover's Farewell

SLOWLY through the tomb-still streets I go—
  Morn is dark, save one swart streak of gold—
Sullen rolls the far-off river's flow,
  And the moon is very thin and cold.

Long and long before the house I stand
  Where sleeps she, the dear, dear one I love—
All undreaming that I leave my land,
  Mute and mourning, like the moon above!

Wishfully I stretch abroad mine arms
  Towards the well-remembered casement-cell—
Fare thee well! Farewell thy virgin charms!
  And thou stilly, stilly house, farewell!

And farewell the dear dusk little room,
  Redolent of roses as a dell,
And the lattice that relieved its gloom—
  And its pictured lilac walls, farewell!

Forth upon my path! I must not wait—
  Bitter blows the fretful morning wind:
Warden, wilt thou softly close the gate
  When thou knowest I leave my heart behind?

from

To My Native Land

i

AWAKE! arise! shake off thy dreams!
  Thou art not what thou wert of yore:
Of all those rich, those dazzling beams,
  That once illum'd thine aspect o'er
Show me a solitary one
Whose glory is not quenched and gone.

The harp remaineth where it fell,
  With mouldering frame and broken chord;
Around the song there hangs no spell—
  No laurel wreath entwines the sword;
And startlingly the footstep falls
Along thy dim and dreary halls.

ii

Thou art forsaken by the earth,
  Which makes a byword of thy name;
Nations, and thrones, and powers whose birth
  As yet is not, shall rise to fame,
Shall flourish and may fail—but thou
Shalt linger as thou lingerest now.

And till all earthly power shall wane,
  And Time's grey pillar, groaning, fall;
Thus shall it be, and still in vain
  Thou shalt essay to burst the thrall
Which binds, in fetters forged by fate,
The wreck and ruin of what once was great.

A Vision of Connaught in the Thirteenth Century

I WALKED entranced
  Through a land of Morn;
The sun, with wondrous excess of light,
  Shone down and glanced
    Over seas of corn
And lustrous gardens aleft and right
  Even in the clime
    Of resplendent Spain,
Beams no such sun upon such a land;
  But it was the time,
    'Twas in the reign,
Of Cáhal Mór of the Wine-red Hand.

  Anon stood nigh
    By my side a man
Of princely aspect and port sublime.

Him queried I—
'O, my Lord and Khan,[1]
What clime is this, and what golden time?'
When he—'The clime
Is a clime to praise,
The clime is Erin's, the green and bland;
And it is the time,
These be the days,
Of Cáhal Mór of the Wine-red Hand!'

Then saw I thrones,
And circling fires,
And a Dome rose near me, as by a spell,
Whence flowed the tones
Of silver lyres,
And many voices in wreathèd swell;
And their thrilling chime
Fell on mine ears
As the heavenly hymn of an angel-band—
'It is now the time,
These be the years,
Of Cáhal Mór of the Wine-red Hand!'

I sought the hall,
And, behold!—a change
From light to darkness, from joy to woe!
King, nobles, all,
Looked aghast and strange;
The minstrel-group sate in dumbest show!
Had some great crime
Wrought this dread amaze,
This terror? None seemed to understand
'Twas then the time
We were in the days,
Of Cáhal Mór of the Wine-red Hand.

[1] *Ceann*, the Gaelic title for a chief.

I again walked forth;
But lo! the sky
Showed fleckt with blood, and an alien sun
Glared from the north,
And there stood on high,
Amid his shorn beams, a skeleton!
It was by the stream
Of the castled Maine,
One Autumn eve, in the Teuton's land,
That I dreamed this dream
Of the time and reign
Of Cáhal Mór of the Wine-red Hand!

The Nameless One

BALLAD

ROLL forth, my song, like the rushing river,
That sweeps along to the mighty sea;
God will inspire me while I deliver
My soul of thee!

Tell thou the world, when my bones lie whitening
Amid the last homes of youth and eld,
That there was once one whose veins ran lightning
No eye beheld.

Tell how his boyhood was one drear night-hour,
How shone for *him*, through his griefs and gloom,
No star of all heaven sends to light our
Path to the tomb.

Roll on, my song, and to after ages
  Tell how, disdaining all earth can give,
He would have taught men, from wisdom's pages,
    The way to live.

And tell how trampled, derided, hated,
  And worn by weakness, disease, and wrong,
He fled for shelter to God, who mated
    His soul with song—

With song which alway, sublime or vapid,
  Flowed like a rill in the morning beam,
Perchance not deep, but intense and rapid
    A mountain stream.

Tell how this Nameless, condemned for years long
  To herd with demons from hell beneath,
Saw things that made him, with groans and tears, long
    For even death.

Go on to tell how, with genius wasted,
  Betrayed in friendship, befooled in love,
With spirit shipwrecked, and young hopes blasted,
    He still, still strove.

Till, spent with toil, dreeing death for others,
  And some whose hands should have wrought for *him*
(If children live not for sires and mothers,)
    His mind grew dim.

And he fell far through that pit abysmal
  The gulf and grave of Maginn and Burns,
And pawned his soul for the devil's dismal
    Stock of returns.

But yet redeemed it in days of darkness
  And shapes and signs of the final wrath,
When death, in hideous and ghastly starkness,
          Stood on his path.

And tell how now, amid wreck and sorrow,
  And want, and sickness, and houseless nights,
He bides in calmness the silent morrow,
          That no ray lights.

And lives he still, then? Yes! Old and hoary
  At thirty-nine, from despair and woe,
He lives enduring what future story
          Will never know.

Him grant a grave to, ye pitying noble,
  Deep in your bosoms! There let him dwell!
He, too, had tears for all souls in trouble,
          Here and in hell.

Sonnet

Bird that discoursest from yon poplar bough,
  Outweeping night, and in thy eloquent tears
  Holding sweet converse with the thousand spheres
That glow and glisten from Night's glorious brow—
Oh! may thy lot be mine! that, lonely now,
  And doomed to mourn the remnant of my years,
  My song may swell to more than mortal ears,
And sweet as in thy strain be poured my vow!
Bird of the poet's paradise! by thee

Taught where the tides of feeling deepest tremble,
Playful in gloom, like some sequestered sea,
I, too, amidst my anguish would dissemble,
And turn misfortune to such melody
That my despair thy transports would resemble!

Love

SPIRIT of wordless love! that in the lone
Bowers of the poet's museful soul doth weave
Tissues of thought, hued like the skies of eve
Ere the last glories of the sun hath shone!
How soon, almost before our hearts have known
The change, above the ruins of thy throne
Whose trampled beauty we would fain retrieve
By all earth's thrones beside, we stand and grieve!
We weep not, for the world's chill breath hath bound
In triple ice the fountain of our tears,
And ever-mourning memory thenceforth rears
Her altars upon desecrated ground,
And always, with a low despairful sound,
Tolls the disastrous bell of all our years!

Siberia

IN Siberia's wastes
The Ice-wind's breath
Woundeth like the toothèd steel;
Lost Siberia doth reveal
Only blight and death.

Blight and death alone.
No Summer shines.
Night is interblent with Day.
In Siberia's wastes alway
The blood blackens, the heart pines.

In Siberia's wastes
No tears are shed,
For they freeze within the brain.
Nought is felt but dullest pain,
Pain acute, yet dead;

Pain as in a dream,
When years go by
Funeral-paced, yet fugitive,
When man lives, and doth not live,
Doth not live—nor die.

In Siberia's wastes
Are sands and rocks.
Nothing blooms of green or soft,
But the snow-peaks rise aloft
And the gaunt ice-blocks.

And the exile there
Is one with those;
They are part, and he is part,
For the sands are in his heart,
And the killing snows.

Therefore, in those wastes
None curse the Czar.
Each man's tongue is cloven by
The North Blast, that heweth nigh
With sharp scymitar.

And such doom each drees,
  Till, hunger-gnawn,
And cold-slain, he at length sinks there,
Yet scarce more a corpse than ere
  His last breath was drawn.

from

Twenty Golden Years Ago

i

O, THE rain, the weary, dreary rain,
  How it plashes on the window-sill!
Night, I guess too, must be on the wane,
  Strass and Gass around are grown so still.
Here I sit, with coffee in my cup—
  Ah! 'twas rarely I beheld it flow
In the taverns where I loved to sup
    Twenty golden years ago!

Twenty years ago, alas!—but stay,
  On my life, 'tis half-past twelve o'clock!
After all, the hours *do* slip away—
  Come, here goes to burn another block!
For the night, or morn, is wet and cold,
  And my fire is dwindling rather low:—
I had fire enough, when young and bold,
    Twenty golden years ago!

Dear! I don't feel well at all, somehow:
  Few in Weimar dream how bad I am;
Floods of tears grow common with me now,
  High-Dutch floods, that Reason cannot dam.
Doctors think I'll neither live nor thrive

If I mope at home so—I don't know—
Am I living *now?* I *was* alive
Twenty golden years ago.

Wifeless, friendless, flagonless, alone,
Not quite bookless, though, unless I chuse,
Left with nought to do, except to groan,
Not a soul to woo, except the Muse—
O! this, this is hard for *me* to bear,
Me, who whilome lived so much *en haut*,
Me, who broke all hearts like chinaware
Twenty golden years ago!

ii

Did I paint a fifth of what I feel,
O, how plaintive you would ween I was!
But I won't, albeit I have a deal
More to wail about than Kerner has!
Kerner's tears are wept for withered flowers,
Mine for withered hopes; my Scroll of Woe
Dates, alas! from Youth's deserted bowers,
Twenty golden years ago!

iii

Tick-tick, tick-tick!—Not a sound save Time's,
And the windgust, as it drives the rain—
Tortured torturer of reluctant rhymes,
Go to bed, and rest thine aching brain!
Sleep!—no more the dupe of hopes or schemes;
Soon thou sleepest where the thistles blow—
Curious anticlimax to thy dreams
Twenty golden years ago!

The Dying Enthusiast

BALLAD

SPEAK no more of life,
What can life bestow,
In this amphitheatre of strife,
All times dark with tragedy and woe?
Knowest thou not how care and pain
Build their lampless dwelling in the brain,
Ever, as the stern intrusion
Of our teachers, time and truth,
Turn to gloom the bright illusion,
Rainbowed on the soul of youth?
Could I live to find that this is so?
Oh! no! no!

As the stream of time
Sluggishly doth flow,
Look how all of beaming and sublime,
Sinks into the black abysm below.
Yea, the loftiest intellect,
Earliest on the strand of life is wrecked.
Nought of lovely, nothing glorious,
Lives to triumph o'er decay;
Desolation reigns victorious—
Mind is dungeon-walled by clay;
Could I bear to feel mine own laid low?
Oh! no! no!

Restless o'er the earth
Thronging millions go:
But behold how genius, love, and worth,
Move like lonely phantoms to and fro.
Suns are quenched, and kingdoms fall,

But the doom of these outdarkens all!
Die they then? Yes, love's devotion,
  Stricken, withers in its bloom;
Fond affections, deep as ocean,
  In their cradle find their tomb:
Shall I linger, then, to count each throe?
Oh! no! no!

Prison-bursting death!
  Welcome be thy blow!
Thine is but the forfeit of my breath,
  Not the spirit! nor the spirit's glow.
Spheres of beauty—hallowed spheres,
Undefaced by time, undimmed by tears,
Henceforth hail! oh, who would grovel,
  In a world, impure as this?
Who would weep, in cell or hovel,
  When a palace might be his?
Wouldst thou have me the bright lot forego?
Oh! no! no!

Disaster

I KNEW that Disaster
  Would shadow thy morning, and must;
The fair alabaster
  Is easily trampled to dust.
If the bright lake lay stilly
  When whirlwinds rose to deform,
If the life of the lily
  Were charmed against every storm,
Thou mightest, though human,
  Have smiled through the saddest of years—

Thou mightest, though Woman,
  Have lived unacquainted with tears.

Weep, hapless forsaken!
  In my lyrical art I can find
No spell that may waken
  The glow of young hope in thy mind.
Weep, fairest and frailest!
  Since bitter, though fruitless, regret
For the loss thou bewailest
  Hath power to win tears from thee yet;
Weep, while from their fountain
  Those drops of affliction can roll—
The snows on the mountain
  Will soon be less cold than thy soul.

Not always shall Sorrow
  As a scimitar pierce to thy core;
There cometh a morrow
  When its tyranny daunteth no more
Chill Habitude, steeling
  The breast, consecrates it to Pride,
And the current of Feeling
  Is locked like a firm winter-tide,
And the stricken heart pillows
  Itself in repose upon Pain,
And cares roll in billows
  O'er the hull of the soul still in vain.

But the crumbling palace
  Is lovely through ruin and ill,
And the wineless chalice
  Sheds light on the banquet still;
And as odours of glory
  Exhale from the patriot's shroud,
As the mountain, though hoary

And barren, still kisses the cloud,
So may thine affections
Live on, though their fervour be past,
And the heart's recollections
May hallow their shrine to the last!

The Night is Falling

THE night is falling in chill December,
The frost is mantling the silent stream,
Dark mists are shrouding the mountain's brow;
My soul is weary: I now
Remember
The days of roses but as a dream.

The icy hand of the old Benumber,
The hand of Winter is on my brain,
I try to smile, while I inly grieve:
I dare not hope or believe
That Summer
Will ever brighten the earth again,

So, gazing gravewards, albeit immortal,
Man cannot pierce through the girdling Night
That sunders Time from Eternity,
Nor feel this death-valse to be
The portal
To realms of glory and Living Light.

Volto Sciolto e Pensieri Stretti

Lock up thy heart within thy breast alway,
  And wear it not as bait upon thy face,
For there be more devouring beasts of prey
  Than haunt the woods, among the human race.

Enthusiasm

Not yet trodden under wholly,
  Not yet darkened,
    Oh, my spirit's flickering lamp, art thou!
Still, alas! thou wanest—though but slowly;
  And I feel as though my heart had hearkened
    To the whispers of despondence now.

Yet the world shall not enthral me—
  Never! never!
    On my briary pathway to the grave
Shapes of pain and peril may appal me,
Agony and ruin may befal me—
  Darkness and dismay may lower ever,
    But, cold world, I will not die thy slave!

Underneath my foot I trample
  You, ye juggles—
    Pleasure, passion, thirst of power and gold!
Shall I, dare I, shame the bright example,
  Beaming, burning in the deeds and struggles
    Of the consecrated few of old?

Sacred flame—which art eternal!
  Oh! bright essence!

Thou, Enthusiasm! forsake me not!
Oh, though life bereft of all her vernal
Beauty, ever let thy magic presence
Shed its glory round my clouded lot.

The Mariner's Bride

From the Spanish

Look, Mother! the Mariner's rowing
His galley a-down the tide;
I'll go where the mariner's going,
And be the mariner's bride!

I saw him one day through the wicket,
I opened the gate and we met—
As a bird in the fowler's net
Was I caught in my own green thicket.
O mother, my tears are flowing,
I've lost my maidenly pride—
I'll go if the mariner's going,
And be the mariner's bride!

This Love the tyrant evinces,
Alas! an omnipotent might,
He darkens the mind like night,
He treads on the necks of Princes!
O mother, my bosom is glowing,
I'll go whatever betide;
I'll go where the mariner's going,
And be the mariner's bride!

Yes! mother, the spoiler has reft me
Of reason and self-control;
Gone, gone is my wretched soul,

And only my body is left me!
The winds, O mother, are blowing,
  The ocean is bright and wide;
I'll go where the mariner's going;
  And be the mariner's bride.

The Karamanian Exile

From the Turkish

I SEE thee ever in my dreams,
    Karaman!
Thy hundred hills, thy thousand streams,
    Karaman! O Karaman!
As when thy gold-bright morning gleams,
As when the deepening sunset seams
With lines of light thy hills and streams,
    Karaman!
So thou loomest on my dreams,
    Karaman! O Karaman!

The hot bright plains, the sun, the skies,
    Karaman!
Seem death-black marble to mine eyes,
    Karaman! O Karaman!
I turn from summer's blooms and dyes;
Yet in my dreams thou dost arise
In welcome glory to my eyes,
    Karaman!
In thee my life of life yet lies,
    Karaman!
Thou still art holy in mine eyes,
    Karaman! O Karaman!

Ere my fighting years were come,
Karaman!
Troops were few in Erzerome,
Karaman! O Karaman!
Their fiercest came from Erzerome,
They came from Ukhbar's palace dome,
They dragged me forth from thee, my home,
Karaman!
Thee, my own, my mountain home,
Karaman!
In life and death, my spirit's home,
Karaman! O Karaman!

O, none of all my sisters ten,
Karaman!
Loved like me my fellowmen,
Karaman! O Karaman!
I was mild as milk till then,
I was soft as silk till then;
Now my breast is as a den,
Karaman!
Foul with blood and bones of men,
Karaman!
With blood and bones of slaughtered men,
Karaman! O Karaman!

My boyhood's feelings newly born,
Karaman!
Withered like young flowers uptorn,
Karaman! O Karaman!
And in their stead sprang weed and thorn;
What once I loved now moves my scorn;
My burning eyes are dried to horn,
Karaman!
I hate the blessed light of morn,
Karaman!

It maddens me, the face of morn,
Karaman! O Karaman!

The Spahi wears a tyrant's chains,
Karaman!
But bondage worse than this remains,
Karaman! O Karaman!
His heart is black with million stains;
Thereon, as on Kaf's blasted plains,
Shall never more fall dews and rains
Karaman!
Save poison-dews and bloody rains,
Karaman! O Karaman!
Hell's poison dews and bloody rains,
Karaman! O Karaman!

But life at worst must end ere long,
Karaman!
Azreel[1] avengeth every wrong,
Karaman! O Karaman!
Of late my thoughts rove more among
Thy fields; o'ershadowing fancies throng
My mind, and texts of bodeful song,
Karaman!
Azreel is terrible and strong,
Karaman!
His lightning sword smites all ere long,
Karaman! O Karaman!

There's care to-night in Ukhbar's halls,
Karaman!
There's hope too, for his trodden thralls,
Karaman! O Karaman!
What lights flash red along yon walls?
Hark! hark!—the muster-trumpet calls!—

[1] The angel of death.

I see the sheen of spears and shawls,
          Karaman!
The foe! the foe!—they scale the walls,
          Karaman!
To-night Muràd or Ukhbar falls,
          Karaman! O Karaman!

JOHN FRANCIS
O'DONNELL
1837–1874

JOHN FRANCIS O'DONNELL

1837–1874

JOHN FRANCIS O'DONNELL was born at Limerick in 1837. He took early to writing, became a professional journalist, and contributed to many long-forgotten Irish magazines and papers under a variety of pen-names. He learned shorthand so that his pen could keep pace with his inspiration, and he would turn out a column of verse as rapidly as a column of prose. In 1861 he went to London where he met Charles Dickens. Dickens seems to have taken to O'Donnell as a man, and to have admired his poetry—much of which he printed in *All the Year Round.* At about this time O'Donnell married a Miss Jones, an Irish girl, by whom he had several children. In 1864 he joined the staff of *The Tablet*, and from then until 1873 he contributed to *Chambers's Journal*, *Fun* under Tom Hood the younger, *The Boston Pilot*, and *The Illustrated Magazine*—nor is this list exhaustive. In the autumn of 1873 he obtained a job, worth between two and three hundred a year, in the office of the Agent-General for New Zealand. He and his family were delighted by this change of fortune. He did not enjoy it long, however, for he died on May 7th, 1874.

A selection of O'Donnell's poems—about a third of the then available material—was edited by his friend Richard Dowling and published in London in 1891. It consists of seventy-seven poems, and it is from these that the following selection has in turn been made. He was certainly a minor poet—smaller even than Irwin—but he knew his place and he filled it honestly. In looking for reasonable comparisons, Ebenezer Elliott comes to mind—and how rewarding a poet Elliott can be is now known, alas, only to a few who follow the byways of English poetry.

Irish poetry of the nineteenth century is but a network of such byways—bohreens we should call them—though we try sometimes to mark some of them on the map as main thoroughfares. Between Tom Moore and Yeats, then, if we would travel at all, it is down these small roads we must go. And anyhow, there are times when a lane has charms that many a main road lacks.

One of the first things one notices about O'Donnell is his enormous facility—it carries him along like a wave, well beyond the right stopping-place. He probably never drew breath to consider, and seldom troubled to correct, so that one finds quietly meaningless lines like 'I saw not the vacant shadow on the floor', or mildly inflated lines like 'Hewn in some quarry vast and fair'.

Another obvious thing is his versatility—Keats, Tennyson, Swinburn, Browning, these were the poets he particularly liked, and he could produce very creditable poems of his own in their various manners. But the poems were his own—they were in no sense empty imitations. And at the time, his compatriots, or as many of them as were writing verse, were for the most part being carried away by Byron and Scott. For it must be remembered that the influence all round was an English one even among those who were aware of a Gaelic literature. And it must also be remembered that the time-lag for Ireland is at least fifty years.

But the chief point about O'Donnell is his delight in natural objects, his ability to use his eyes. This is curiously rare among us. For reasons that it would be interesting to try and trace, there is nothing in Ireland in the smallest degree comparable to the great Natural

History tradition of England. Consequently we have, apart from T. C. Irwin and J. F. O'Donnell, no rural poet comparable with—I will not say John Clare—but with Robert Bloomfield or Thomas Gisborne or James Hurdis.

Thomas Davis had urged contributors to *The Nation*, in which famous paper O'Donnell's early poems had appeared, 'not to live influenced by wind and sun and tree, but by the passion and deeds of the past'. But O'Donnell felt so strongly for all that Davis would have had him turn from—'The yellow matted mignonette', 'The hollyhocks against the sun', 'The beauty of the golden moss'—and he so wanted to get them all into his poems, that he sometimes blurs his outlines with a clutter of imagery.

In the following selections many of the poems are not given in full because of O'Donnell's over-facility.

J. F. O'DONNELL

BIBLIOGRAPHY

The Emerald Wreath, 1865.
Memories of the Irish Franciscans, 1871.
Poems, 1891.

from

In the Twilight

I ROW in my boat in the twilight, half-purple, half-grey,
overhead;
(Oh, cool is the plash of the water; and green is the
weed on the oar);
Before me the river runs burning, as if the white lilies
had bled,
And the track of the keel runs in lightnings that beat
on the base of the shore,
Whilst the woods by the banks in the sunset, are
flaming with fire to the core.

It darkens! the trees lock above me, they sway from
their roots and embrace:
O God, what a peace in this silence! what rest in this
sycamore gloom!
Looking down on the hurrying river, it gives back no
face to my face:
Yet 'tis Earth, for, high up in the branches, there
shivers a bird's startled plume—
'Tis Earth, though the air and the water be black
with the blackness of Doom!

The Lilies

I WALKED amid the lilies, at the morn,
And they were fair,
With trembling chalices that banqueted
On sun and air.

In the cool depths of the green inland lake
I saw them rise,
Chilly and white as stars that break and break
Through autumn skies.

At eventide, slow pacing, I returned;
Ah! sad to see!
Gone were the bright inhabitants of morn,
That welcomed me!
What keel of summer skiff, red-beaked and slow,
Had ridden o'er
My white lake-garden, blotting out its lights,
'Twixt Shore and Shore?

No answer and no answer. Lucid sprites,
Where'er you be,
The spring is flying backward o'er the hills,
Be patient ye.
I hear the wind-swirled trumpeters of March
On wave and plain;
Be patient, spring is coming quick, and ye
Shall rise again.

Geraldine's Garden

THIS is the garden; its twenty paths,
Drawn from the dial, merrily run
Down where the autumn's undermaths
Lie speckled with shadows of leaf and sun;
Here you may count them one by one:
The stooping stems of the lime and larch,
The violet haze that folds their roots,
And, out through the great laburnum arch,
The orchard croft, and its fire of fruits.

There are no steps in the garden yet,
No sounds, save the bird in the lilac hedge,
No trailing vesture of violet
Touching the yellowing long box edge,
Or bending the reeds by the fountain's ledge.
For Geraldine comes in the afternoon,
When the copper-beech shadow tempers the glare,
And the luminous phantom of the moon
Is thin and white in the sultry air.

Sweet, ere the wicket shall give you grace
To pass and enter, I pluck this rose,
First of the summer, that in the space
Of the ivied gable tenderly blows,
As a pearl through your twisted tresses glows.
I shall pluck it, and leave it here
Down on the pathway—who knows you'll stray,
With some sweet purpose not over clear,
Out from the beeches, and down this way!

Should you see it, as you come down,
Through the whispering lilacs all alone;
A gleam of gold on your purple gown,
Your hair by the orchard wind back-blown—
In beautiful disorder strown.
Should you see it, my fancy is:
You may take it in careless mood—
Careless at first, then guess and guess,
Till a happy tumult shakes all your blood.

There am I dreaming; and here you are!
Let me hide in the cloister of the yew,
Where not a glimmer of sun or star
Can trickle the matted branches through,
No, nor a wink of the sultry blue.
Here you come with your airy grace,

Your dainty footfall and sidelong glance,
Whilst over the bloom of your pure, sweet face,
Fifty shadows coquet and dance.

You pass my rose. If it could but speak!
Now you return and pause awhile,
And, over the damask of your cheek,
Slowly ripples a tender smile;
What if one watched you all the while!
Where is the sin if one takes a rose,
Idly cast from a garden seat?
Oh, flattering wind, that comes and goes,
One effort, and blow it straight at her feet.

Were I a woman I'd take the flower,
You are a woman, why, take it then;
How know you 'tis not a fairy dower
Downward dropped from a random rain
Of blossoms hurrying over the plain
To Queen Mab's nuptials? O, love, accept
The earliest rose the garden bears,
It blew up there where the swallows slept
Under the thatch, in the cool spring airs.

'Tis hers! it lies on her beauteous breast!
There where my head and my heart would lie,
In one sweet trance of delicious rest,
Careless how ran the seasons by,
What waxed or waned in the changing sky!
'Tis hers! and she quits the garden seat,
My heart beats louder than I can breathe;
'Tis hers! it lies on her bosom's beat,
And a thought I can guess is underneath.

JOHN FRANCIS O'DONNELL

April

How many pipes have dittied unto thee,
Rain-bringer, swathing the blue peaks in mist,
Whose blossom-lights are lit on wold and lea,
Before the tempestings of March have ceast
To stir the heavens! Thy south wind comes and goes,
And periwinkles twinkle in the grass,
And oxlips faint amid the meadows cool:
Mayhap, the fiery-arched laburnum blows,
Whilst through the emerald darkness thou dost pass,
With swallows skirring round the breezy pool.

With thee, ripe dawnings, saffron streaked with white,
Float from the sunrise; and the happy lark,
Leaving the clover-buds to dew and night,
Catches thy voice betwixt the light and dark.
By hooded porches, looking to the sun,
The almond stirreth, and the wallflowers blush,
Ascetic ivies pulse through stem and frond;
The jasmine bells, unfolding one by one,
Take to their amber hearts a phantom flush;
And long-haired willows whiten by the pond.

Season of broken cloud and misty heat,
How the green lanes find echoes for thy horn,
Blown over purple moorlands, to the beat
Of nodding marigolds in marsh and corn!
And thou hast benedictions for the birds,
Couched in the red dead nettles, where they sit
Choiring for seed-time; the poor robin shrills
A pipe of welcome; or, amid the herds,
The martens chirrup greetings, as they flit
Along the barren reaches of the hills.

Lo! as the day behind the chestnuts dies,
  And yonder cloud dissolves, half rain, half bloom,
Thy bow is bended in the weeping skies,
  Thy shadowy splendour bridges the vast gloom
'Twixt sunset and the stars. A mournful drowse
  Falls on the flockless meadows—a low swoon
    Tingles along the windless woodlands' rim;
The twilight thickens in the lampless house;
  And, merged in vapour, the half-risen moon
    Leans on the trunkèd forests, vague and dim.

Drifting

FLOAT, little bark, down yonder stream,
  By many a margin fringed with bloom
Of lilies, amber-leaved and wan,
  And poplars fair with silver gleam;
  Float round yon island in the sun,
Slide slowly through the winking gloom
Of many an immemorial wood,
Whose trunks make cloisters for the flood.

Blow southern wind, and fill her wake
  With creamy swirlings, faint and sweet—
Go, break the sunlight on her sail;
  Loosen the blossom in the brake,
  And waft, from primrose plot and vale,
Their odours rich and exquisite
Go, little bark, the shining west.
Shall find thy prow a nook of rest.

Speed, happy lovers, stream and breeze
  Glide with ye towards the peaceful night
O babble softly in her ear,

Dark-violet river, till she sees
The golden-hornèd star appear,
Suspent in azure mist and light,
And hears, across the sobbing foam,
Bell-voices and the songs of home.

Float on, float on! The heavens are fair,
The last flame burns amid the leaves,
The last bird pipes on yonder bough,
The last crow blackens the rich air,
The cistus drowses on the eaves,
The lustrous freshet trickles slow;
The earth has lost the sun, and lo!
Around the oaks the brown bats go.

My Jack

ALONG the roof-line, sharp and red,
The black crows stand against the sky,
And windy clamourings are bred
Within the elm trees standing nigh.
Hard clinks the chapel's evening bell,
The mill-wheel answers dreamily;
Whilst from the deep carnation sky
A glory rolls down field and fell:
It smites the mountain to the north,
It burns upon the window free,
Where Jack stands up, with eyes of mirth
And clapping hands, to welcome me.

Dear lad, again, the wild gold hair
Makes ringlets in the autumn wind,
And in those eyes, so blue and fair,
The sweet, fresh soul has grown more kind

How quaintly, too, those arms are set—
  In indolent, and frank repose,
  Upon the long green box, where grows
The wild thyme mixed with mignonette!
O happy shout! the choiring lark,
  Caged coyly by the glinting pane,
Ne'er uttered, between light and dark,
  A blither, a more natural strain.

Come down, and dance into my arms,
  My heart shall have full holiday;
Come, let us range by smoking farms,
  And poppied girths of wheat and hay.
The scythe is glittering in the grass,
  The weeds are burning on the hill,
  The blackbird's voice is scarcely still—
He keeps a song for Candlemas.
O hasten, ere the stars are up,
  And bring the moonrise in their wake;
Haste ere the lily folds its cup,
  And vanishes into the lake.

Your hand in mine, your mouth to mine,
  The perfect, pure-lipped rosy shell
That on the feast of Valentine,
  Seven months ago, bade me farewell!
Ah, Jack, that voice was in my ear
  When in the night-time by the Main
  The German house-tops hissed with rain,
The chimneys shuddered far and near.
Against the clouds the old house rose,
  Behind it spread the rolling wolds,
And you stood in the privet close
  Among the yellow marigolds.

That dream is fact; we too again
  By long belovèd hedges walk,
And separation's bitter pain
  Dies in the music of your talk.
The stifled pang, the injured sense,
  The shame of doubt, the wrong of sin,
  Turn into benedictions in
Your clear sun-lighted innocence.
Look, there's the sun behind the wood,
  The clouds one puff of golden gloom;
Now for the night's divinest mood—
  Low laughters and the lamp-lit room.

from

A July Dawn

WE left the city, street and square
  With lamplights glimmering through and through,
And turned us toward the suburb, where—
  Full from the east—the fresh wind blew.

One cloud stood overhead the sun—
  A glorious trail of dome and spire—
The last star flickered, and was gone;
  The first lark led the matin choir.

Wet was the grass beneath our tread,
  Thick-dewed the bramble by the way;
The lichen had a lovelier red,
  The elder-flower a fairer grey.

And there was silence on the land,
  Save when, from out the city's fold,

Stricken by Time's remorseless wand,
  A bell across the morning tolled.

The beeches sighed through all their boughs;
  The gusty pennons of the pine
Swayed in a melancholy drowse,
  But with a motion sternly fine.

One gable, full against the sun,
  Flooded the garden-space beneath
With spices, sweet as cinnamon,
  From all its honeysuckled breadth.

Then crew the cocks from echoing farms,
  The chimney-tops were plumed with smoke,
The windmill shook its slanted arms,
  The sun was up, the country woke!

from

To Spring

FROM the grey wicket of the morn,
  Under the shadow-braided skies,
  With violet twilights in thine eyes,
Thou walk'st across the fresh, green corn.

I see thy pathway in the dark,
  Thy sweet feet print the fields with light
  With primroses and snowdrops white,
And silver on the larch tree's bark.

I know thy coming. Underneath
  The black and leafless lattices,

There comes the moan of blowing trees,
The wallflower's faint ascetic breath.

I know thy coming—for the air
Blows soft upon the sleeted pane,
And drips the eaves with amber rain,
And scatters odours everywhere.

Far down, amid the shallows dank
Of the cold freshets, mallow-blooms
Are broadening in the willow glooms,
And cowslips flame on brae and bank.

from

Happy Christmases

I

In the December weather, grey and grim,
In the December twilight, keen and cold,
Stood the farmhouse on the green-reached hill
Piled with thatched roofs, mellowed into gold;
Under the dark eaves trailed the famished vines,
Blood-ribbed skeletons of autumn days,
And the quaint windows, looking to the downs,
Flickered and darkened in the ruddy blaze.

Three leagues around, the meadows to the moon
Yearned like a silver dreamland, faint and white,
Below the deep-ploughed road a little pool
Glimmered breezily in the tender light.
The great ash caught the glory as it dropped
From bough to bough fantastically fair,

And the stars looked into its leafless heart,
  Through shifting vapours and translucent air.

Wild looked the gardens round the drowsy house,
  The laurel sparkled in the sifting frost;
But the white gables, where the roses grew,
  In the dank atmosphere of fog, were lost;
The wicket swang with a perturbèd cry,
  The mighty watch-dog crossed the dial floor;
My heart beat as I stroked his shaggy head—
  My heart throbbed as I stood beside the door.

In the sweet Christmas light that filled the porch,
  As with a glory round a saint she stood,
Welcomes innumerable were on her lips,
  And her cheeks reddened with tumultuous blood.
My own, my darling one, my life, my love,
  That made the common ways of earth divine;
'Twas sweet to stand beneath the balmy roof,
  Three fingers of thy gloveless hand in mine.

II

. . . . . .

Down looked the moon, but looked no more
Upon the silent river shore,
Or on the hilltops faint and hoar.

Down into London's struggling gloom,
Down on the city of the Doom,
A scarf of cloud around her bloom.

Below the bridge the black ships lay,
The thin lamps gleamed from quay to quay,
The thin masts trembled in the grey.

. . . . . .

Upon the bridge I stood alone,
Listening to the slow waves' moan,
Lapping the weedy buttress stone.

Friendless and homeless, 'twas to me
A sort of Christmas company
To watch the swirls glide to the sea;

To see the starlight glimmer grim,
Across the currents vague and dim,
And wish that I could go with them.

. . . . . .

III

'Twas summer time, the radiant world of June
Fell on the dreamful earth,
Within—'twas coolest shadow; the red broom
  Lay piled upon the hearth.

Through the slim spaces in the lattice breadth
  The sun sloped from the eaves;
The very atmosphere waxed tremulous
  With the green stir of leaves,

With airy whispers from the distant woods,
  Around the moorland reach—
The whisper of the fainting lilac boughs,
  The low voice of the beech.

The subtle melodies the hot gusts sucked
  From the quaint woodland bridge,
That shone a perfect circle in the brook,
  Beyond the last wold ridge.

And when the birds sang and the echoes blew
  And beat upon the blind,
That shook, a purple languor, in the sun,
  And rose with the sweet wind,

Again for me the old world charm revived;
  It seemed as after death
One woke from sleep upon a fairer earth—
  The dreamland of our faith.

Beside each other in the porch we sat,
  The quaint old-fashioned place,
Built up of knotted boughs and peakèd roofs,
  And rich in country grace.

Between us and the roadway stretched the lawn;
  The wicket was not seen,
For the laburnums raised their slender trunks
  And branching firs between.

Long on the grass the gable shadows stretched,
  And then the chimneys threw
Their grim phantasmal shadows on the sward,
  That dim and dimmer grew.

. . . . . .

So it was all confest; my own was mine,
  And I in peace was blest;
A tender hand upon my shoulder lay,
  A face was on my breast.

. . . . . .

Dark grew the dial, but we little recked
  How the sweet minutes ran;
Or how the dusk was posting up the east,
  A faint star caravan.

JOHN FRANCIS O'DONNELL

By the Turnstile

THERE's light in the west, o'er the rims of the walnut
Low croons the stream, in the meadows below,
Shrill sings the robin, a-top of the briar,
Black, through the golden dusk, darkens the crow.
O love, from the hamlet, that gleams in the sallows,
Come up through the pastures—come upwards and smile,
That your dear face may shine twenty roods through the twilight,
And sprinkle with starbeams the stones of the stile.
Come hither, come hither,
'Tis midsummer weather;
Airy-paced, violet-eyed, dainty-lipped lisper,
For into your pink ear, sweetheart, if you let me,
If but for a moment, I'd hurriedly whisper.

O daisies that glitter in long tangled grasses,
White wastes of delight that stream fair to the moon,
Unprison your lids, though the dank dew is falling,
And catch the sweet footsteps that hasten here soon.
There's a candle a-gleam in the grey cottage lattice,
There's a shadow that comes 'twixt the light and the pane,
And a dear little head slily peers through the casement,
Turns backward, and leaves me the shadow again.
Come hither, come hither,
'Tis midsummer weather;
The windmill has stopped, dear, ah! that is our token,
For ere the night falls through yon great arch of planets,
One quick little word in your ear must be spoken.

There's an echo that comes from the dusk of the
    paddock—
  The echoes of feet that are tripping and walking,
There's a murmur that creeps through the heart of the
    pasture,
  O love, is it you, or the daisies, are talking?
'Tis she, for the wild mint, scarce crushed by her
    footstep,
  Gives out all its odour—that's all it can give her—
And the stile that I've sat by since six in the evening,
  Turns round, ay it does, of itself to receive her.
        Come hither, come hither,
        'Tis midsummer weather;
Now answer me this, by the round moon above me,
Do you?—well, after all, what's the use of being
  talking?
Sure you wouldn't come hither if you didn't love me?

from

May

OPEN, sweet flowers, your eyes,
  Earth's awake,
Rain droppeth from the skies,
The songs of throstles rise,
  In field and brake.
Come churchyard marigold,
  Flower of the sun,
    O pansies bloom,
O lilies break the fold,
  Unbosom one by one,
    And come!

Shy daisies of the mead,
  Quick, be up,
And let your lids be red,
Round every yellow head,
  And dew-charged cup.
Puce honeysuckles blow—
  Blow in the grass;
    Mint, from the gloom,
Breathe out your odorous woe,
  As nymphs and shepherds pass,
    And come!

Primroses, moist and pale,
  Sun the hedge,
Spread sunshine down the vale,
Climb over park and pale.
  The brooklets sedge
Is dark without your light.
  Naiads do cry,
    And bitterns boom,
Through all the grey daylight,
  Till the sweet sun doth die,
    Come, come!

from

Ossian

i

SPOKE my heart in the dearth of the night, of the evil, the terrible night:
  What boots it to thee, O descendant of poets, and sages, and kings,

That thou wearest a garment fine-threaded with issues
of blackness and light—
That in courts thy harp rings?

Thou hast seen all the glamour of Tara, the musters of
shield-covered men,
The fires, the rejoicings, the tumults, the trophies,
the long spoils of Meath—
Hast seen the processions march sunward—the flame
of their spears on the plain;
Yet their guerdon was Death!

To death have gone down the pale victors—the bearers
of sparth-given scars;
They sleep coldly, mutely, for ever, the cromlechs
their silent abodes;
Where be they? Ah, vainly I question the mutable eyes
of the stars,
And the shrines of the Gods.

There are pastures full fat in the heavens; red deer that
are swift as the cloud,
When rolls from Hy-Brasil the tempest, and, inland,
the forests grow dim;
There are women delightful and fragrant, by sunshines
of saffron o'erbowed—
Yet who has seen them?

ii

I've rhymed to the chieftains and sages; at councils and
camp-fires I've sung,
Or, heated with mead, flung my hands where the
moon in the skies stood at bay

Of the blood-boltered brands of the sun; in the Gods' ear my psalters have rung,
But no answer made they.

The swift, sharp rejoicings of life, and its gladsome contentions are dead;
I lean as a pine thunder-rift on the sands of a wave-channelled shore,
The salts and the breathings of brine make its trunk fearful orange and red:
But for bloom! Nevermore.

At midnight the grey curtain shakes; deep at midnight a hand parts its fold,
And a stark, cold Intelligence looks with a stare of request in my face,
That face is as old as a million of ages a million times told—
'Tis the Spectre of Space.

The world knows me not, and I know not the world that perhaps may know me—
A Thing undefinable, ghostly, a Thing void of meaning or date.
Soul be calm: there's a flame on the land, and a voice on the crests of the sea,
Say to Patrick, I wait.

from

Adare

THE morn comes freshly from the east,
It strikes with fire the upland ridge,

And pours a shaft of gold between
  The midmost shadows of the bridge,
  Where, late at eve, shall dance the midge.
Flame fills the immemorial tree,
  Which keeps its chestnuts for the time
When harvest banquets through the world,
  And the hot breezes flow in rhyme.

Soft sleeps the village in the maze
  Of dreamy elm and sycamore;
Soft slides the river's rosy tide
  Through blossomed sedges by the shore,
  Rushes, and pendent willows hoar.
The little boat moored in the cove
  Takes no pulsation from the stream,
But shadowed on the water lies,
  The lovely image of a dream.

I leave the village to its rest—
  White walls with ivy diapered,
Brown roofs that in the springtime give
  Asylum to the happy bird,
  Whose wing the southern air has stirred;
And wandering down the grassy marge
  Of Mague, amidst its Paradise,
Turn one green bend of lawn, and, lo!
  Three Hundred Years confront mine eyes.

Three Hundred Years in channelled stones,
  Hewn in some quarry vast and fair,
But touched with melancholy grey—
  That habit of our Irish air—
  Which slays, but still knows when to spare.
Chancel, quadrangle, tower are here,
  Gaunt cloisters, roof and mullions riven,

With that clear interspace through which
  Souls, tired of flesh, looked out to heaven.

I see it all—the choir, the stalls,
  The broad east window, smote with blood—
(Bright as six rainbows ribbonèd)—
  St Francis' brown-robed brotherhood,
  Each with his crucifix of wood.
Slowly the instant pageant fades;
  Ruin returns to leaf and stone;
A shadow rises from my brain,
  And I am, with the sun, alone.

The Spring

Now blows the white rose round our garden pales,
  Now by the wicket, breathes the scented briar;
Now flowers the happy lilac in the sun,
  Now the laburnum wakes in gusts of fire;
    But never, never shall they bloom for me.

High on the uplands, the brown woods are touched
  By gentle visitings of morning rain;
The cowslip in the budding hedgerows teems,
  The sun-eyed daisies whiten half the plain;
    Ah never, never shall they bloom for me.

Thou com'st no more to build below our eaves,
  Long-wingèd swallow, for they are no more!
Poor redbreast, thou hast ceased to shrill thy heart
  In friendly shadows by our open door!
    Ah never, never shall ye sing for me.

Dear mother, thou hast ceased at morn to pass,
By leafy lattices, to watch us sleep;
Thy palms are fettered with the salt seaweed,
Thy head is rocking in unfathomed deep;
Ah never, never wilt thou come to me.

O home, O friends, O long familiar haunts—
Chapel, and brook, and wood, and mossy bridge;
The fisher bending by the shallow stream,
The windmill whirring on the glebe-land's ridge;
Ah! never, never shall you shine for me.

Sad are our memories, sad, unbidden tears,
Deep mingled ecstasies of peace and pain,
Sad are the thoughts that glimmer round our hearts,
The odours of wild-flowers in falling rain,
Ah! bitter, bitter are my thoughts to me!

Good-bye! and I could say unnumbered times,
To friend, and stream, and tree—good-bye, good-bye!
Only remains to comfort us a while
Love, like a late light in a darkening sky,
Ah love, in sorrow, thou abid'st with me.

A Spinning Song

My love to fight the Saxon goes
And bravely shines his sword of steel,
A heron's feather decks his brows,
And a spur on either heel;

His steel is blacker than the sloe,
And fleeter than the falling star;
Amid the surging ranks he'll go
And shout for joy of war.

Tinkle, twinkle, pretty spindle, let the white wool drift and dwindle,
Oh! we weave a damask doublet for my love's coat of steel.
Hark! the timid, turning treadle crooning soft, old-fashioned ditties
To the low, slow murmur of the brown round wheel.

My love is pledged to Ireland's fight;
My love would die for Ireland's weal,
To win her back her ancient right,
And make her foemen reel.
Oh, close I'll clasp him to my breast
When homeward from the war he comes;
The fires shall light the mountain's crest,
The valley peal with drums.

Tinkle, twinkle, pretty spindle, let the white wool drift and dwindle,
Oh! we weave a damask doublet for my love's coat of steel.
Hark! the timid, turning treadle crooning, soft, old-fashioned ditties
To the low, slow murmur of the brown round wheel.

JOHN FRANCIS O'DONNELL

from

Limerick Town

HERE I've got you, Philip Desmond, standing in the market-place,
'Mid the farmers and the corn sacks, and the hay in either space,
Near the fruit stalls, and the women knitting socks and selling lace.

There is High Street up the hillside, twenty shops on either side,
Queer, old-fashioned, dusky High Street, here so narrow, there so wide,
Whips and harness, saddles, signboards, hanging out in quiet pride.

Up and down the noisy highway, how the market people go!
Country girls in Turkey kerchiefs—poppies moving to and fro—
Frieze-clad fathers, great in buttons, brass and watch-seals all a-show.

Merry, merry are their voices, Philip Desmond, unto me,
Dear the mellow Munster accent, with its intermittent glee;
Dear the blue cloaks, and the grey coats, things I long have longed to see.

Even the curses, adjurations, in my senses sound like rhyme,

And the great, rough-throated laughter of that peasant
in his prime,
Winking from the grassbound cart-shaft, brings me
back the other time.

Not a soul, observe you, knows me, not a friend a hand
will yield,
Would they know, if to the landmarks all around them
I appealed?
Know me! If I died this minute, dig for me the Potter's
field?

Bricks wan grey, and memories greyer, and our faces
somehow pass
Like reflections from the surface of a sudden darkened
glass.
Live you do, but as a unit of the undistinguished mass.

'Pshaw! you're prosy.' Am I prosy? Mark you then
this sunward flight:
I have seen this street and roof tops ambered in the
morning's light,
Golden in the deep of noonday, crimson on the marge
of night.

Continents of gorgeous cloudland, argosies of blue and
flame,
With the sea-wind's even pressure, o'er this roaring
faubourg came.
This is fine supernal nonsense. Look, it puts my cheek
to shame.

Come, I want a storm of gossip, pleasant jests and
ancient chat;
At that dusky doorway yonder my grandfather smoked
and sat,

Tendrils of the wind-blown clover sticking in his
broad-leafed hat.

There he sat and read the paper. Fancy I recall him
now!
All the shadow of the house front slanting up from
knee to brow;
Critic he of far convulsions, keen-eyed judge of sheep
and cow.

Now he lives in GOD's good judgments. Ah, 'twas
much he thought of me,
Laughing gravely at my questions, as I sat upon his
knee—
As I trifled with his watch seal, red carbuncle fair to
see.

from

Reminiscences of a Day

WICKLOW

O DIM delicious heaven of dreams—
The land of boyhood's dewy glow—
Again I hear your torrent streams
Through purple gorge and valley flow,
Whilst fresh the mountain breezes blow.
Above the air smites sharp and clear—
The silent lucent spring it chills—
But underneath, moves warm amidst
The bases of the hills.

With scalps fire-charged, or violet
The grim peaks pierce the open sky;

There may the storm at midnight fret
  Its strength in moans of agony,
  Whilst tempest-shaped the clouds roll by
Pale lightnings leap from scar to scar,
  Between the hurtlings of the rains,
And four-fold thunders peal throughout
      The loud rejoicing glens.

But not to-night, O lovely land,
  Bear'st thou the colour of the storm;
The wind that fans my cheek is bland
  And delicate, and sweet, and warm.
  No wracks portending ill deform
The starry azure of those skies,
  Where Dian flames a fiery crest,
Bernice's hair across the north—
      Orion down the west.

The cloud that helms the mountain's brow,
  The cataract that leaps and cries,
Have long-lost meanings—voices—now
  For manhood's wakened ears and eyes.
  Forbid it God I should despise
The other meanings, long since lost
  'Mid the thronged cities' smoking fold—
Vague intimations that made time
      A very time of Gold.

LESSER POETS

ANONYMOUS

Castle Hyde

As I roved out on a summer's morning
  Down by the banks of Blackwater side,
To view the groves and the meadows charming,
  The pleasant gardens of Castle Hyde;
'Tis there I heard the thrushes warbling,
  The dove and partridge I now describe;
The lambkins sporting on ev'ry morning,
  All to adorn sweet Castle Hyde.

The richest groves throughout this nation
  And fine plantations you will see there;
The rose, the tulip, the rich carnation,
  All vying with the lily fair.
The buck, the doe, the fox, the eagle,
  They skip and play by the river side;
The trout and salmon are always sporting
  In the clear streams of sweet Castle Hyde.

There are fine walks in these pleasant gardens,
  And seats most charming in shady bowers.
The gladiators both bold and darling
  Each night and morning do watch the flowers.
There's a church for service in this fine arbour
  Where nobles often in coaches ride
To view the groves and the meadow charming,
  The pleasant gardens of Castle Hyde.

There are fine horses and stall-fed oxes,
  And dens for foxes to play and hide;

Fine mares for breeding and foreign sheep there
  With snowy fleeces in Castle Hyde.
The grand improvements they would amuse you,
  The trees are drooping with fruit of all kind;
The bees perfuming the fields with music,
  Which yields more beauty to Castle Hyde.

If noble princes from foreign nations
  Should chance to sail to this Irish shore,
'Tis in this valley they would be feasted
  As often heroes have been before.
The wholesome air of this habitation
  Would recreate your heart with pride.
There is no valley throughout this nation
  In beauty equal to Castle Hyde.

I rode from Blarney to Castlebarnet,
  To Thomastown, and sweet Doneraile,
To Kilshannick that joins Rathcormack,
  Besides Killarney and Abbeyfeale;
The flowing Nore and the rapid Boyne,
  The river Shannon and pleasant Clyde;
In all my ranging and serenading
  I met no equal to Castle Hyde.

I Know Where I'm Going

I KNOW where I'm going, she said,
  And I know who's going with me;
I know who I love—
  But the dear knows who I'll marry.

Feather beds are soft,
  And painted rooms are bonny,

But I'll forsake them all
To go with my love Johny;

Leave my dresses of silk,
My shoes of bright green leather,
Combs to buckle my hair,
And rings for every finger.

O some say he's black,
But I say he's bonny—
The fairest of them all,
My winsome handsome Johny.

I know where I'm going, she said,
And I know who's going with me;
I know who I love—
But the dear knows who I'll marry.

The Night Before Larry was Stretched

THE night before Larry was stretched
The boys they all paid him a visit;
A bait in their sacks, too, they fetched;
They sweated their duds till they riz it:
For Larry was ever the lad,
When a boy was condemned to the squeezer,
Would fence all the duds that he had
To help a poor friend to a sneezer,
And warm his gob 'fore he died.

The boys they came crowding in fast,
They drew all their stools round about him,
Six glims round his trap-case were placed,
He couldn't be well waked without 'em.

When one of us asked could he die
  Without having duly repented,
Says Larry, 'That's all in my eye,
  And first by the clergy invented,
    To get a fat bit for themselves.'

'I'm sorry, dear Larry,' says I,
  'To see you in this situation;
And, blister my limbs if I lie,
  I'd as lieve it had been my own station.'
'Ochone! it's all over,' says he,
  'For the neckcloth I'll be forced to put on,
And by this time tomorrow you'll see
  Your poor Larry as dead as a mutton,
    Because, why, his courage was good.

'And I'll be cut up like a pie,
  And my nob from my body be parted.'
'You're in the wrong box, then,' says I,
  'For blast me if they're so hard-hearted:
A chalk on the back of your neck
  Is all that Jack Ketch dares to give you;
Then mind not such trifles a feck,
  For why should the likes of them grieve you?
    And now boys come tip us the deck.'

The cards being called for, they played,
  Till Larry found one of them cheated;
A dart at his napper he made
  (The boy being easily heated):
'Oh, by the hokey, you thief,
  I'll skuttle your nob with my daddle!
You cheat me because I'm in grief,
  But soon I'll demolish your noddle,
    And leave you your claret to drink.'

Then the clergy came in with his book,
He spoke him so smooth and so civil;
Larry tipped him a Kilmainham look,
And pitched his bag wig to the devil;
Then sighing, he threw back his head
To get a sweet drop of the bottle,
And pitiful sighing, he said:
'Oh, the hemp will be soon round my throttle,
And choke my poor windpipe to death.

'Though sure it's the best way to die,
Oh, the devil a better a-livin',
For sure when the gallows is high
Your journey is shorter to Heaven;
But what harasses Larry the most,
And makes his poor soul melancholy,
Is to think of the time when his ghost
Will come in a sheet to sweet Molly—
Oh, sure it will kill her alive.'

So moving these last words he spoke,
We all vented our tears in a shower;
For my part I thought my heart broke,
To see him cut down like a flower.
On his travels we watched him next day;
Oh, the throttler! I thought I could kill him;
But Larry not one word did say,
Nor changed till he came to 'King William'
Then, musha! his colour grew white.

When he came to the nubbling chit,
He was tucked up so neat and so pretty,
The rumbler jogged off from his feet,
And he died with his face to the city;
He kicked, too—but that was all pride,
For soon you might see twas all over;

Soon after, the noose was untied;
  And at darky we waked him in clover,
    And sent him to take a ground sweat.

The Rakes of Mallow

BEAUING, belling, dancing, drinking,
Breaking windows, damning, sinking,
Ever raking, never thinking,
      Live the rakes of Mallow.

Spending faster than it comes,
Beating waiters, bailiffs, duns,
Bacchus' true-begotten sons,
      Live the rakes of Mallow.

One time naught but claret drinking,
Then like politicians thinking
To raise the sinking-funds when sinking,
      Live the rakes of Mallow.

When at home with dadda dying
Still for Mallow water crying;
But where there's good claret plying,
      Live the rakes of Mallow.

Living short but merry lives;
Going where the devil drives;
Having sweethearts but no wives,
      Live the rakes of Mallow.

Racking tenants, stewards teasing,
Swiftly spending, slowly raising,

Wishing to spend all their lives in
Raking as in Mallow.

Then to end this raking life,
They get sober, take a wife,
Ever after live in strife,
And wish again for Mallow.

The Gay Old Hag

WILL you come a boating, my gay old hag,
Will you come a boating, my tight old hag,
Will you come a boating, down the Liffey floating?
I'll make a pair of oars of your two long shins.

Crush her in the corner the gay old hag,
Crush her in the corner the tight old hag,
Crush her in the corner and keep her snug and warm,
Put powder in her horn, she's a fine old hag.

Napoleon's on dry land, says the gay old hag,
Napoleon's on dry land, says the tight old hag,
Napoleon's on dry land, with a sword in his right hand,
He's a gallant Ribbon man, says the gay old hag.

My mother's getting young, says the gay old hag,
My mother's getting young, says the gay old hag,
My mother's getting young and she'll have another son
To make the orange run, says the gay old hag.

Remember '98, says the gay old hag,
When our Boys you did defeat, says the gay old hag,

Then our Boys you did defeat, but we'll beat you out
compleat,
Now you're nearly out of date, says the fine old hag.

The Orange Lily O

Oh did you go to see the show,
Each rose and pink-a-dilly O,
To feast your eyes upon the prize
Won by the Orange Lily O.
The Viceroy there so debonair,
Just like a daffydilly O,
And Lady Clarke blithe as a lark,
Approached the Orange Lily O.

Then heigho the lily O,
The royal loyal lily O.
Beneath the sky what flower can vie
With Erin's Orange Lily O?

The elated Muse, to hear the news,
Jumped like a Connacht filly O,
As gossip fame did loud proclaim
The triumph of the lily O:
The lowland field may roses yield,
Gay heaths the highlands hilly O,
But high or low, no flowers can show
Like the glorious Orange Lily O.

Then heigho the lily O,
The royal loyal lily O.
There's not a flower in Erin's bower
Can match the Orange Lily O.

CECIL FRANCES ALEXANDER

St. Simon and St. Jude's Day

LIKE two pale stars at distance seen
  When silver dews are on the lawn,
And misty shadows lie between
  The silent earth and breaking dawn;

So bright, so dimly seen the two
  Whose names the Church has loved to own,
So pure in Heaven's eternal blue,
  Of man below so little known.

She only saith from age to age
  That one wrote down a burning word
That lives along the e[illegible],
  And one was zealous for the Lord.

And when men call Christ's roll of fame,
  His chosen twelve in church or cot,
They speak the zealot Simon's name,
  And Judas who betrayed Him not.

But all the rest to human ken
  Is dark or dimly understood,
So small is the applause of men,
  So great the silence of the good.

WILLIAM ALEXANDER

Frost-Morning

THE morn is cold. A whiteness newly-brought
Lightly and loosely powders every place,
The panes among yon trees that eastward face
Flash rosy fire from the opposite dawning caught,—
As the face flashes with a splendid thought,
As the heart flashes with a touch of grace
When heaven's light comes on ways we cannot trace,
Unsought, yet lovelier than we ever sought.
In the blue northern sky is a pale moon,
Through whose thin texture something doth appear
Like the dark shadow of a branchy tree.—
Fit morning for the prayers of one like me,
Whose life is in midwinter, and must soon
Come to the shortest day of all my year!

JOHN ANSTER

Sonnet

If I might choose where my tired limbs shall lie
When my task here is done, the oak's green crest
Shall rise above my grave—a little mound,
Raised in some cheerful village cemetery.
And I could wish that, with unceasing sound,
A lonely mountain rill was murmuring by
In music through the long soft twilight hours.
And let the hand of her whom I love best
Plant round the bright green grave those fragrant flowers
In whose deep bells the wild-bee loves to rest;
And should the robin from some neighbouring tree
Pour his enchanted song—oh softly tread!
For sure if aught of earth can soothe the dead
He still must love that pensive melody.

MARY BALFOUR

In Ringlets Curl'd Thy Tresses Flow

In ringlets curl'd thy tresses flow,
  And bright and sparkling are thine eyes,
Time in thy absence lingers slow,
  When measur'd by a lover's sighs.
Had sacred rites once crown'd my love,
  With bounding steps the fields I'd tread,
Oh, grief! that we no longer rove
  Where Truigha's lonely green woods spread.

Oh! would that on thy bosom laid,
  While Erin's sons are hush'd to rest,
I might beneath the green-wood shade
  Breathe the pure raptures of thy breast!
Sweet blooming flower! thy sex's pride,
  To me a guiding star thou art,
And Heaven itself will sure preside
  O'er love that fills a virtuous heart.

My charmer! let us haste away
  To Truigha's woods our footsteps bend,
Where streams through water-cresses play,
  And Uchais lovely plains extend;
There holly berries glowing red,
  With nuts and apples sweet abound,
Green rushes there shall strew our bed,
  And warblers chaunt their lov'd notes round.

The Dew each Trembling Leaf Inwreath'd

THE dew each trembling leaf inwreath'd,
The red-breast sweetly sung,
The balmy air with fragrance breath'd
From bow'rs with roses hung:
The setting sun still faintly gleam'd,
And swift and sweet the moments flew
With her, whose smile too artless seem'd,
To hide a heart untrue.

But now o'er dreary scenes I range,
Where once such beauties shone,
Yet blooming nature knows no change,
Alas! 'tis all my own.
The rose still holds its lovely form,
The dew still sparkles on the tree,
But, oh! the smile that gave the charm
No longer beams for me!

STOPFORD AUGUSTUS BROOKE

A Moment

TO-DAY chance drove me to the wood,
  Where I have walked and talked with her
Who lies in the earth's solitude.
  The soft west wind, the minister
Of Love and Spring, blew as of old
Across the grass and marigold,
  And moved the waters of the pool,
  And moved my heart a moment—Fool!
Do I not know her lips are cold.

Lines

IN the day the sun is darkened,
  And the moon as blood,
And the earth is swept to ruin
  On the avenging flood,
Come to me—Then give thyself
  To my arms and kiss;
We shall not know that all is lost,
  So great shall be our bliss.

WILLIAM CARLETON

Sir Turlough; or, The Churchyard Bride

THE bride she bound her golden hair—
    Killeevy, O Killeevy!
And her step was light as the breezy air
When it bends the morning flowers so fair,
    By the bonnie green woods of Killeevy.

And oh, but her eyes they danced so bright,
    Killeevy, O Killeevy!
As she longed for the dawn of tomorrow's light,
Her bridal vows of love to plight
    By the bonnie green woods of Killeevy.

The bridegroom is come with youthful brow,
    Killeevy, O Killeevy!
To receive from his Eva her virgin vow;
'Why tarries the bride of my bosom now?'
    By the bonnie green woods of Killeevy.

A cry! a cry! 'twas her maidens spoke,
    Killeevy, O Killeevy!
'Your bride is asleep, she has not woke,
And the sleep she sleeps will never be broke'
    By the bonnie green woods of Killeevy.

Sir Turlough sank down with a heavy moan,
    Killeevy, O Killeevy!
And his cheek became like the marble stone;
'Oh the pulse of my heart is for ever gone!'
    By the bonnie green woods of Killeevy.

The *keen* is loud, it comes again,
Killeevy, O Killeevy!
And rises sad from the funeral train,
As in sorrow it winds along the plain,
By the bonnie green woods of Killeevy.

And oh but the plumes of white were fair,
Killeevy, O Killeevy!
When they fluttered all mournful in the air,
As rose the hymns of the requiem there,
By the bonnie green woods of Killeevy.

There is a voice but one can hear,
Killeevy, O Killeevy!
And it softly pours, from behind the bier,
Its note of death on Sir Turlough's ear,
By the bonnie green woods of Killeevy.

The *keen* is loud, but the voice is low,
Killeevy, O Killeevy!
And it sings its song of sorrow slow,
And names young Turlough's name with woe,
By the bonnie green woods of Killeevy.

Now the grave is closed and the mass is said,
Killeevy, O Killeevy!
And the bride she sleeps in her lonely bed,
The fairest corpse among the dead,
By the bonnie green woods of Killeevy.

The wreaths of virgin white are laid,
Killeevy, O Killeevy!
By virgin hands o'er the spotless maid;
And the flowers are strewn, but they soon will fade,
By the bonnie green woods of Killeevy.

'Oh go not yet—not yet away,
Killeevy, O Killeevy!
Let us feel that life is near our clay,'
The long-departed seem to say
By the bonnie green woods of Killeevy.

But the tramp and the voices of life are gone,
Killeevy, O Killeevy!
And beneath each cold forgotten stone
The mouldering dead sleep on alone,
By the bonnie green woods of Killeevy.

But who is he that lingereth yet?
Killeevy, O Killeevy!
The fresh green sod with his tears is wet
And his heart in the bridal grave is set,
By the bonnie green woods of Killeevy.

Oh who but Sir Turlough the young and brave,
Killeevy, O Killeevy!
Should bend him o'er that bridal grave,
And to his death-bound Eva rave?
By the bonnie green woods of Killeevy.

'Weep not, weep not,' said a lady fair,
Killeevy, O Killeevy!
'Should youth and valour thus despair
And pour their vows to the empty air?'
By the bonnie green woods of Killeevy.

There's charmed music upon her tongue,
Killeevy, O Killeevy!
Such beauty, bright and warm and young,
Was never seen the maids among
By the bonnie green woods of Killeevy.

A laughing light, a tender grace,
Killeevy, O Killeevy!
Sparkled in beauty round her face,
That grief from mortal heart might chase,
By the bonnie green banks of Killeevy.

'The maid for whom thy salt tears fall,
Killeevy, O Killeevy!
Thy grief or love can ne'er recall;
She rests beneath that grassy pall,
By the bonnie green woods of Killeevy.

'My heart it strangely cleaves to thee,
Killeevy, O Killeevy!
And now that thy plighted love is free,
Give its unbroken pledge to me
By the bonnie green woods of Killeevy.'

The charm is strong upon Turlough's eye,
Killeevy, O Killeevy!
His faithless tears are already dry,
And his yielding heart has ceased to sigh
By the bonnie green woods of Killeevy.

'To thee,' the charmed chief replied,
Killeevy, O Killeevy!
I pledge my love o'er my buried bride;
Oh come and in Turlough's halls abide,
By the bonnie green woods of Killeevy.

Again the funereal voice came o'er,
Killeevy, O Killeevy!
The passing breeze, as it wailed before,
Streams of mournful music bore,
By the bonnie green woods of Killeevy.

'If I to thy youthful heart am dear,
    Killeevy, O Killeevy!
One month from hence thou wilt meet me here
Where lay thy bridal Eva's bier
    By the bonnie green woods of Killeevy.'

He pressed her lips as the words were spoken,
    Killeevy, O Killeevy!
And his banshee's wail, now far and broken,
Cried for Death as he gave the token
    By the bonnie green woods of Killeevy.

'Adieu, adieu,' said the lady bright,
    Killeevy, O Killeevy!
And she slowly passed like a thing of light
Or a morning cloud from Sir Turlough's sight
    By the bonnie green woods of Killeevy.

Now Sir Turlough has death in every vein,
    Killeevy, O Killeevy!
And there's fear and grief o'er his wide domain,
And gold for those who will calm his brain,
    By the bonnie green woods of Killeevy.

'Come haste thee, leech; right swiftly ride,
    Killeevy, O Killeevy!
Sir Turlough the brave, Green Truagh's pride,
Has pledged his love to the churchyard bride
    By the bonnie green woods of Killeevy.'

The leech groaned loud: 'Come tell me this,
    Killeevy, O Killeevy!
By all thy hopes of weal and bliss,
Has Sir Turlough given the fatal kiss
    By the bonnie green woods of Killeevy?'

'The banshee's cry is loud and long,
    Killeevy, O Killeevy!
At eve she weeps her funeral song,
And it floats on the twilight breeze along,
    By the bonnie green woods of Killeevy.'

Then the fatal kiss is given. The last,
    Killeevy, O Killeevy!
Of Turlough's race and name is past,
His doom is sealed, his die is cast,
    By the bonnie green woods of Killeevy.

Now the month is closed and Green Truagh's pride,
    Killeevy, O Killeevy!
Is married to Death; and side by side
He slumbers now with his churchyard bride,
    By the bonnie green woods of Killeevy.

JOHN KEEGAN CASEY

The Rising of the Moon

A.D. 1798

'OH! then tell me, Shawn O'Ferrall,
  Tell me why you hurry so?'
'Hush, ma bouchal, hush and listen,'
  And his cheeks were all a-glow.
'I bear ordhers from the captain,
  Get you ready quick and soon,
For the pikes must be together
  At the risin' of the moon.'

'Oh! then tell me, Shawn O'Ferrall
  Where the gatherin' is to be?'
'In the ould spot by the river,
  Right well known to you and me.
One word more—for signal token
  Whistle up the marching tune,
With your pike upon your shoulder
  By the risin' of the moon.'

Out from many a mud-wall cabin
  Eyes were watching thro' that night,
Many a manly chest was throbbing
  For the blessed warning light.
Murmurs passed along the valleys
  Like the banshee's lonely croon,
And a thousand blades were flashing
  At the risin' of the moon.

There beside the singing river
  That dark mass of men was seen,

Far above the shining weapons
  Hung their own beloved green.
'Death to every foe and traitor!
  Forward! strike the marchin' tune,
And hurrah, my boys, for freedom!
  'Tis the risin' of the moon.'

Well they fought for poor old Ireland
  And full bitter was their fate
(Oh! what glorious pride and sorrow
  Fill the name of Ninety-Eight.)
Yet, thank God, e'en still are beating
  Hearts in manhood's burning noon,
Who would follow in their footsteps
  At the risin' of the moon!

Maire My Girl

OVER the dim blue hills
  Strays a wild river,
Over the dim blue hills
  Rests my heart ever.
Dearer and brighter than
  Jewels and pearl,
Dwells she in beauty there,
  Maire my girl.

Down upon Claris heath
  Shines the soft berry,
On the brown harvest tree
  Droops the red cherry.
Sweeter thy honey lips,
  Softer the curl

Straying adown thy cheeks
Maire my girl.

'Twas on an April eve
That first I met her;
Many an eve shall pass
Ere I forget her.
Since my young heart has been
Wrapped in a whirl,
Thinking and dreaming of
Maire my girl.

She is too kind and fond
Ever to grieve me,
She has too pure a heart
Ever to deceive me.
Were I Tyrconnel's chief
Or Desmond's Earl,
Life would be dark, wanting
Maire my girl.

Over the dim blue hills
Strays a wild river,
Over the dim blue hills
Rests my heart ever;
Dearer and brighter than
Jewels or pearl,
Dwells she in beauty there
Maire my girl!

GEORGE CROLY

Approach of Evening

NIGHT'S wing is on the east—the clouds repose
Like weary armies of the firmament,
Encamped beneath their vanes of pearl and rose,
Till the wind's sudden trumpet through them sent,
Shakes their pavilions, and their pomps are blent
In rich confusion. Now the air is filled
With thousand odours, sighed by blossoms bent
In closing beauty, where the dew distilled
From Evening's airy urns their purple lips has chilled.

Twilight has come in saffron mists embowered
For the broad sun on the Atlantic surge,
Now sparkling in the fiery flashes showered
From his swift wheels—the forest vapours urge
Their solemn wings above—white stars emerge
From the dark east, like spires of mountain snows
Touched by the light upon th' horizon's verge;
Just rising from her sleep, the young Moon shows,
Supine upon the clouds, her cheeks suffused with rose.

This is the loveliest hour of all that Day
Calls upwards through its kingdom of the air.
The sights and sounds of earth have died away;
Above, the clouds are rolled against the glare
Of the red west—high volumed waves that war
Against a diamond promontory's side,
Crested with one sweet solitary star
That, like a watch-fire trembles on the tide,
Brightening with every shade that on its surge doth
ride.

GEORGE CROLY

An Aestuary

A CALM EVENING

Look on these waters, with how soft a kiss
They woo the pebbled shore then steal away
Like wanton lovers,—but to come again
And die in music! There the bending skies
See all their stars,—and the beach-loving trees,
Osiers and willows, and the watery flowers,
That wreathe their pale roots round the ancient stones.
Make pictures of themselves.

JOHN PHILPOT CURRAN

The Deserter's Lamentation

If sadly thinking,
And spirits sinking,
Could more than drinking
  Our griefs compose—
A cure for sorrow
From care I'd borrow;
And hope tomorrow
  Might end my woes.

But since in wailing
There's naught availing,
For Death, unfailing,
  Will strike the blow;
Then, for that reason,
And for the season,
Let us be merry
  Before we go!

A wayworn ranger,
To joy a stranger,
Through every danger
  My course I've run.
Now, death befriending,
His last aid lending,
My griefs are ending,
  My woes are done.

No more a rover,
Or hapless lover,

Those cares are over—
    'My cup runs low;'
Then, for that reason,
And for the season,
Let us be merry
Before we go!

THOMAS OSBORNE DAVIS

Oh! for a Steed

OH! for a steed, a rushing steed, and a blazing scimitar,
To hunt from beauteous Italy the Austrian's red
hussar;
To mock their boasts,
And strew their hosts,
And scatter their flags afar.

Oh! for a steed, a rushing steed, and dear Poland
gathered around,
To smite her circle of savage foes, and smash them
upon the ground;
Nor hold my hand
While, on the land,
A foreigner foe was found.

Oh! for a steed, a rushing steed, and a rifle that never
failed,
And a tribe of terrible prairie men, by desperate valour
mailed,
Till 'stripes and stars'
And Russian czars,
Before the Red Indian quailed.

Oh! for a steed, a rushing steed, with the Greeks at
Marathon,
Or a place in the Switzer phalanx, when the Morat
men swept on,
Like a pine-clad hill,
By an earthquake's will
Hurled the valleys upon.

Oh! for a steed, a rushing steed, when Brian smote
down the Dane,
Or a place beside great Aodh O'Neill, when Bagenal
the bold was slain,
Or a waving crest
And a lance in rest,
With Bruce upon Bannoch plain.

Oh! for a steed, a rushing steed, on the Curragh of
Kildare,
And Irish squadrons skilled to do, as they are ready to
dare—
A hundred yards,
And Holland's guards
Drawn up to engage me there.

Oh! for a steed, a rushing steed, and any good cause at
all,
Or else, if you will, a field on foot, or guarding a
leaguered wall
For freedom's right;
In flushing fight
To conquer if then to fall.

from

The Welcome

COME in the evening, or come in the morning,
Come when you're looked for, or come without
warning;
Kisses and welcome you'll find here before you,
And the oftener you come here the more I'll adore you.

Light is my heart since the day we were plighted,
Red is my cheek that they told me was blighted;
The green of the trees looks far greener than ever,
And the linnets are singing, 'true lovers! don't sever.'

. . . . . .

from

The Geraldines

I

The Geraldines! the Geraldines!—'tis full a thousand years
Since, 'mid the Tuscan vineyards, bright flashed their battle-spears;
When Capet seized the crown of France, their iron shields were known,
And their sabre-dint struck terror on the banks of the Garonne:
Across the downs of Hastings they spurred hard by William's side,
And the grey sands of Palestine with Moslem blood they dyed;
But never then, nor thence, till now, has falsehood or disgrace
Been seen to soil Fitzgerald's plume, or mantle in his face.

II

The Geraldines! The Geraldines!—'tis true, in Strongbow's van,
By lawless force, as conquerors, their Irish reign began;

And, oh! through many a dark campaign they proved their prowess stern,
In Leinster's plains, and Munster's vales, on kind, and chief, and kerne;
But noble was the cheer within the halls so rudely won,
And generous was the steel-gloved hand that had such slaughter done;
How gay their laugh, how proud their mien, you'd ask no herald's sign
Among a thousand you had known the princely Geraldine.

III

These Geraldines! these Geraldines!—not long our air they breathed;
Not long they fed on venison in Irish water seethed;
Not often had their children been by Irish mothers nursed;
When from their full and genial hearts an Irish feeling burst!
The English monarchs strove in vain, by law, and force, and bribe,
To win from Irish thoughts and ways this 'more than Irish' tribe;
For still they clung to fosterage, to *breitheamh*, cloak, and bard:
What king dare say to Geraldine, 'your Irish wife discard'?

. . . . . .

VI

True Geraldines! brave Geraldines!—as torrents mould the earth,
You channelled deep old Ireland's heart by constancy and worth:

When Ginckle 'leaguered Limerick, the Irish soldiers gazed
To see if in the setting sun dead Desmond's banner blazed?
And still it is the peasant's hope upon the Cuirreach's mere,
'They live, who'll see ten thousand men with good Lord Edward here'—
So let them dream till brighter days, when, not by Edward's shade,
But by some leader true as he, their lines shall be arrayed!

VII

These Geraldines! these Geraldines;—rain wears away the rock,
And time may wear away the tribe that stood the battle's shock;
But ever, sure, while one is left of all that honoured race,
In front of Ireland's chivalry is that Fitzgerald's place:
And, though the last were dead and gone, how many a field and town,
From Thomas Court to Abbeyfeile, would cherish their renown,
And men would say of valour's rise, or ancient power's decline,
''Twill never soar, it never shone, as did the Geraldine.'

VIII

The Geraldines! the Geraldines!—and are there any fears
Within the sons of conquerors for full a thousand years?

Can treason spring from out a spil bedewed with
  martyrs' blood?
Or has that grown a purling brook, which long rushed
  down a flood?—
By Desmond swept with sword and fire,—by clan and
  keep laid low,—
By Silken Thomas and his kin,—by sainted Edward,
  no!
The forms of centuries rise up, and in the Irish line
Command their son to take the post that fits the
  Geraldine.

The Sack of Baltimore

I

THE summer sun is falling soft on Carbery's hundred
  isles—
The summer sun is gleaming still through Gabriel's
  rough defiles—
Old Inisherkin's crumbled fane looks like a moulting
  bird,
And in a calm and sleepy swell the ocean tide is heard;
The hookers lie upon the beach; the children cease
  their play;
The gossips leave the little inn; the households kneel to
  pray—
And full of love, and peace, and rest—its daily labour
  o'er—
Upon that cosy creek there lay the town of Baltimore.

II

A deeper rest, a starry trance, has come with midnight there;
No sound, except that throbbing wave, in earth, or sea, or air.
The massive capes, and ruined towers, seem conscious of the calm;
The fibrous sod and stunted trees are breathing heavy balm.
So still the night, those two long barques, round Dunashad that glide,
Must trust their oars—methinks not few—against the ebbing tide—
Oh! some sweet mission of true love must urge them to the shore—
They bring some lover to his bride, who sighs in Baltimore!

III

All, all asleep within each roof along that rocky street,
And these must be the lover's friends, with gently gliding feet—
A stifled gasp! a dreamy noise! 'the roof is in a flame!'
From out their beds, and to their doors, rush maid, and sire, and dame—
And meet, upon the threshold stone, the gleaming sabre's fall,
And o'er each black and bearded face the white or crimson shawl—
The yell of 'Allah' breaks above the prayer, and shriek and roar—
Oh, blessed God! the Algerine is lord of Baltimore!

IV

Then flung the youth his naked hand against the
shearing sword;
Then sprung the mother on the brand with which her
son was gored;
Then sunk the grandsire on the floor, his grand-babes
clutching wild;
Then fled the maiden moaning faint, and nestled with
the child;
But see, yon pirate strangled lies, and crushed with
splashing heel,
While o'er him in an Irish hand there sweeps his
Syrian steel—
Though virtue sink, and courage fall, and misers yield
their store,
There's *one* hearth well avengèd in the sack of Balti-
more!

V

Mid-summer morn, in woodland nigh, the birds began
to sing—
They see not now the milking maids—deserted is the
spring!
Mid-summer day—this gallant rides from distant
Bandon's town—
These hookers crossed from stormy Skull, that skiff
from Affadown;
They only found the smoking walls, with neighbours'
blood besprent,
And on the strewed and trampled beach awhile they
wildly went—
Then dashed to sea, and passed Cape Clear, and saw
five leagues before
The pirate galleys vanishing that ravaged Baltimore.

VI

Oh! some must tug the galley's oar, and some must
tend the steed—
This boy will bear a Scheik's chibouk, and that a Bey's
jerreed.
Oh! some are for the arsenals, by beauteous Darda-
nelles;
And some are in the caravan to Mecca's sandy dells.
The maid that Bandon gallant sought is chosen for the
Dey—
She's safe—he's dead—she stabbed him in the midst
of his Serai;
And, when to die a death of fire, that noble maid they
bore,
She only smiled—O'Driscoll's child—she thought of
Baltimore.

VII

'Tis two long years since sunk the town beneath that
bloody band,
And all around its trampled hearths a larger concourse
stand,
Where, high upon a gallows tree, a yelling wretch is
seen—
'Tis Hackett of Dungarvan—he, who steered the
Algerine!
He fell amid a sudden shout, with scarce a passing
prayer,
For he had slain the kith and kin of many a hundred
there—
Some muttered of MacMurrough, who brought the
Norman o'er—
Some cursed him with Iscariot, that day in Baltimore.

Lament for the Death of Owen Roe O'Neill

TIME.—10*th November* 1649. SCENE.—*Ormond's Camp, County Waterford.* SPEAKERS.—*A veteran of Owen O'Neill's clan, and one of the horsemen, just arrived with an account of his death.*

I

'Did they dare, did they dare, to slay Owen Roe O'Neill?'
'Yes, they slew with poison him, they feared to meet with steel.'
May God wither up their hearts! May their blood cease to flow!
May they walk in living death, who poisoned Owen Roe!

II

'Though it break my heart to hear, say again the bitter words.'
'From Derry, against Cromwell, he marched to measure swords:
But the weapon of the Sacsanach met him on his way,
And he died at Clough Oughter, upon St. Leonard's day.

III

'Wail, wail ye for the Mighty One! Wail, wail ye for the Dead!
Quench the hearth, and hold the breath—with ashes strew the head.
How tenderly we loved him! How deeply we deplore!
Holy Saviour! but to think we shall never see him more.

IV

'Sagest in the council was he, kindest in the hall!
Sure we never won a battle—'twas Owen won them all.
Had he lived—had he lived—our dear country had
been free;
But he's dead, but he's dead, and 'tis slaves we'll ever
be.

V

'O'Farrell and Clanrickarde, Preston and Red Hugh,
Audley, and MacMahon, ye are valiant, wise, and
true;
But—what, what are ye all to our darling who is gone?
The Rudder of our Ship was he, our Castle's corner
stone!

VI

'Wail, wail him through the Island! Weep, weep for
our pride!
Would that on the battle-field our gallant chief had
died!
Weep the victor of Benburb—weep him, young men
and old;
Weep for him, ye women—Your Beautiful lies cold!

VII

'We thought you would not die—we were sure you
would not go,
And leave us in our utmost need to Cromwell's cruel
blow—
Sheep without a shepherd, when the snow shuts out
the sky—
Oh! why did you leave us, Owen? Why did you die?

VIII

'Soft as woman's was your voice, O'Neill! bright was your eye,
Oh! why did you leave us, Owen? Why did you die?
Your troubles are all over, you're at rest with God on high,
But we're slaves, and we're orphans, Owen!—why didst thou die?'

SIR AUBREY DE VERE

The Landrail

DEAR, wakeful bird! I bid thine accents hail,
  When, like the voice of May, thy startling note
Comes wandering up the moonlit, grassy vale,
  Or hill of springing corn, or reedy moat;
  Dearer I love thee than the classic throat,
Melodious, of the poet's nightingale,
  When her aerial numbers wildly float,

Like fairy music, o'er some haunted dale.
'Tis thine to wake a sweeter harmony,
Thrilling the viewless chords of memory:—
  To come upon the heart in silent hours,
Touching each trembling pulse deliciously;
  Recalling vows of youth, Hope's budding flowers,
  And visions of pure love in amaranthine bowers!

Kilmallock

WHAT ruined shapes of feudal pomp are there,
In the cold moonlight fading silently?
The castle, with its stern, baronial air,
Still frowning, as accustomed to defy;
The Gothic street, where Desmond's chivalry
Dwelt in their pride; the cloistered house of prayer;
The gate-towers, mouldering where the stream moans
  by,
Now, but the owl's lone haunt, and fox's lair.
Here once the pride of princely Desmond flushed;

His courtiers knelt, his mailed squadrons rushed;
And saintly brethren poured the choral strain:
Here Beauty bowed her head, and smiled and
 blushed:—
Ah, of these glories what doth now remain?
The charnel of yon desecrated fane!

Castleconnell

BROAD, but not deep, along his rock chafed bed,
In many a sparkling eddy winds the flood.
Clasped by a margin of green underwood:
A castled crag, with ivy garlanded,
Sheer, o'er the torrent frowns: above the mead
De Burgho's towers, crumbling o'er many a rood,
Stand gauntly out in airy solitude
Backed by yon furrowed mountain's tinted head.
Sounds of far people, mingling with the fall
Of waters, and the busy hum of bees,
And larks in air, and throstles in the trees,
Thrill the moist air with murmurs musical.
While cottage smoke goes drifting on the breeze;
And sunny clouds are floating over all.

The Rock of Cashel

ROYAL and saintly Cashel! I would gaze
 Upon the wreck of thy departed powers,
 Not in the dewy light of matin hours,
Nor the meridian pomp of summer's blaze,
But at the close of dim autumnal days,

When the sun's parting glance, through slanting showers,
Sheds o'er thy rock-throned battlements and towers
Such awful gleams as brighten o'er Decay's
Prophetic cheek. At such a time, methinks,
There breathes from thy lone courts and voiceless aisles
A melancholy moral, such as sinks
On the lone traveller's heart, amid the piles
Of vast Persepolis on her mountain stand,
Or Thebes half buried in the desert sand.

EDWARD DOWDEN

The Singer

'THAT was the thrush's last good-night,' I thought,
And heard the soft descent of summer rain
In the drooped garden leaves; but hush! again
The perfect iterence,—freer than unsought
Odours of violets dim in woodland ways,
Deeper than coiled waters laid a-dream
Below mossed ledges of a shadowy stream,
And faultless as blown roses in June days.
Full-throated singer! art thou thus anew
Voiceful to hear how round thyself alone
The enriched silence drops for thy delight
More soft than snow, more sweet than honey-dew?
Now cease: the last faint western streak is gone,
Stir not the blissful quiet of the night.

WILLIAM DRENNAN

Branch of the Sweet and Early Rose

BRANCH of the sweet and early rose
  That in the purest beauty blows,
So passing sweet to smell and sight,
  On whom shalt thou bestow delight?

Who in the dewy evening walk
  Shall pluck thee from the tender stalk?
Whose temples blushing shalt thou twine,
  And who inhale thy breath divine?

Aspiration

O! HOW I long to be at rest!
No more oppressing, or opprest,
To sink asleep, on nature's nursing breast!

In Earth's green cradle to be laid,
Where larks may build, where lambs have play'd,
And a clear stream may flow, and soothe my hovering
  shade.

The twilight mem'ry loves to spread,
Haply may linger o'er my head,
And half illume the long departed dead.

JOHN SWANWICK DRENNAN

Epigrams

I. LOVE

FOR Love is like a plant that clings
Most closely unto rugged things,
And ever clasps with fondest stress
Deformity and barrenness.

II. L'AMITIE ET L'AMOUR

With nought to hide or to betray
  She eyed me frank and free.
But, oh, the girl that looked away
  Was dearer far to me!

III

Love signed the contract blithe and leal,
Time shook the sand, Death set the seal.

IV. AVARO

Avaro sick is seen to shiver,
  Some presage dread his soul engrossing;
Is it of the Infernal River?
  No, but the obolus for crossing.

V

A golden casket I designed
  To hold a braid of hair;
My Love was false, and now I find
  A coil of serpents there.

VI. A SPINOZAISM.

Of the divine and human thought
How different are the sums;
For what man thinks is often nought
But what God thinks becomes.

VII

The Metaphysic Sphynx that preys on us
Is not appeased by offerings to the eye;
Science would soothe her with his 'This' and 'Thus,'
But she remains insatiate with her 'Why?'

Not Gone Yet

'WAVE ye, dark tresses! clust'ring, or apart,
Contrast your beauty with the snowy brow;
Ringlets no more are fetters for my heart,
Nor doth it tremble with their motion now.
Smile, ye bright eyes! your wanton beams no more
Shall wrongfully divert a glance of mine;
My bark is turn'd from Love's illusive shore,
And its false lights now unregarded shine.'
But whilst the mariner in boastful joy,
Again afloat, his sails is shaking out,
Lo! at the helm there stands a Winged Boy,
And silently the ship is put about.

Perdita

FROM the dusk forest or the dark'ning strand,
    Why dost thou come,
Trembling and chill, as if a spectre's hand
    Had warned thee home?
Oft hast thou lingered on the hills afar,
    And roamed the heath,
To win, thou said'st, the lustre of the star
    The night-flower's breath;
Oft hast thou loosed upon the twilight shore
    Thy lonely sail,
But ne'er returning met my kiss before
    Thus still and pale.
Hath some deceptive planet mock'd thy vow
    With sudden blight?
'Yes, Mother, I *have* felt upon my brow
    Disastrous light!'
Or didst thou in the tangled forest grass
    A serpent wake,
With venom 'neath his shining folds? Alas,
    It was a snake!
Haply some bright-eyed vampire that hath crept
    Thy sleep upon
Thus hueless left thy cheek? ''Twas so,' she wept,
    ''Twas such an one!'
Or, is it the beguilement that thus mute
    Thou seek'st to smother,
Of treach'rous berry or false-rinded fruit?
    ''Tis poison, Mother.'
Such feign'd mishap, such heedless enterprise,
    Might well befall;

But I can read in those averted eyes
    A worse than all;
Maiden, is Love the cause of thy despair?
    She bow'd her head,
Shook down the shining shadow of her hair,
    And nothing said.

On the Telescopic Moon

A LIFELESS solitude—an angry waste,
Searing our alien eyes with horrors bare;
No fertilizing cloud—no genial air
To mitigate its savageness of breast;
The light itself all undiffusive there;
Motionless terror clinging to the crest
Of steepmost pinnacles; as by despair
Unfathomable caverns still possessed!
How shall we designate such world forlorn?
What nook of Heaven abhors this portent dark?
Lo! where the *Moon* reveals her gentle ray,
Waking the nightingale's and poet's lay;
Speeding benign the voyager's return;
And lighting furtive kisses to their mark!

GEORGE FOX

The County of Mayo

From the Irish

On the deck of Patrick Lynch's boat I sat in woeful plight
Through my sighing all the weary day, and weeping all the night.
Were it not that full of sorrow from my people forth I go,
By the blessed sun! 'tis royally I'd sing thy praise, Mayo!

When I dwelt at home in plenty, and my gold did much abound,
In the company of fair young maids the Spanish ale went round
'Tis a bitter change from those gay days that now I'm forced to go,
And must leave my bones in Santa Cruz, far from my own Mayo.

They are altered girls in Irrul now; 'tis proud they're grown and high,
With their hair-bags and their top-knots—for I pass their buckles by;
But it's little now I heed their airs, for God will have it so,
That I must depart for foreign lands, and leave my sweet Mayo.

'Tis my grief that Patrick Loughlin is not Earl of Irrul
still,
And that Brian Duff no longer rules as Lord upon the
hill,
And that Colonel Hugh MacGrady should be lying
cold and low,
And I sailing, sailing swiftly from the county of Mayo.

GERALD GRIFFIN

Ancient Lullaby

DARKNESS o'er the world is creeping,
Slumber while the heavens are weeping,
While the kerns their watch are keeping,
And all eyes beside are sleeping.

Heaven's dark curtains now are closing,
The wild winds in peace reposing;
Now the harper old is prosing,
While his chieftain's eyes are dozing.

Heavy is the humming number:
Let the witch that scatters slumber,
In her passage halt and murmur,
Till her dews thy lids encumber.

Dull and dim the moon is gleaming,
Drowsy is the owlet's screaming,
Sullen sounds and gloomy seeming
Soon shall mingle in thy dreaming.

Aileen Aroon

WHEN like the early rose,
Aileen aroon!
Beauty in childhood blows,
Aileen aroon!
When like a diadem

Buds blush around the stem,
Which is the fairest gem?
Aileen aroon!

Is it the laughing eye?
Aileen aroon!
Is it the timid sigh?
Aileen aroon!
Is it the tender tone,
Soft as the string'd harp's moan?
Oh, it is truth alone,
Aileen aroon!

When, like the rising day,
Aileen aroon!
Love sends his early ray,
Aileen aroon!
What makes his dawning glow,
Changeless through joy or woe?
Only the constant know,
Aileen aroon!

I know a valley fair,
Aileen aroon!
I knew a cottage there,
Aileen aroon!
Far in that valley's shade
I knew a gentle maid,
Flower of the hazel glade,
Aileen aroon!

Who in the song so sweet?
Aileen aroon!
Who in the dance so neat?
Aileen aroon!
Dear were her charms to me,

Dearer her laughter free,
Dearest her constancy,
Aileen aroon!

Were she no longer true,
Aileen aroon!
What should her lover do?
Aileen aroon!
Fly with his broken chain
Far o'er the sounding main,
Never to love again,
Aileen aroon!

Youth must with time decay,
Aileen aroon!
Beauty must fade away,
Aileen aroon!
Castles are sacked in war,
Chieftains are scattered far,
Truth is a fixed star,
Aileen aroon!

I Love My Love in the Morning

I LOVE my love in the morning,
For she like morn is fair—
Her blushing cheek, its crimson streak,
Its clouds, her golden hair.
Her glance, its beam, so soft and kind;
Her tears, its dewy showers;
And her voice, the tender whispering wind
That stirs the early bowers.

I love my love in the morning,
  I love my love at noon,
For she is bright, as the lord of light,
  Yet mild as autumn's moon:
Her beauty is my bosom's sun,
  Her faith my fostering shade,
And I will love my darling one
  Till even the sun shall fade.

I love my love in the morning,
  I love my love at even;
Her smile's soft play is like the ray
  That lights the western heaven:
I loved her when the sun was high,
  I loved her when he rose;
But best of all when evening's sigh
  Was murmuring at its close.

SIR WILLIAM ROWAN HAMILTON

A Prayer

O BROODING Spirit of Wisdom and of Love,
  Whose mighty wings even now o'ershadow me,
  Absorb me in thine own immensity,
And raise me far my finite self above!
  Purge vanity away, and the weak care
That name or fame of me may widely spread,
And the deep wish keep burning in their stead,
  Thy blissful influence afar to bear,—
Or see it borne! Let no desire of ease,
  No lack of courage, faith, or love, delay
  Mine own steps on that high thought-paven way
In which my soul her clear commission sees:
  Yet with an equal joy let me behold
  Thy chariot o'er that way by others rolled.

JAMES KENNEY

The Green Leaves all turn Yellow

A SAGE once to a maiden sung,
  While summer leaves were growing;
Experience dwelt upon his tongue,
  With love her heart was glowing:
'The summer bloom will fade away,
  And will no more be seen;
These flowers, that look so fresh and gay,
  Will not be ever green—
    For the green leaves all turn yellow.

''Tis thus with the delights of love,
  The youthful heart beguiling;
Believe me, you will find them prove
  As transient—though as smiling:
Not long they flourish, ere they fade,
  As sadly I have seen;
Yes, like the summer flowers, fair maid,
  Oh! none are ever green—
    For the green leaves all turn yellow.'

WILLIAM LARMINIE

The Nameless Doon

WHO were the builders? Question not the silence
That settles on the lake for evermore,
Save when the sea-bird screams and to the islands
The echo answers from the steep-cliffed shore.
O half-remaining ruin, in the lore
Of human life a gap shall all deplore
Beholding thee; since thou art like the dead
Found slain, no token to reveal the why,
The name, the story. Some one murdered
We know, we guess; and gazing upon thee,
And, filled with thy long silence of reply,
We guess some garnered sheaf of tragedy;—
Of tribe or nation slain so utterly
That even their ghosts are dead, and on their grave
Springeth no bloom of legend in its wildness;
And age by age weak washing round the islands
No faintest sigh of story lisps the wave.

HENRY LUTTRELL

from

Advice to Julia

After the Wedding

CUPIDS in vain around them hover,
Unless—the conjuration over
Which makes a husband of a lover—
Four conscious horses, strong and supple,
Whisk from the door the happy couple,
And lodge them in that deep retreat
Impregnable—a country-seat;
There, haply in the sultry season,
Condemned without one earthly reason
To struggle through a week's warm weather
In hopeless solitude together . . .
Surely 'twere kinder not to banish
These turtles,—not to bid them vanish
At once into some rustic den,
Far from the cheerful haunts of men,
Till they are reconciled and broke
A little to the nuptial yoke.
Launched in a life so strange and new,
Society should help them through,
As training makes young colts less wild,
Or as a go-cart props a child
Until, by practice steady grown,
Its infant limbs can move alone.
  Say, why should grots and shrubberies hide
A lawful bridegroom and a bride?
Why must they, lost in shady groves,
Fit shelter for unlicensed loves,

Steal from th' approving world and seek
A long probationary week
Of close retirement as profound
As if they both were under ground?
Twelve hours of every four-and-twenty
Left to themselves, methinks, were plenty.
Then why to villas hurry down,
When these, fond pair, are yours in town?
   Be counselled.—Stir not, near or far,
But stay, I charge you, where you are.
The dream of passion soon or late
Is broken—don't anticipate.

EDWARD LYSAGHT

Garnyvillo

HAVE you been at Garnyvillo?
  Have you seen at Garnyvillo
Beauty's train trip o'er the plain
  With lovely Kate of Garnyvillo?
Oh! she's pure as virgin snows,
  E'er they light on woodland hill-o;
Sweet as dew-drop on wild rose
  Is lovely Kate of Garnyvillo!

Philomel, I've listened oft
  To thy lay, nigh weeping willow—
Oh, the strain's more sweet, more soft,
  That flows from Kate of Garnyvillo!
        Have you been, &c.

As a noble ship I've seen
  Sailing o'er the swelling billow,
So I've marked the graceful mien
  Of lovely Kate of Garnyvillo;
        Have you been, &c.

If poets' prayers can banish cares,
  No cares should come to Garnyvillo;
Joy's bright rays shall gild her days,
  And dove-like peace perch on her pillow.
      Charming maid of Garnyvillo!
      Lovely maid of Garnyvillo!
      Beauty, grace, and virtue wait
      On lovely Kate of Garnyvillo!

FRANCIS SYLVESTER MAHONY

The Bells of Shandon

'Sabbata pango,
Funera plango,
Solemnia clango'
Inscrip. on an old Bell

WITH deep affection
And recollection
I often think of
  Those Shandon bells,
Whose sounds so wild would
In the days of childhood
Fling round my cradle
  Their magic spells.
On this I ponder
Where'er I wander,
And thus grow fonder
  Sweet Cork, of thee;
With thy bells of Shandon,
That sound so grand on
The pleasant waters
  Of the river Lee.

I've heard bells chiming
Full many a clime in,
Tolling sublime in
  Cathedral shrine,
While at a glib rate
Brass tongues would vibrate—
But all their music
  Spoke naught like thine;

For memory dwelling
On each proud swelling
Of the belfry knelling
  Its bold notes free,
Made the bells of Shandon
Sound far more grand on
The pleasant waters
  Of the river Lee.

I've heard bells tolling
Old 'Adrian's Mole' in,
Their thunder rolling
  From the Vatican,
And cymbals glorious
Swinging uproarious
In the gorgeous turrets
  Of Notre Dame;
But thy sounds were sweeter
Than the dome of Peter
Flings o'er the Tiber,
  Pealing solemnly;—
O! the bells of Shandon
Sound far more grand on
The pleasant waters
  Of the river Lee.

There's a bell in Moscow,
While on tower and kiosk, O!
In Saint Sophia
  The Turkman gets,
And loud in air
Calls men to prayer
From the tapering summit
  Of tall minarets.
Such empty phantom
I freely grant them;

But there is an anthem
More dear to me,—
'Tis the bells of Shandon
That sound so grand on
The pleasant waters
Of the river Lee.

In Mortem Venerabilis Andreae Prout Carmen

SWEET upland! where, like hermit old, in peace sojourn'd
This priest devout;
Mark where beneath thy verdant sod lie deep inurn'd
The bones of Prout!
Nor deck with monumental shrine or tapering column
His place of rest,
Whose soul, above earth's homage, meek yet solemn,
Sits mid the blest.
Much was he prized, much loved; his stern rebuke
O'er-awed sheep-stealers;
And rogues feared more the good man's single look
Than forty Peelers.
He's gone; and discord soon I ween will visit
The land with quarrels;
And the foul demon vex with stills illicit
The village morals.
No fatal chance could happen more to cross
The public wishes;
And all the neighbourhood deplores his loss
Except the fishes;
For he kept Lent most strict, and pickled herring
Preferred to gammon.

Grim Death has broke his angling-rod; his berring
Delights the salmon.
No more can he hook up carp, eel, or trout,
For fasting pittance,—
Arts which Saint Peter loved, whose gate to Prout
Gave prompt admittance.
Mourn not, but verdantly let shamrocks keep
His sainted dust;
The bad man's death it well becomes to weep,—
Not so the just.

The Attractions of a Fashionable Irish Watering-Place

THE town of Passage
Is both large and spacious,
And situated
Upon the say.
'Tis nate and dacent
And quite adjacent
To come from Cork
On a summer's day:
There you may slip in
To take a dipping,
Fornent the shipping
That at anchor ride.
Or in a wherry
Come o'er the ferry,
To Carrigaloe,
On the other side.

Mud cabins swarm in
This place so charming,

With sailor garments
  Hung out to dry;
And each abode is
Snug and commodious.
With pigs melodious
  In their straw-built sty.
It's there the turf is,
And lots of murphies,
Dead sprats and herrings
  And oyster-shells;
Nor any lack, O!
Of good tobacco—
Though what is smuggled
  By far excels.

There are ships from Cadiz,
And from Barbadoes,
But the leading trade is
  In whisky-punch;
And you may go in
Where one Molly Bowen
Keeps a nate hotel
  For a quiet lunch.
But land or deck on,
You may safely reckon,
Whatever country
  You came hither from,
On an invitation
To a jollification,
With a parish priest
  That's called 'Father Tom.'

Of ships there's one fixed
For lodging convicts
A floating 'stone jug'
  Of amazing bulk;

The hake and salmon,
Playing at backgammon,
Swim for divarsion
All round this 'hulk';
There 'Saxon' jailors
Keep brave repailors
Who soon with sailors
Must anchor weigh
From the em'rald island
Ne'er to see dry land
Until they spy land
In sweet Bot'ny Bay.

Ad Leuconoen

Love, mine! seek not to grope
Through the dark windings of Chaldaean witchery,
To learn your horoscope,
Or mine, from vile adepts in fraud and treachery,
My Leuconoe! shun
Those sons of Babylon.

Far better 'twere to wait,
Calmly resign'd, the destined hour's maturity,
Whether our life's brief date
This winter close, or through a long futurity
For us the sea still roar
On yon Tyrrenean shore.

Let Wisdom fill the cup:—
Vain hopes of lengthened days and years felicitous
Folly may treasure up;
Ours be the day that passeth—unsolicitous

Of what the next may bring.
Time flieth as we sing!

Solvitur Acris Hiems

Now Winter melts beneath
Spring's genial breath,
And Zephyr
Back to the water yields
The stranded bark—back to the fields
The stabled heifer—
And the gay rural scene
The shepherd's foot can wean
Forth from his homely hearth, to tread the meadows green.

Now Venus loves to group
Her merry troop
Of maidens
Who, while the moon peeps out,
Dance with the Graces round about
Their queen in cadence;
While far, 'mid fire and noise,
Vulcan his forge employs,
Where Cyclops grim aloft their ponderous sledges poise.

Now maids, with myrtle-bough
Garland their brow—
Each forehead
Shining with flowerets deck'd;
While the glad earth, by frost uncheck'd,
Buds out all florid;—
Now let the knife devote,

In some still grove remote,
A victim-lamb to Faun; or, should he list, a goat.

Death's undiscerning foot
Knocks at the hut;
The lowly
As the most princely gate.
O favour'd friend! on life's brief date
To count were folly;
Soon shall, in vapours dark,
Quench'd be thy vital spark,
And thou, a silent ghost, for Pluto's land embark.

Where at no gay repast,
By dice's cast
King chosen,
Wine-laws shalt thou enforce,
But weep o'er joy and love's warm source
For ever frozen;
And tender Lydia lost,
Of all the town the toast,
Who then, when thou art gone, will fire all bosoms most!

RICHARD ALFRED MILLIKIN

The Groves of Blarney

THE Groves of Blarney
They look so charming
Down by the purling,
  Of sweet silent streams.
Being banked with posies
That spontaneous grow there,
Planted in order
  By the sweet 'Rock Close'.
'Tis there the daisy
And the sweet carnation,
The blooming pink
  And the rose so fair.
The daffodowndilly,
Likewise the lily,
All flowers that scent
  The sweet, fragrant air.

'Tis Lady Jeffers
That owns this station;
Like Alexander,
  Or Queen Helen fair,
There's no commander
In all the nation,
For emulation,
  Can with her compare.
Such walls surround her,
That no nine-pounder
Could dare to plunder
  Her place of strength;

But Oliver Cromwell
Her he did pommell,
And made a breach
  In her battlement.

There's gravel walks there
For speculation
And conversation
  In sweet solitude.
'Tis there the lover
May hear the dove, or
The gentle plover
  In the afternoon;
And if a lady
Would be so engaging
As to walk alone in
  Those shady bowers,
'Tis there the courtier
He may transport her
Into some fort, or
  All underground.

For 'tis there's a cave where
No daylight enters,
But cats and badgers
  Are for ever bred;
Being mossed by nature,
That makes it sweeter
Than a coach-and-six or
  A feather bed.
'Tis there the lake is,
Well stored with perches,
And comely eels in
  The verdant mud;
Besides the leeches,
And groves of beeches,

Standing in order
   For to guard the flood.

There's statues gracing
This noble place in—
All heathen gods
   And nymphs so fair;
Bold Neptune, Plutarch,
And Nicodemus,
All standing naked
   In the open air!
So now to finish
This brave narration,
Which my poor genii
   Could not entwine;
But were I Homer,
Or Nebuchadnezzar,
'Tis in every feature
   I would make it shine.

CAROLINE ELIZABETH SARAH NORTON

Love Not

Love not, love not! ye hapless sons of clay!
  Hope's gayest wreaths are made of earthly flowers—
Things that are made to fade and fall away
  Ere they have blossom'd for a few short hours.
                  Love not!

Love not! the thing ye love may change:
  The rosy lip may cease to smile on you,
The kindly-beaming eye grow cold and strange,
  The heart still warmly beat, yet not be true.
                  Love not!

Love not! the thing you love may die,
  May perish from the gay and gladsome earth;
The silent stars, the blue and smiling sky,
  Beam o'er its grave, as once upon its birth.
                  Love not!

Love not! oh warning vainly said
  In present hours as in the years gone by;
Love flings a halo round the dear one's head,
  Faultless, immortal, till he change or die.
                  Love not!

GEORGE OGLE

Mailligh Mo Stor

As down by Banna's banks I strayed,
One evening in May,
The little birds, in blithest notes,
Made vocal every spray;
They sung their little notes of love,
They sung them o'er and o'er.
Ah! gradh mo chroidhe, mo cailin og,
'Si Mailligh mo stor.

The daisy pied, and all the sweets
The dawn of Nature yields—
The primrose pale, and violet blue,
Lay scattered o'er the fields;
Such fragrance in the bosom lies
Of her whom I adore.
Ah! gradh mo chroidhe, &c.

I laid me down upon a bank,
Bewailing my sad fate,
That doomed me thus the slave of love
And cruel Molly's hate;
How can she break the honest heart
That wears her in its core?
Ah! gradh mo chroidhe, &c.

You said you loved me, Molly dear!
Ah! why did I believe?
Yet who could think such tender words
Were meant but to deceive?
That love was all I asked on earth—

Nay, heaven could give no more.
Ah! gradh mo chroidhe, &c.

Oh! had I all the flocks that graze
On yonder yellow hill,
Or lowed for me the numerous herds
That yon green pasture fill—
With her I love I'd gladly share
My kine and fleecy store.
Ah! gradh mo chroidhe, &c.

Two turtle-doves, above my head,
Sat courting on a bough;
I envied them their happiness,
To see them bill and coo.
Such fondness for me once was shown,
But now, alas! 'tis o'er.
Ah! gradh mo chroidhe, &c.

Then fare thee well, my Molly dear!
Thy loss I e'er shall moan;
Whilst life remains in my poor heart,
'Twill beat for thee alone:
Though thou art false, may heaven on thee
Its choicest blessings pour.
Ah! gradh mo chroidhe, mo cailin og,
'Si Mailligh mo stor.

The Banks of Banna

SHEPHERDS, I have lost my love,—
Have you seen my Anna?
Pride of every shady grove
On the Banks of Banna.

I for her my home forsook,
  Near yon misty mountain,
Left my flocks, my pipe, my crook,
  Greenwood shade, and fountain.

Never shall I see them more
  Until her returning;
All the joys of life are o'er—
  Gladness chang'd to mourning.
Whither is my charmer flown?
  Shepherds, tell me whither?
Woe is me, perhaps she's gone
  For ever and for ever!

STANDISH JAMES O'GRADY

Lough Bray

Now Memory, false, spendthrift Memory,
  Disloyal treasure-keeper of the soul,
This vision change shall never wring from thee
  Nor wasteful years, effacing as they roll.
O steel-blue lake, high cradled in the hills!
  O sad waves, filled with little sobs and cries!
White glistening shingle, hiss of mountain rills,
  And granite-hearted walls blotting the skies,
Shine, sob, gleam, gloom for ever! Oh, in me
  Be what you are in Nature—a recess—
To sadness dedicate and mystery,
  Withdrawn, afar, in the soul's wilderness.
Still let my thoughts, leaving the worldly roar
Like pilgrims, wander on thy haunted shore.

JOHN O'KEEFFE

Jingle

AMO, amas,
I love a lass,
As cedar tall and slender;
Sweet cowslip's face
Is her nominative case,
And she's of the feminine gender.
Horum quorum,
Sunt divorum,
Harum, scarum, Divo,
Tag rag, merry derry, periwig and bobtail
Hic, hoc, harum, genitivo.

GEORGE PETRIE

Do You Remember that Night

From the Irish

Do you remember that night
When you were at the window,
With neither hat nor gloves
Nor coat to shelter you?
I reached out my hand to you,
And you ardently grasped it;
I remained in converse with you
Until the lark began to sing.

Do you remember that night
That you and I were
At the foot of the rowan-tree,
And the night drifting snow?
Your head on my breast,
And your pipe sweetly playing?
Little thought I that night
That our love ties would loosen!

Beloved of my inmost heart,
Come some night, and soon,
When my people are at rest,
That we may talk together.
My arms shall encircle you
While I relate my sad tale,
That your soft, pleasant converse
Hath deprived me of heaven.

The fire is unraked,
The light unextinguished,

GEORGE PETRIE

The key under the door,
Do you softly draw it.
My mother is asleep,
But I am wide awake;
My fortune in my hand,
I am ready to go with you.

THOMAS WILLIAM ROLLESTON

The Dead at Clonmacnois

From the Irish of Angus O'Gillan

IN a quiet-water'd land, a land of roses,
Stands Saint Kieran's city fair,
And the warriors of Erinn in their famous generations
Slumber there.

There beneath the dewy hillside sleep the noblest
Of the Clan of Conn,
Each below his stone; his name in branching Ogham
And the sacred knot thereon.

There they laid to rest the Seven Kings of Tara,
There the sons of Cairbrè sleep—
Battle-banners of the Gael, that in Kieran's plain of crosses
Now their final hosting keep.

And in Clonmacnois they laid the men of Teffia
And right many a lord of Breagh;
Deep the sod above Clan Creidè and Clan Connall,
Kind in hall and fierce in fray.

Many and many a son of Conn the Hundred-Fighter
In the red earth lies at rest;
Many a blue eye of Clan Colman the turf covers,
Many a swan-white breast.

THOMAS WILLIAM ROLLESTON

The Grave of Rury

CLEAR as air, the western waters
evermore their sweet unchanging song
Murmur in their stony channels
round O'Conor's sepulchre in Cong.

Crownless, hopeless, here he lingered;
felt the years go by him like a dream,
Heard the far-off roar of conquest
murmur faintly like the singing stream.

Here he died, and here they tomb'd him,
men of Fechin, chanting round his grave.
Did they know, ah, did they know it,
what they buried by the babbling wave?

Now above the sleep of Rury
holy things and great have passed away;
Stone by stone the stately Abbey
falls and fades in passionless decay.

Darkly grows the quiet ivy,
pale the broken arches glimmer through;
Dark upon the cloister-garden
dreams the shadow of the ancient yew.

Through the roofless aisles the verdure
flows, the meadow-sweet and foxglove bloom;
Earth, the mother and consoler,
winds soft arms about the lonely tomb.

Peace and holy gloom possess him,
last of Gaelic monarchs of the Gael,
Slumbering by the young, eternal
river-voices of the western vale.

JAMES STUART

from

Morna's Hill

A DISTANT PROSPECT OF THE CITY OF ARMAGH

As round the pine-clad top of Morna's hill
Slowly I wind, what varied scenes appear
In glorious prospect? Whether o'er the plains
Mantled in green, the eye delighted roves,
Or where yon spires peep o'er the sloping hills,
And glitter in the sun; or where aloft,
Thy column Rokeby, lifts its head in air,
High o'er the verdant pines, transmitting down
To latest years, thy friendship and thy name!
Or thine, O Molyneux, that stands sublime,
With form majestick, o'er thy waving woods,
Raised to thy country's glory in the day
Of Erin's fame. How lovely bloom the groves
Whose bending tops play wanton in the gale,
Mingling their varied hues! Bright through the vales
The streams soft gliding, wind their devious course,
Deep'ning the tender verdure of the fields,
And mantling ev'ry blossom of the spring
In robes of humid lustre . . .
  Nor wants the glowing landscape many a charm
Transmitted down through Time's revolving years
To dignify the scene. The sacred mound,
Where waves the wild grass o'er the prostrate heads
Of heroes now no more. The convex cairne
That crowns the heath-clad hill, where silent sleeps

The mighty Fion; and the antique rath
Within whose circular entrenchments stood
Secure embattled hosts; ere Science taught
The sons of war to sweep the tented field
With murderous cannon. Contemplation loves
To dwell upon these objects; and the soul,
Deep-musing, turns to deeds of ancient days,
And snatches, from the annals of the world,
A sadly-pleasing, melancholy joy.

RICHARD CHENEVIX TRENCH

Sonnet

I STOOD beside a pool, from whence ascended,
Mounting the cloudy platforms of the wind,
A stately heron; its soaring I attended,
Till it grew dim, and I with watching blind—
When lo! a shaft of arrowy light descended
Upon its darkness and its dim attire;
It straightway kindled them, and was afire,
And with the unconsuming radiance blended.

And bird, a cloud, flecking the sunny air,
It had its golden dwelling 'mid the lightning
Of those empyreal domes, and it might there
Have dwelt for ever, glorified and bright'ning,
But that its wings were weak—so it became
A dusky speck again, that *was* a winged flame.

Elegy

THIS winter eve how soft! how mild!
How calm the earth! how calm the sea!
The earth is like a weary child,
And ocean sings its lullaby.

A little ripple in mine ear!
A little motion at my feet!

They only make the quiet here,
  Which they disturb not, more complete.

I wander on the sands apart,
  I watch the sun, world-wearied, sink
Into his grave:—with tranquil heart
  Upon the loved and lost I think.

EDWARD WALSH

Mairgread ni Chealleadh

AT the dance in the village
Thy white foot was fleetest;
Thy voice 'mid the concert
Of maidens was sweetest;
The swell of thy white breast
Made rich lovers follow;
And thy raven hair bound them,
Young Mairgread ni Chealleadh.

Thy neck was, lost maid!
Than the *ceanabhan* whiter;
And the glow of thy cheek
Than the *monadan* brighter;
But death's chain hath bound thee,
Thine eyes glazed and hollow,
That shone like a sunburst,
Young Mairgread ni Chealleadh.

No more shall mine ear drink
Thy melody swelling;
Nor thy beamy eye brighten
The outlaw's dark dwelling;
Or thy soft heaving bosom
My destiny hallow,
When thine arms twine around me,
Young Mairgread ni Chealleadh.

The moss couch I brought thee
To-day from the mountain,

Has drank the last drop
Of thy young heart's red fountain—
For this good *skian* beside me
Struck deep and rung hollow
In thy bosom of treason,
Young Mairgread ni Chealleadh.

With strings of rich pearls
Thy white neck was laden,
And thy fingers with spoils
Of the Sassenach maiden;
Such rich silks enrob'd not
The proud dames of Mallow—
Such pure gold they wore not
As Mairgread ni Chealleadh.

Alas! that my loved one
Her outlaw would injure—
Alas! that he e'er proved
Her treason's avenger!
That this right hand should make thee
A bed cold and hollow,
When in Death's sleep it laid thee
Young Mairgread ni Chealleadh!

And while to this lone cave
My deep grief I'm venting,
The Saxon's keen bandog
My footsteps is scenting;
But true men await me
Afar in Duhallow.
Farewell, cave of slaughter,
And Mairgread ni Chealleadh.

Mo Craoibhin Cno

My heart is far from Liffey's tide
And Dublin town;
It strays beyond the southern side
Of Knockmealdown,
Where Cappoquin hath woodlands screen,
Where Avonmore's waters flow,
Where dwells unsung, unsought, unseen,
Mo craoibhin cno,
Low clustering in her leafy green
Mo craoibhin cno!

The high-bred dames of Dublin town
Are rich and fair,
With wavy plume and silken gown,
And stately air;
Can plumes compare thy dark brown hair?
Can silks thy neck of snow?
Or measur'd pace thine artless grace,
Mo craoibhin cno,
When harebells scarcely show thy trace,
Mo craoibhin cno?

I've heard the songs by Liffey's wave
That maidens sung—
They sung their land the Saxon's slave,
In Saxon tongue—
Oh! bring me here that Gaelic dear
Which cursed the Saxon foe,
When thou didst charm my raptured ear,
Mo craoibhin cno!
And none but God's good angels near,
Mo craoibhin cno!

I've wandered by the rolling Lee!
    And Lene's green bowers—
I've seen the Shannon's wide-spread sea,
    And Limerick's towers—
And Liffey's tide, where halls of pride
  Frown o'er the flood below;
My wild heart strays to Avonmore's side,
    Mo craoibhin cno!
With love and thee for aye to bide,
    Mo craoibhin cno!

WILLIAM WILKINS

The Magazine Fort, Phœnix Park, Dublin

INSIDE its zig-zag lines the little camp is asleep,
Embalm'd in the infinite breath of the greensward, the river, the stars.
Round the staff, the yellow leopards of England, weary of wars,
Curl and uncurl, to the murmurous voice of the greenwood deep.
On the lonely terrace their watch the shadowy sentinels keep,
Each bayonet a spire of silver—high over the silvery jars
Of the streamtide, swooning in starlight adown its foam-fretted bars
To the city, that lies in a shroud as of ashes under the steep.
To the south are the hills everlasting; eastward the sea-capes and isles;
Inland, the levels of emerald stretch for a hundred miles.

NOTES

ANONYMOUS. With the decay of the Irish language there grew up, towards the end of the eighteenth and all through the nineteenth centuries an extensive popular poetry—political songs, street songs, romantic ballads, and more sophisticated songs of ribaldry and drinking. The six anonymous poems that I have included are characteristic samples; their number could have been greatly increased without much reducing the general quality.

Castle Hyde. This is the model which Milliken set himself to outdo in extravagance when he wrote 'The Groves of Blarney'.

I know where I'm going. From Co. Antrim. The words are probably nineteenth century; the well-known tune is traditional.

The Night Before Larry was Stretched. This poem was for long ascribed to a clergyman of the Church of Ireland, Dean Burrowes.

The Rakes of Mallow. This, like the previous poem, has an eighteenth-century atmosphere. But in Ireland eighteenth-century ways of life continued, as did eighteenth-century architecture, beyond the middle of the nineteenth century.

The Gay Old Hag. One of the mystical names for Ireland. The poem, a version of the Shan Van Vocht, is taken from a Dublin broadside.

The Orange Lily O. A floral emblem second only to the Shamrock in the affection of Ulster Protestants. It keeps green the immortal memory of King William III.

ALEXANDER, CECIL FRANCES (1818–1895). Born at Dublin. She created some confusion about the date, as she liked to be thought ten years younger than she was. Her father was a Major Humphreys and she married William Alexander the Archbishop. She is best known for her popular hymns—'All things bright and beautiful', 'There is a green hill far away', 'St. Patrick's Breastplate'. The poem here included is not so commonly found in hymn-books.

ALEXANDER, WILLIAM (1824–1911). Born at Derry; educated at Tonbridge and Oxford where he came under Newman's influence. He was Bishop of Derry, and later Archbishop of Armagh and Primate of all Ireland. He wrote much verse and much theology. He was the husband of Mrs. Alexander the hymn-writer.

ANSTER, JOHN (1789–1867). Born at Carleville, Co. Cork; died in Dublin. He was educated at Trinity College, Dublin, where, in 1850, he was appointed Regius Professor of Civil Law. Anster is remembered as one of the first and best translators of Goethe. He also published several books of original verse in Dublin and Edinburgh.

BALFOUR, MARY (b. 1780 c.). Daughter of a Derry clergyman who was a friend of the Earl Bishop of Derry. She was a schoolmistress at various places in Ulster; published a book of poems at Belfast in 1810; and produced a poetic melodrama there in 1814.

BROOKE, STOPFORD AUGUSTUS (1832–1916). Born in Donegal, a descendant of Henry Brooke, the author of *The Fool of Quality*. He resigned his orders in the

Church of England to become a fashionable Unitarian preacher. Late in life he was intimate with a Water-sprite or Naiad called Louisa whom he had found at a German spa and with whom he lived at his house in Surrey. Brooke's biographer is reticent on the circumstances of this association; but Brooke himself seems to have thought it neither surprising nor discreditable.

CARLETON, WILLIAM (1794–1869). Born in Tyrone of peasant stock. He was educated at a 'Hedge School' where a good grounding in Latin and mathematics was to be had. He was almost a great writer of fiction; and, like the novelist George Moore he became a convert to Protestantism. He received a Civil List pension for the last twenty years of his life. The ballad of *Sir Turlough* is founded on a Monaghan legend.

CASEY, JOHN KEEGAN (1846–1870). Born near Mullingar in Westmeath. He wrote for the *Nation* under the name of 'Leo', and published a book of poems in 1866. In the next year he was arrested as a Fenian, but was later released. He published a second book of poems in 1869, shortly before his death from consumption. It was thought that his death was hastened by imprisonment and he was given a spectacular funeral.

The Rising of the Moon is well known from Lady Gregory's use of it in her play of the same name. Apart from this and *Maire, My Girl*, his poems have been grossly overvalued, presumably for political reasons.

CROLY, GEORGE (1780–1860). Born in Dublin; educated at Trinity College, Dublin; Rector of St.

Stephen's, Wallbrook. He was, as Allibone says, 'one of the most voluminous writers of the day. Works of Theology, History, Politics, Fiction, Poetry, etc., streamed from his pen'. He died suddenly whilst walking in Holborn. As a poet he is more neglected than he should be.

CURRAN, JOHN PHILPOT (1750–1817). Born at Newmarket, Co. Cork, died at Brompton, near Cheltenham. He was one of the most distinguished and attractive politico-legal characters of his time.

Because of Curran's dates, his poem would hardly find place in this book were it not the earliest example in English of a manner regarded as peculiarly Irish.

DAVIS, THOMAS OSBORNE (1815–1845). Born at Mallow, Co. Cork, of Welsh-Irish parentage. He was educated at Trinity College, Dublin; was called to the Irish Bar; had a very active political career; and died of scarlet fever.

Most of Davis's poetry was intended as propaganda. Even his engagement to Annie Hutton induced no love poems of interest. But the poems here given show his vivid historical imagination, though they do not indicate his intellectual power.

The sack of Baltimore, on which the poem is founded, occurred on June 19th, 1631.

The Welcome: Unfortunately the rest of the poem does not live up to the promise of its opening.

The Geraldines: The Fitzgerald family, Earls of Desmond and Kildare, were the most patriotic of the Norman-Irish nobility. Stanzas 4 and 5 have been omitted. The last line of the poem refers to William Smith O'Brien, a rebel of 1848 and a Geraldine on his mother's side.

DE VERE, SIR AUBREY, second Baronet (1788–1846). Born in Limerick; educated at Harrow with Byron. He wrote several dull poetic plays and some good sonnets. He was the father of Aubrey De Vere, and one of the more enlightened landlords of his time.

Sir Aubrey de Vere is our most conscious and conscientious topographical poet. Of the places described in these three poems, Cashel only remains as he saw it; though (thanks to the Board of Works) it is tidier, and by so much less romantic, than it was then. The rapids of Castleconnell have been shorn of much of their impressiveness by the Shannon Hydro-Electric Scheme. As for Kilmallock, long celebrated as the 'Baalbek of Ireland', its destruction has been completed more recently still. The last of its fine sixteenth-century stone houses was pulled down in 1942 to make way for a cinema.

Cashel is also the subject of a fine set piece in prose in Mahaffy's *Rambles and Studies in Greece*. The text of de Vere's sonnet here given is that of 1842.

DOWDEN, EDWARD (1843–1913). Born at Cork. He was Professor of English Literature at Dublin University, the first biographer of Shelley, and in poetry and criticism a minor counterpart to Matthew Arnold.

DRENNAN, WILLIAM (1754–1820). Born in Belfast, the son of a Presbyterian minister. Educated at Glasgow and Edinburgh; practised as a Doctor in Belfast and Newry. Drennan was an early member of the Volunteers and one of the founders of the United Irishmen. He was prosecuted for seditious libel in 1794, and was successfully defended by Curran. He died in Belfast.

DRENNAN, JOHN SWANWICK (1809–1893). Born at his grandfather's house in Shropshire. He was the son of William Drennan, the United Irishman; was educated at Dublin and Paris; practised medicine at Leeds; retired to Belfast sometime after 1845; and spent the rest of his long life there.

FOX, GEORGE (1809–c. 1880). Born in Belfast. He was a brilliant conversationalist and a keen student of the Irish language. As a young man he emigrated to British Guiana and is presumed to have died there. Sir Samuel Ferguson dedicated a book to him in 1880.

The County of Mayo seems certainly to be by Fox, though it is his only known poem and was at first thought to be by Ferguson.

GRIFFIN, GERALD (1803–1839). Born in Limerick. He went to London in 1823 and wrote *The Collegians*, a novel which was dramatized by Boucicault as *The Colleen Bawn* and is also the foundation of Benedict's opera *The Lily of Killarney*. Griffin became very much depressed and joined the Christian Brothers. He died, worn out by fasting, in the North Monastery, Cork.

Griffin's long poem, *Shanid Castle*, has some merit; but his fame as a poet rests mainly on *Aileen Aroon*—the best and best-known of many *Aileen Aroons* by many other authors. The air to which they were all written is known in England as 'Robin Adair', and was much admired by Handel.

HAMILTON, SIR WILLIAM ROWAN (1805–1865). The Astronomer-Poet of Ireland. He discovered or invented Quaternions. Aubrey De Vere reports Wordsworth as saying that Coleridge and Sir W. R.

Hamilton were the only men he had met to whom he would apply the term *wonderful*.

KENNEY, JAMES (1780–1849). A prolific and successful dramatist who also wrote a few poems. He died on the day on which a performance was given for his benefit at Drury Lane Theatre.

LARMINIE, WILLIAM (1850–1900). Born at Castlebar, Co. Mayo; educated at Trinity College, Dublin, and became a civil servant in London. He retired in 1887 and lived the rest of his life in Ireland. He is of interest for his Gaelic use of assonance in English verse.

LUTTRELL, HENRY (1766–1851). Born in Dublin; probably a natural son of Lord Carhampton. He was a member of the Irish Parliament for Clonmines, Co. Wexford, but retired to London after the Union. He lived and died in Brompton Square.

LYSAGHT, EDWARD (1763–1810). Born at Brickhill, Co. Clare; educated at Trinity College, Dublin, and at Oxford. He was called to the Bar and settled in Dublin where he gained a great reputation as a wit. He was a vigorous opponent of the Union, yet he could write with charity of Lord Clare:

> Cold is thy heart, hush'd is thy voice;
>   Around thy sacred urn
> Rapine and fraud and guilt rejoice,
>   While truth and justice mourn.

He was known as 'pleasant Ned Lysaght'.

MAHONY, FRANCIS SYLVESTER (1804–1866). Born in Cork of an old local family; educated at Amiens and the Irish College at Rome. He entered the Society of Jesus and was for a short time master of Rhetoric in Clongoweswood College, but he was dismissed and retired to Italy where he was expelled from the Society. He occasionally said Mass in the chapel of the Bavarian Legation in London. He contributed to *Fraser's Magazine* over the pen-name 'Father Prout'. Father Mahony was a considerable wit and a great linguist. He travelled in the Balkans and the Levant, finally settling in Paris where he died. He wrote verse in English, Greek, Latin, French, Italian, and Irish.

MILLIKIN, RICHARD ALFRED (1767–1815). Born at Castle Martyr, Co. Cork; educated at Midleton; practised Law in Dublin and Cork. He founded a fine art society in Cork, published a long poem, *The River Side* in 1807, and a novel in 1810. He was a kindly man and was known as 'Honest Dick Millikin'.

The Groves of Blarney. This poem is in the same metre, derived from the Gaelic, as Curran's *Deserter's Lamentation* and as the anonymous *Sweet Castle Hyde*, in competition with which it was written. The parade of learning, the inconsequence, and the decorative use of words not fully understood, hark back to the proverbial grandiloquence of the hedge-schoolmasters. Fr. Mahony added a stanza:

> There is a stone there,
> That whoever kisses,
> Oh! he never misses
> To grow eloquent;
> 'Tis he may clamber
> To a lady's chamber,
> Or become a member

Of parliament.
A clever spouter
He'll soon turn out, or
An out-and-outer,
To be let alone.
Don't hope to hinder him,
Or to bewilder him,
Sure he's a pilgrim
From the Blarney Stone!

NORTON, CAROLINE ELIZABETH SARAH (1808–1877). Granddaughter of Richard Brinsley Sheridan and sister of Lady Dufferin. She was the model for Meredith's *Diana of the Crossways*. She married Mr. George Norton, a blackguard. Most of her verse resembles that of her contemporary and in some sense her compatriot Felicia Hemens. She and Allingham were among the first to recognize the genius of the Dorset poet William Barnes.

OGLE, GEORGE (1742–1814). Born in Wexford. He was an active and patriotic politician, and a prolific and popular song-writer. Though very much an eighteenth-century writer, he is included here because *Mailligh Mo Stor* is the first Anglo-Irish poem of any merit.

O'GRADY, STANDISH JAMES (1846–1915). Born at Barehaven; educated at Trinity College, Dublin. O'Grady gained a high reputation as a prose writer by his romances of Irish history and legend.

O'KEEFE, JOHN (1747–1833). Born in Dublin; studied painting under West at the Royal Dublin Society; took to writing plays and acting at the Smock-Alley

Theatre. After 1778 he lived mostly in London. From 1820 he received a royal pension.

PETRIE, GEORGE (1789–1866). Born in Dublin. He was an artist, a topographer, an antiquary, and a collector of Irish music; and also the first accurate investigator of Irish archaeology.

ROLLESTON, THOMAS WILLIAM (1857–1920). Born at Shinrone, the son of a judge; educated at St. Columba's College and Trinity College, Dublin. He lived much on the Continent. His verse is, on the whole, undistinguished; but *The Dead at Clonmacnois* is, I think, the best Irish poem of the nineteenth century.

STUART, JAMES (1764–1840). Born in Armagh; educated at the Royal School, Armagh, and at Trinity College, Dublin. He was called to the Bar; was first editor of the *Newry Telegraph*; and wrote a *History of Armagh* which has not yet been superseded. He died at Belfast.

TRENCH, RICHARD CHENEVIX (1807–1886). Born in Dublin; Archbishop of Dublin from 1864 to 1884; died in London. He was a Cambridge friend of Tennyson who dedicated *The Palace of Art* to him. He is best known for his *Study of English Words* and *English Past and Present*.

WALSH, EDWARD (1805–1851). Born at Derry, where his father, a Cork militiaman, was stationed. He was a schoolmaster in Cork and Waterford, and collected folklore and Gaelic poetry. At the time of his death he was schoolmaster to the Cork Work-house.

WILKINS, WILLIAM (1852–1915). Born at Zante in Greece; educated at Dundalk Grammar School and Trinity College, Dublin. In 1879 he was appointed headmaster of the Dublin High School, where W. B. Yeats was one of his pupils. His *Songs of Study* was published in 1881.

INDEX OF FIRST LINES

A beauty all stainless, a pearl of a maiden *page* 229
A golden casket I designed 341
A lifeless solitude—an angry waste 344
A March wind sang in a frosty wood 82
A plenteous place is Ireland 127
A roadside inn this summer Saturday 205
A sage once to a maiden sung 352
A sunset's mounded cloud 41
Adieu to Ballyshannon! where I was bred and born 32
All landscapes are this land 43
Along the roof-line, sharp and red 273
Amo, amas 373
Among the mountain skirts a league away 49
An isle of trees full foliaged in a meadow 204
And from a northern coast the lovers watched 44
As down by Banna's banks I strayed 369
As I roved out on a summer's morning 297
As round the pine-clad top of Morna's hill 378
At my casement I sat by night 78
At noon she left her cavern cell 165
At the dance in the village 382
Avaro sick is seen to shiver 341
Awake! arise! shake off thy dreams 241
Awake thee, my Bessy, the morning is fair 65
Awakened, I beheld through dewy leaves 202

Bare winter owns the earth at last 161
Beauing, belling, dancing, drinking 302
Bird that pipest on the bough 132
Black texture of the leafy trees 45
Blow, summer wind, from yonder ocean blow 207

Branch of the sweet and early rose *page* 340
Broad but not deep, along this rock-chafed bed 337
But haste we! 'Tis that merry time of year 51
By the shore, a plot of ground 15

Clear as air, the western waters 377
Come in the evening, or come in the morning 325
Come see the Dolphin's anchor forged 128
Crom Cruach and his sub-gods twelve 113
Cupids in vain around them hover 354

Darkness o'er the world is creeping 347
Dear wakeful bird! I bid thine accents hail 336
Did they dare, did they dare, to slay Owen Roe O'Neill 333
Do you remember that night 374
Down looked the moon 278
Dumb are the heavens: sphere controlling sphere 164

Earth's night is where she rolls 44
Ellen Bawn, O Ellen Bawn 230

Fall, snow, and cease not! Flake by flake 90
Fare well to Fair Alba 137
Finn on the mountain found the mangled man 117
Float, little bark, down yonder stream 272
Flowers I would bring if flowers would make you fairer 101
For love is like a plant that clings 341
Forgive me that I love you as I do 100
Four ducks on a pond 53
From the dusk forest or the dark'ning strand 342
From the grey wicket of the morn 276

Give me my harp and let me sing a song 136
Gloomy with wind and driving cloud, the night 197
Grey-faced spirit! let us sit 158

Had I been worthy of the love you gave *page* 101
Have you been at Garnyvillo? 356
He found me sitting among flowers 98
Here I've got you, Philip Desmond 290
Here the white-ray'd anemone is born 39
Hold on, hold on, while yet ye can 92
Hours I remember lonely and lovely to me 197
How hard is my fortune 69
How many pipes have dittied unto thee 271

I go to knit two clans together 77
I heard a woman's voice that wailed 85
I knew that Disaster 252
I know where I'm going, she said 298
I love my love in the morning 349
I love you, pretty maid, for you are young 94
I once was a guest at a nobleman's wedding 18
I ride through a dark, dark Land by night 238
I row in my boat in the twilight 267
I saw her once, one little while 237
I see Him: on thy lap He lies 105
I see thee ever in my dreams 257
I sit at eve within the curtain's fold 199
I stood beside a pool, from whence ascended 380
I walk of grey noons by the old canal 206
I walked amid the lilies, at the morn 267
I walked entranced 242
I walked in the lonesome evening 31
I walked through Ballinderry in the springtime 140
I'd wed you without herds 124
If I might choose where my tired limbs shall lie 307
If sadly thinking 322
In a quiet-watered land, a land of roses 376
In ringlets curl'd thy tresses flow 308
In the day the sun is darkened 310

In the December weather, grey and grim *page* 277
In the night, in the night, O my Country 85
Inside its zig-zag lines the little camp is asleep 386
Into the wood at close of rainy day 202
Ione, fifteen years have o'er you passed 95
Island of bitter memories, thickly sown 50
It is a bleak December noon 207

Lady—the lyre thou bid'st me take 62
Lift up the drooping head 231
Like two pale stars at distance seen 305
Lo! from the woodland skirting the old town 169
Lock up thy heart within thy breast alway 255
Look forth and say, 'Lo, on the left 142
Look, Mother! the mariner's rowing 256
Look on those waters, with how soft a kiss 321
Love, mine! seek not to grope 362
Love not, love not! ye hapless sons of clay! 368
Love signed the contract blithe and leal 341
Loved for themselves, too. Oft as I behold 135

My dreams were doleful and drear 184
My heart is far from Liffey's side 384
My love to fight the Saxon goes 288

Near where the riotous Atlantic surge 46
Nestled into a hollow of the downs 45
Night's wing is on the east—the clouds repose 320
No longer soiled with stain of earth 143
Not yet trodden under wholly 255
Now blows the white rose round your garden pales 287
Now early sink away the starry Twins 51
Now fare you well! my bonny ship 42
Now Memory, false spendthrift Memory 372

Now Winter melts beneath *page* 363
Now, winter's dolorous days are o'er, and through 206

O brooding Spirit of Wisdom and of Love 351
O crystal Well 192
O did you go to see the show 304
O dim delicious heaven of dreams 292
O English mother, in the ruddy glow 43
O for a steed, a rushing steed 324
O how I long to be at rest 340
O lovely Mary Donnelly 19
O many a day have I made good ale in the glen 70
O Mary dear, oh Mary fair 122
O my Dark Rosaleen 217
O my fair Pastheen is my heart's delight 121
O spirit of the Summertime! 30
O, strew the way with rosy flowers 239
O, the rain, the weary, dreary rain 249
O, then tell me Shawn O'Ferrall 317
O where are you going so early? he said 10
O woman of Three Cows, agra! 225
October, and the skies are cool and grey 30
Of the divine and human thought 342
On the deck of Patrick Lynch's boat 345
On the floor of the low, white-clouded seas 193
Once I had passed the shortened autumn day 187
Once more, through God's high will and grace 88
One evening walking out, I o'ertook a modest colleen 38
Open sweet flowers, your eyes 282
Over the dim blue hills 318

Paul, let thy faces from the canvas look 134
Primeval night had repossessed 104

Pure is the dewy gem that sleeps *page* 61
Put your head, darling, darling, darling 125

Regions of soft clear air, of cold green leaves 201
Remote from smoky cities, aged and grey 201
Royal and saintly Cashel! I would gaze 337

Seek up and down, both fair and brown 9
Shepherds, I have lost my love 370
Since hopeless of thy love I go 126
Slowly through the tomb-still streets I go 240
Softly, O midnight Hours 97
Solomon! where is thy throne? 236
South-westward, where th'autumnal sun went down 50
Speak no more of life 251
Spoke my heart in the dearth of the night 283
Summer vapours, soft and white 187
Sweet Sunday Bells! 37
Sweet upland! where, like hermit old 359

Take a blessing from my heart 227
That was the thrush's last good-night 339
The apple ripens under yellowing leaves 203
The blue waves are sleeping 63
The bride she bound her golden hair 311
The crags lay dark in strange eclipse 81
The dew each trembling leaf inwreathed 309
The fairy King was old 18
The Geraldines! the Geraldines! 326
The girl I love is comely, straight and tall 68
The Groves of Blarney 365
The hamlet Ballytullagh, small and old 47
The lions of the hill are gone 138
The little Black Rose shall be red at last 87
The Metaphysic Sphynx that preys on us 342

The mighty mountain plains have we two trod *page* 102
The moon comes freshly from the east 285
The moon is cold. A whiteness newly brought 306
The night a spongy dimness fill'd 44
The night before Larry was stretched 299
The night is falling in chill December 254
The noisy sparrows in our clematis 21
The North wind clanged on the sharp hill-side 80
The objects of the summer scene entone 196
The rainbow o'er the sea of afternoon 200
The rough green wealth of wheaten fields that sway 200
The summer sun is falling soft 329
The sun upon Ivera 66
The town of Passage 360
The vast and solemn company of clouds 31
The wing'd seeds with decaying wings 45
There is an order by a northern sea 86
There was a long old road anear the town 178
There was lifted up one voice of woe 223
There's light in the west, o'er the ruins of walnut 281
They err who say this long-withdrawing line 135
This is the garden, its twenty paths 268
This winter eve how soft! how mild! 380
'Tis pleasant, stretched on grassy lawn 153
'Tis the rose of the desert 61
'Tis where the road-side rivulet expands 52
To-day chance drove me to the wood 310
'Twas summer time, the radiant world of June 279
Two leaps the water from its race 46
Two women loved him, shapes of Heaven 170

Up the airy mountain 16
Up the sea-saddened valley at evening's decline 83
Upon an upland orchard's sunny side 203
Urania! Voice of Heaven, sidereal Muse 92

Wave ye, dark tresses! clustering or apart *page* 342
We left the city, street and square 275
We seem to tread the self-same street 79
What ruined shapes of feudal pomp are these 336
When each bright star is clouded 64
When e'er I see soft hazel eyes 125
When I had turned Catullus into rhyme 204
When, like the early rose 347
When on the level summer seas 168
When the spinning room was here 53
Where in the summer-warm woodlands 208
Where is my Chief, my Master 219
Where mountains round a lonely dale 40
Who feels not, when the Spring once more 102
Who were the builders? Question not the silence 353
Whose were they, those voices 84
Why have you risen, to stand with naked feet 186
Will you come a boating, my gay old hag 303
With deep affection 357
With grief and mourning I sit to spin 12
With nought to hide or to betray 341
With witch-like branches, barren, bleak, and drear 195

Ye two fair trees that I so long have known 205
You drop a tear for those that die 99